The Importance of Being Irish

The Importance of Being IRISH

by ALAN BESTIC

WILLIAM MORROW AND COMPANY, INC.

New York ▥ *1969*

Printed in the United States of America at
The Haddon Craftsmen, Inc., Scranton, Pennsylvania

Library of Congress Catalog Card Number 76-83532

CONTENTS

To Joan and Jim Brophy, who gave me a bridgehead in Balbriggan from which to launch raids into the hinterland, but who are in no whit responsible for the subsequent skirmishes or the wounds therefrom.

PROLOGUE

ASKING an Irishman to write a book about Ireland is like telling a cannibal chef that he must cook his grannie for special guests. He tries hard to justify whatever professionalism he has acquired. He bastes her and turns her and prepares to drench her in his very special sauce. One moment he turns off the heat and the next he throws on a few more logs, prodding her from time to time with a spear to see how she is coming along. Over and over again he tells himself that he is an artist and that art is loyal only to art. Yet constantly he is conscious of a shrewd, wicked old eye, peering at him with supercilious venom and unctuous martyrdom over the rim of the cauldron.

If, like myself, he has been away from the tribe for fifteen years, schizophrenia sets in early. Now he feels sorry for what he is doing. Now he is dunking her back into the gravy, telling her to stop bubbling over nothing, that it would be much worse to be cooked by a total stranger.

In my case, grannie has changed considerably in the time that I have been away. She has grown fatter, more prosperous. The tears, many of which were genuine and justified, do not roll so readily down her cheeks. She has tarted herself up so much that a stranger might have difficulty in recognizing her and might feel secretly sorry, indeed, that she no longer seems to be teetering on the edge of the grave. There is nothing worse than to be cheated out of a good and long-anticipated funeral.

I, on the other hand, am thoroughly delighted to see her looking so well, though it does not help the schizophrenia. I gaze at her and sometimes I wonder whether this sharp old chick and I are related at all. At other times I feel very close to her—closer than I was before I left home. One minute I write: 'We Irish. . . .' A sentence later, it is: 'The Irish. . . .'

The dish, however, is ready now. For better or for worse, the long hours over the hot stove are over. The result is Gaelic Granny with a dopple of whipped cream on her blue-rinsed hair.

I hope that she is tender. I hope that you enjoy her. I hope that all her other grand-children will know that I have cooked with loving care.

Woking, Surrey
7 October 1968

ALAN BESTIC

1 THE NEW IRELAND

ONCE upon a time it was easy to explain the Irish to the non-Irish. The whole tedious business could be wrapped up in a couple of handy, deep-frozen sentences, which could be thawed, garnished delicately and served up again and again. These sentences meant everything and nothing, their digestibility depending upon the audience, the mood, the hour of night, the state of sobriety and occasionally the direction of the wind.

I used to be able to assume a soberly detached, carefully casual air of deep cynicism and say (preferably over the left shoulder): 'Inside every Irishman there are a thousand Irishmen fighting to get out.' In the more intellectual circles, this little package deal slid down the assembled throats like a dozen of Galway oysters. It had the advantage of being reasonably true, but, more important, it was snapped up as yet another example of Irish wit and/or mystic profundity. This reputation for wit, I believe, has sprung from the fact that we use far more words than most and that somewhere along the line some of them must be witty, even by accident.

The mystic profundity bit is a little more difficult to explain, but the fact remains that all Irish people are supposed to be born with it, as those from less fortunate races are born with crinkly faces and an ability to cry. The English adhere particularly strongly to this quaint theory; and the above definition is greeted more often that not in England by someone saying through a briar pipe held in tightly clenched teeth: 'These Irish are as fey as hell, old boy, but, by God, they can put their finger on the *truth!*' The conversation then breaks up in a disorder of obscure quotations from Wilde and Shaw, whereupon all Irish present take to the boats mainly because (if they are anything like myself) they have not read nearly enough of these excellent Celts.

I had, of course, a longer and more complicated definition, which was guaranteed to stone the assembled company into momentary silence before driving the conversation into more meaningful channels, such as the weather or sex or Mao Tse-tung, or the importance of being anything else but Irish. With emotional sincerity, conveyed by shouting and arm-waving, I would say: 'The Irish are devious and naïve, aggressive and gentle, turbulent and dreamy, irreverent and religious, happy and sad, lousy lovers and lusty, kind and bitter, respectable, disrespectful, cruel, soft-hearted, polite, caustic, hypocritical, frank, lazy, tireless, dogmatic, amenable, narrow, tolerant, a people of strong weaknesses and lukewarm hates.'*

As they say in certain Dublin theatrical circles: 'Folly that!'† The whole twisted catalogue, of course, had a heavy veneer of truth, perhaps because in some ways it was a description of people everywhere.

All that, however, was once upon a time. No longer can the subject be dispatched so facilely. With a perversity exceeding even that with which the rest of the world has credited them for so long, the Irish have complicated the issue hopelessly by shattering a dozen or so of the images which, for one reason or another, so many people found so fascinating. They have had a revolution. There is nothing, I admit, unusual about that. Revolutions have been a popular and respectable hobby among the Irish for seven or eight hundred years and my only regret is that so many of them failed. What made (and makes, for it is going on still) this effort so odd was (and is) its nature. Right from the beginning, it was quiet. Not a shot was fired, not a barricade manned, not even a shillelagh, made in Hong Kong, waved for the benefit of the tourist trade. It was an English-type revolution, lacking only the stiff upper lip, a device which the Irish have spurned as of no practical use. Personally I have always found a trembling lower lip much more effective and so have most of my fellow-countrymen.

This revolution of the sixties has made it clear that the Irish are not a wobbling blancmange of poor, priest-ridden, blinded dreamers. That was a popular picture in both the United States and Britain and, though we protested shrilly about it, there was an element of truth in it. Today, however, it is no longer compulsory for white-haired Irish mothers to die of tuberculosis in crumbling thatched cottages, while balding chickens peck at their feet.

In the cities and towns, the open-sore tenements, which roused the decent, ribald wrath of Seán O'Casey, with their stench of stale cabbage and the rustle of rats, have dwindled in number, though they still exist.

No priest rampages through the whin bushes after a Saturday night dance, flushing out the lovers who are bringing the evening to a logical conclusion. Instead the younger clergy are raising their voices

* For example: 'I hate that fellah!' Anglice: 'That chap and I do not see eye to eye on some points.'

† In Dublin 'follow' is pronounced sometimes 'folly'. Please do not ask me why.

in protest about social conditions, identifying themselves with the people on a scale hitherto unknown and long overdue.

One brave cleric, indeed, Father Michael Sweetman, a Jesuit, shared a platform in Dublin recently with Mick O'Riordan of the Workers' Party, which is what the Irish call their tiny Communist party. Better housing was their common cause. I remember watching a mob, straight from twelve o'clock Mass, kicking the same Workers' Party boys, Mick among them, up and down O'Connell Street in Dublin just for being there, while the police conveyed their approval by their inactivity; and that was not so very long ago, either.

The blind of censorship is being raised, quietly again, English fashion, for to do it any other way would be to needle the narrow few into shrill and probably effective protest. Long-banned authors, Irish and otherwise, have their wares displayed on the bookstalls now; and so far there has been no untoward epidemic of rape, which would seem to indicate that the Irish are not the inflammable, impressionable band of sex-maniacs that the Establishment for so long seemed to think they were.

Sex is discussed openly and sensibly in the newspapers and on television nowadays, giving the lie to a theory, held for so long, that all Irish babies were found under cabbages. This change has come as a considerable relief to frustrated Irish newspaper sub-editors, denied for years the use of such a handy, short word in headings. Now they are sprinkling it about like snuff at a wake, yet so divorced had I (and most others outside Ireland) become from the raw realities that I was staggered, when I returned to Ireland to work on this book, to see in the *Sunday Press* the heading: TEACH YOUR CHILDREN ABOUT SEX . . . by the Rev. G. Thomas Fehily.

I soon learned that Father Fehily was one of the more progressive minds abroad in Ireland, one of the new frontiersmen. At the time, however, that heading merely jolted my mind back to the days when I had worked for the *Irish Press*, which is from the same stable as the *Sunday Press*. An epidemic of gastro-enteritis was killing babies by the hundred in Dublin. I interviewed a woman doctor who told me that the death rate could be slashed, the epidemic halted, perhaps, if only mothers would breast-feed their children. The assistant editor of the newspaper changed the phrase 'breast-feeding' to 'feeding the children themselves'. When I protested, he said: 'That other phrase is in-delicate.' When I said that his alternative was confusing, and reminded him that lives were at stake, he walked away. 'Feeding the children themselves' it was. The blinds were as thick as that.

But no longer. The old, dreary temples of my day are rusting and tilting and falling. History is respected now, but not worshipped. It is no longer a mortal sin to remove one's eyes for a moment from the saga of the 1916 rebellion to look outwards and ahead. To suggest that Ireland had no more heroes than any other nation no longer leaves one open to a charge of treason. Yet once upon a time, if the sermon from the Celtic Mount was to be believed, there were not enough villains around to make up a poker school.

No more, it seems, need we keep on gouging open our wounds, waving them round our heads and thrusting them in the faces of startled, uninterested foreigners. Cromwell is off the menu. It now is not merely possible to have an Englishman as a friend, but to let one's sister marry him, Anglican faith and all.

The other day, for instance, I was buying a bottle of whiskey in an off-licence. (That 'e' in the operative word, incidentally, is correct. It is dropped only when writing about Scotch or other Irish-type whiskies.) The eighteen-year-old lad who was serving me lapsed immediately and automatically into political chat, which, come to think of it, his English or American counterparts would have been unlikely to do.

'Tell me, Mr Bestic,' he said, 'why were we fighting the British for the past fifty years?'

'That,' I said, 'is a question I used to ask about fifteen years ago and it wasn't very good for my popularity rating.'

'I mean I thought we beat them in 1921,' he went on. 'Shouldn't we have been doing business with them since then?'

It was, I admit, a somewhat over-simplified and not exactly accurate picture of that half-century; but the thought behind it was sound enough.

The most important change of all, however, has come in the Irish attitude to the Irish. We now are inclining to believe that we are almost like other people, warts and all; and we are ready to admit as much to non-Irish, even to emigrants, who have returned temporarily. In my earlier forays back to my native land I used to make the mistake of taking up the conversation more or less where I had dropped it when I was a tax-paying resident. I was an innocent lad. I would trot out my tiny criticisms of this and that and would not notice that the backs of necks were turning puce, that signs of volcanic eruption were rampant.

Then there would be the gush of verbal lava, short, sharp, searing: 'Holy God, you're in London as long as a wet day and you think you can come back and run the country!'

We are less sensitive now. We know we can make mistakes. No longer do we believe what for decades our mentors encouraged us to believe—that God made Ireland first as a sort of prototype world and was so delighted with the result that he produced all the other countries as Mark Two Irelands, only to find that he had botched the job through carelessness or laziness, or an over-confidence that sprang from having achieved perfection too soon.

So much for the revolution—too much, maybe, but my eyes are still out on sticks from staring at the result. So much for the effect; but what about the cause? What has jerked us up to something near maturity after a long, dreary adolescence, addled with emerald-green pimples? There are many factors, of course, but three of the most important, I believe, are television, packaged holiday tours and money.

The first change brought about by television was in the skyline of Dublin. Shrewd salesmen were quick to realize that pictures from wicked British transmitters in Wales could be picked up by Irish saints and scholars, if they planted their aerials on top of towering masts. Soon these masts were sprouting over the neat, prim semi-detacheds of suburbia and over the sprawling blocks of Dublin Corporation housing estates, like naked beanstalks, the grid on top swallowing in and spewing out the alien culture and perhaps chewing away at some of the roots of censorship too. Up they went everywhere, these long, thin poles, even over the pubs, and for a while the conversation, as important as the drink, was hushed, smothered by the cottonwool of 'Gunlaw' and 'The Lucy Show'.

The Irish, in fact, took to television as if it had been invented especially for them. They did not accept it uncritically, however, did not swallow it as a soporific, like a cup of cocoa at bedtime. Even though they paid no licence fees, being removed from British jurisdiction by bloody history, they wrote sharp criticism of the programmes to the B.B.C. and the commercial companies. Nor did they concentrate on horse operas and the frothier funnies. They absorbed the current affairs programmes, the discussions, the news and the interpretation of this news. They saw another world because not even the most conscientious supporter of censorship could go around putting paper bags over the heads of the sets; and they wanted to see more.

The announcement that Ireland was to have its very own television station was not greeted with the rapturous cheers which might have been expected. In the first place it meant the end of the good old days of licence-free viewing. Secondly, the cynical Irish felt that their home-grown programmes would be so pure they would bore a bevy of nuns. There was some basis for this view, for their poor old steam Rádio Éireann had always kept its head bent low for fear of a belt from the crozier. There was little else it could do, of course, because it was shackled by ancient legislation to the Department of Posts and Telegraphs and most civil servants are much holier than bishops.

In 1953 these chains were loosened considerably, though the limbs remained stiff for a while afterwards. The television station—Telefís Éireann, opened in 1960—suffered no such hangover from restraint, however; and for another reason it was more uninhibited from the beginning. Because there were no local experts, foreigners had to be imported to get the wheels turning. These insensitive outsiders were unaccustomed to closed doors and lowered eyes. They went ahead as they would have done in their own countries, which, in fact, were Britain, the United States and Canada; and the Establishment, which, like its sisters elsewhere, loves nothing better than a foreign expert, raised not a murmur.

It may have thought, of course, that once the local lads took over, it could discipline them suitably. If so, it was wrong. The doors were open; the eyes were wide. The local lads and girls, most of them young and enthusiastic, kept them that way. Generally speaking, the home brew, as opposed to the canned import, was excellent, covering subjects which the newspapers had been terrified to touch. It is true that there were protests. The Most Reverend Dr Michael Browne, Bishop of Galway, on one splendid occasion thundered that Telefís Éireann was the spawning-ground for atheistic Communism; but this led to no search for reds beneath the beds of the programme planners. When Father Rom Dodd, now Director of Religious Broadcasts, spoke about homosexuality, some parents complained that the subject was unsuitable for their children. He replied to each of them, saying that, if their children were over twelve, they should have been listening and learning and, if they were under twelve, they should have been in bed at that hour. Nothing dire happened to him, I am happy to report. Far from there being a wild outcry at this brash liberalism, a nationwide plea for protection, there was a chain reaction. Irish newspaper editors, blinking the sand from their eyes, gazed up at television head-quarters and saw to their amazement that it had not been destroyed by thunderbolts. That meant that either the gods' aim was extraordinarily poor—an unlikely theory, as every theologian knows—or that they approved. The newspapermen decided to take a chance, at any rate, and that is why the word 'sex' now can be used in headings by sub-editors.

Packaged holiday tours broadened the vision still further. The Irish already had a great tradition of travel and exploration. A Galway man was said to have been one of Columbus's crew; and even that honour is somewhat tarnished by a firmly held belief that St Brendan, the navigator, discovered America many centuries before Columbus saw the sea. A history of oppression, however, led to an inevitable in-sularity and independence did little to relieve it. While the Englishman despised all foreigners as inferior beings, the Irishman regarded them with some awe because, in the first place, he had not met many, and in the second place, he had a thriving inferiority complex.

Cheap holiday tours, however, soon taught him that Europeans were not that much different from Irish islanders and, incidentally, they led to a hitherto unknown demand for foreign foods and wines in Ireland. The Irishman, unlike the Englishman, does not demand fish and chips abroad. Holidays also nourished the infant notion that other nations had worthwhile ideas, even ideals, even heritages, of which, they had always been taught, Ireland was supposed to have a monopoly.

Neither of these two important developments would have been possible, however, had it not been for the third big change: the arrival of money on the Irish scene. Without money, nobody could have bought television sets or been able to afford holidays abroad even at those cheaper-than-cheap rates. The sight of the stuff hit me minutes after I had set foot again on my native soil. At that time I was still clinging to the quaint old fantasy that everything in general and drink in particular was much cheaper than it was in England. Disillusionment set in with the first large Irish in the airport bar, for it set me back seven shillings. Later I was to learn that Dublin had become one of the more expensive cities in Western Europe, but at that time my only reaction was to wonder how my poor, starving countrymen could afford to drink.

I looked around me. The bar was full. I strained my ears to catch the accents. The majority of them were Irish and, even more surprising, most of the drinkers were young, either in their teens or their early twenties. They were buying all around them, obviously making a night of it; and it was a Thursday night, twelve hours to pay day!

The six-mile drive into the city (Dublin is only a spit away from everything that matters—mountains, sea and the escape hatch of the airport, should the pressures prove too strong) was even more revealing. Cars came at me from all sides—and not just Minis, but great, black, arrogant Mercedes. One of these monsters cut in in front of me and, as I braked hard, I caught myself muttering: 'Where there's Merc, there's brass.'

That drive, incidentally, was a taste of hazards to come. Cars are a necessity in Ireland now, not a luxury, as they were in my day. Unfortunately many Irishmen and women seem bogged in the old horse and carriage era. They drive in the cities as if at any moment they expected to turn a corner and come face to face with a herd of ambling cattle. To someone like myself, geared to the bitter harshness of the British roads, this situation is terrifying. There I knew where I stood and where I died. I had learned from a variety of hair-raising experiences that all Britons, even the mildest, most tolerant of the breed (and of these there are many), become bastards, hard and absolute, once they sat behind a wheel. Pass him on the road and he takes it as a personal insult from a foreign wife-robber. The face contorts. The boot slams down. The joust begins, and too often ends in hospital.

But at least the Briton plays by the rules, not particularly from a sense of duty, but because he loves them and all other laws. He believes, very properly, I suppose, that they are designed to make his life run smoothly; and so he uses his winkers, dips his lights, observes speed limits and would die, roaring, rather than cross a double white line. Anyone who breaks the rules is a cad and deserves to die. Come to think of it, he drives as if he believes that everyone in every other car is a cad and cars in England sometimes stop so that the drivers can get out, stand nose to nose and tell each other so.

This seldom happens in Ireland. If there is a bump or a narrow escape, it is greeted with some hilarity and little ill-feeling. Rules are the children of faceless, long-dead men and as such they should be patted kindly on the head from time to time, but never spoiled. I shall treasure forever the memory of a policeman (officially in Ireland a member of the Garda Síochana, but normally called a guard), dragged in his shirt-sleeves from his dinner in a village by an English tourist who had run into a grass bank. Deeply conscious of the fact that accidents

must be reported, the driver said: 'I came round the bend a little too
sharply and grazed the bank.'

The guard looked at the bank, at the dented wing, at the tourist
with his destroyer escort of a powerful wife and two neat children.

'It's a bad old bank,' he said. 'A lot of cars do hit it.'

For a moment there was silence, while two alien minds shuffled
around in search of common ground. At last the Englishman said:
'Aren't you going to take some notes?' I could see the guard's thoughts
streaking back to the chops and the tinned peas and the potatoes
congealing in his cottage. Courtesy to foreign visitors, no matter
how lunatic, conquered hunger and for a while the guard searched
the pockets of his blue serge trousers, hauling out at last a heap of
old envelopes. With a gentle, hopeful smile, he said to his new guest:
'I suppose you wouldn't have a pin?'

'A pin?'

'A pin. Something to write the notes with.'

The tourist glared at him. Policemen without pens were like stock-
brokers without striped trousers—or any trousers. He whipped the
necessary equipment from an inside pocket, thrust it at the guard and
snapped: 'Be careful of it. It's a Parker 51. Normally I never let anyone
use it.'

Then he began reciting the details of the affair in precise, accident-
reporting language. The guard ground away with the Parker 51 until
the saga ended. Once again there was silence, while they surveyed each
other.

'Well?' said the tourist. 'What are you going to do about it?'

It was a good question. The guard looked down at his grimy, creased
envelopes, frowned as he scrabbled around for some soothing words
to make this quaint, sad man happy, and said at last with a beautiful
smile: 'In due course, I shall make a full report to my superior officers.
And I hope you, your good lady and the children, God bless them, will
have a pleasant journey.'

With that he ambled away in the general direction of the chops.
The Englishman, bouncing with frustration, watched him go in
horror; and then, in a voice shrill with unbelief, shouted: 'Hey! You've
taken my pen!'

The Irish motorist hits banks often enough and makes a fuzzy mental
note to get the old wing mended sometime. He drives happily in the
middle of the road, often at twenty-five miles an hour, and never looks

in the mirror to see if anyone is behind him. He feels a little hurt, if someone blips a horn so that he can pass, but pulls over eventually, sad of face and reluctant. He seldom uses signals and is inclined to be over-come by panic if anyone else does. (Godalmighty, what's that fellah up to!) The dip-switch he regards as an imperfection in the metal and keeps his foot well clear of it. The standard of driving in Ireland, in fact, is diabolical and thorough carnage is avoided only by the fact that when seemingly inevitable death looms, it is chased away by a flash of last-minute, split-second tolerance. However, tolerance does not win all the time. Ireland ranks high in the international accident league table, prepared by the World Health Organization. In the fifteen years up to 1965, it recorded 9 dead and 130 injured for every 100 accidents, coming just behind the league leaders, Poland, which had 11 dead and 93 injured. The order may have changed since then, of course, because many more cars now threaten the Irish roads, signs of a lethal affluence.

Elsewhere, I am happy to say, wealth strikes more gently, though not always pleasantly. I drove down O'Connell Street, psychedelic with a rash of new neon lights, past coffee bars that seemed to have been breeding rapidly since my day, past cinemas (Dublin is said to have the highest film-going population in the world), past new restaurants and across O'Connell Bridge into a maze of bewildering, but sensible, one-way streets, a brave attempt to disentangle a welter of cars in a city built for horse trams. I parked with difficulty and went into a pub that once I had known. I looked for the long bar, but it was gone. Only the outside shell was recognizable, indeed, for the inside had been gutted completely. Here was a new geography, a new aura. There were two or three bars now, flecked with gleaming white coats. Lush carpets snuggled up to each wall and soft, sweet music trickled almost apologetically into the ears, whispering, lest it might offend.

To my surprise, the friend I had arranged to meet was waiting at the bar. Time seldom meant much in Dublin, perhaps because it is such a handy city. Few people mind if someone is late for an appointment. They know they are not being rude deliberately, that they have been held up unavoidably; and they are comfortably confident that they will bump into them anyway somewhere else within the next couple of hours. He greeted me warmly, but quickly. He was doing, he said, a little bit of business, which, in Dublin bar language, means cashing a cheque. He slid it across to the barman, who handed back three fivers and five singles.

'Are you taking off?' I asked. 'Going away somewhere?'

'No. Why?'

'The score. The twenty.'

'Oh, that! No. I'm meeting a couple of people tonight. There'll be nosh and that sort of stuff.'

Suddenly I felt very old and, much worse, very poor. 'I remember the day, Seán,' I said, heavy with cliché, 'when you and I cashed a post-dater for three pounds and split it to carry us over a couple of days.'

He screwed his face into a wealth of age, bent double and said in a quavering falsetto: 'I remember the days, when you could go out with five bob, take a woman to the music hall, have a few scoops, a packet of fags, a horse cab home *. . . and* have change!'

Freely translated, that meant: 'You've been away . . .'

A dark-suited, yellow-faced man with an apologetic walk and a badge in his lapel to show that he had forsworn the demon drink, sidled up to us, selling black-bordered pictures of John and Robert Kennedy. A barman hustled him out, but not half quickly enough for me. I was glad to see Dublin making money, but surely it had not become all that important. We turned back to the bar and Seán ordered a pint of Red Barrel. Here was another change—English draught beer in an Irish pub, where once the pipes would have got themselves knotted if anything but Guinness had flowed through them. When I mentioned as much to Seán, he handed me a copy of the *Irish Times*, open at the page devoted to parliamentary reports. I read:

On the section providing for taxes on beers, Mr T. Mullins inquired why foreign beers were sold in Irish pubs at the same price as home-produced beers. He said that home-produced beers were giving employment to Irish workers in Irish factories and it seemed strange that imported beers should be available at the same price.

Mr Haughey, Minister for Finance, said he understood that the publicans were anxious to maintain the status of Irish beers and for that reason did not sell them any cheaper than the foreign beers. This was purely an excess of patriotism on the part of publicans, who would not like the public to hold Irish beer in any less esteem than foreign beer.

I read it twice. Then I said: 'Was he joking? Does he really mean that Dublin dockers would feel their nation had been slighted, if they were charged twopence less for an Irish pint?'

'I don't know,' said Seán. 'But that class of patriotism obviously pays. A pub that was bought for £15,000 a few years back sold for

£80,000 the other day.' He dug in his pockets and produced a cutting. The heading was: 'Publican Can't Earn Reasonable Living—Hardship for Thousands.' Beneath it was a report of a speech by A. J. Pinkerton, President of the Irish National Vintners' Federation, in which he said: "Thousands of publicans and their families are living on a starvation wage . . .'

That made me feel better. The old place had not really changed so much after all. Its contradictions had never been healthier. I thought of the Irishman with the thousand Irishmen fighting to get out from inside him; and then I thought of the poor, starving publican with his barefoot children, fighting to get out of his pub, even if it meant accepting a pittance of £80,000.

A few of my more prickly fellow-countrymen may criticize me for letting this chapter spend too much time in a pub. They get angry (and I get bored) with the constantly recurring picture in foreign print of the drunken Irishman, maintaining correctly that we have given more to the world than street fights and hangovers. Nevertheless, drink-shops everywhere are the barometer of a nation's economy; and in Ireland today few pubs are cold through lack of customers.

There are other barometers, particularly in Dublin. The newsboy who sold me my evening paper was well-dressed and gave me my change quickly. A few years back he would have been wearing hand-me-downs and would have searched hopelessly and hopefully for the change in the belief that the customer might get tired of waiting and walk away. Who could blame him? Then there were beggars, casual, poor. Now there are only the fully paid up, card-carrying professionals, who clutter the streets and earn a good income. Then wages lasted from Friday until Tuesday. Now I sit in Bewley's Café in Westmoreland Street, red plush seats, and warm, dark wood, defiant in the face of the chrome and Cona brigade and I hear a young girl say to her friend: 'I got that frock for the dance—the twenty-five quid one. Daddy'll be raging.'

But will he? Daddy has money now. He is spending it, admittedly, like a drunken sailor, but who is to blame him? After all, it has not been around before—at least not for seven or eight hundred years. How has it appeared so quickly and in such quantities? That is a complicated story, stuffed with contradictions and brightened here and there by a bit of a minor miracle. If you are sitting comfortably, I shall do my best to explain it as painlessly as possible.

FOR a very long time certain sections of the Irish people held that everything green was splendid and everything foreign was either shoddy, corrupting or fattening. To suggest otherwise was plain unpatriotic, akin to inviting the British back or quoting the thoughts of Mao in church and/or in the Irish language.

In 1932 Éamon de Valéra's newly elected Government seemed to indicate that it subscribed to this theory. It ruled that fifty-one per cent of the capital of every Irish company must be held by an Irish citizen. These citizens had to have a majority on the board of directors. So far as international investors were concerned, Ireland was a closed shop.

A quarter of a century later the shop was in a shambles. Unemployment was appalling and businesses were closing because there were not enough people with money to buy their goods. Over 40,000 young men and women were emigrating every year, a savagely wounding loss to a nation with a population of under 3,000,000.

The Irish were sour with apathy and cynicism.

Then de Valéra, who had always hinted that Ireland should remain slightly aloof from commercialism, materialism and the ugly, mass-produced, plastic way of life, retired from active politics. He was elected President, a suitable honour indeed for a man who had fought so hard, so long and on so many fronts.

Seán Lemass, his deputy and a much younger man, became head of the Government. Very soon afterwards, green became much like any other colour, a matter of choice rather than compulsion. The industrial policy was reversed. Foreign firms were invited to set up business in Ireland. They were enticed to do so, indeed, by offers of factory sites and new buildings, a rich source of labour, grants and alluring tax concessions on all money they made by exporting.

The foreigners rose to these tasty baits. Britons, Germans, Americans, Dutch, Italians, French, Belgians, Swiss, Danes, South Africans, Canadians, Finns, Austrians, Japanese and Monégasque—they all surfaced in this calm, clear pond. Ireland, which had been very near the point of no return, began its revival.

The cynics—there still were plenty of them around—said, of course, that the Government had been forced to abandon its disastrous policy of protection by the sour fruits of its utter failure. Had it not taken drastic evasive action, it would have been left with nobody to govern. The churches would have been empty, and the pulpits, too. Even the clerks in the labour exchanges—and that had been a good, steady job for years in Ireland—would have been away, digging up roads in Kilburn or serving up drinks in Manhattan. Ireland would have been upended on the world.

Seán Lemass, naturally enough, denied these inevitable allegations. Today he still denies them, though he is free from the responsibility of office, having retired for a reason which many world leaders might contemplate. In his room at Leinster House, where the Irish Parliament in which he now is a back-bencher sits, he told me: 'I'm sixty-eight. A man of my years cannot think five years ahead; and to do anything less is futile.'

Thinking five years ahead, rebuilding a sagging country seems to have kept him fit, for he certainly does not look his age. He is a chunky man, with a quick, unexpected smile and an ability to bite on his words while retaining an affable charm. Nor did he sound his age, when I asked him whether he had been forced into scuttling old policies.

'We were not forced to do anything,' he told me. 'Ours was a classic example of industry everywhere. Our industry was protected and then stripped of tariffs to meet the stress of competition. Outside Britain, that has been the normal method of development. By the end of the war it was obvious that we had gone as far as we could in the development of industry for the home market. From then on it would have to be based on the export market.

'It was recognition of that fact that led to the change of policy and to invitations to foreign companies to participate with their capital. In the circumstances then and to a certain extent now, the advantage was not so much bringing know-how and capital into the country, but making available established markets and marketing methods.'

Was there no other way for this comparatively young nation, so jealous of its independence? Could this know-how not have been hired? Could capital not have been raised by recalling the millions which Irish people have invested abroad?

'Capital,' said Seán Lemass, 'was the last of our worries. We had to back it with technical know-how and certainly we could have hired that; but the main advantage of foreign participation has been easy access to export markets. Most companies coming in have had markets which they couldn't supply from their home-based plants. Many have had orders stretching twelve months or two years ahead.'

Just how vital it was to get those orders was made very clear to me later by George Colley, Minister for Industry and Commerce and the man responsible for keeping all the new machinery moving. He spelt out the situation, facing the country and the Government; and certainly it was frightening.

'We had vast unemployment and emigration,' he told me. 'It was bad enough to watch young people leaving because they had no jobs. It was much worse to see men with jobs taking their families out of the country, losing faith. Our job was to stop that rot. Had we attempted to do so alone, it might have taken us fifty years, a hundred years; and by that time there might have been nobody left.'

Whether the Government jumped according to plan, or was pushed by circumstances, however, is of only academic interest now. Its policy has worked with high drama.

Emigration has dived from a peak of nearly 50,000 in 1958 to about 12,000 for 1967, the latest figure available.

Exports have soared in eleven years from £131,000,000 to a record £365,000,000, about £1,000,000 a day. In the last year the rate of growth was three times that of the rest of the world.

Most important of all, apathy has disappeared, and cynicism, of which the Irish have a secret hoard hidden from the world, is withering. Wherever I went throughout the country, I sniffed in the air a tang of vitality that I had never known before. In Galway I found men in their early twenties, buying houses and getting married . . . this in a city where once a bachelor of forty was still a lad. One of the older workers said: 'I remember when it was all we could afford to take a girl to the pictures on a Saturday night.'

They work for a typical new industry, Steinbock, producing fork-lift trucks. Originally it was German, but in 1967 it was taken over by an American company. When they started in Galway in 1960, they had no skilled labour. They took thirty lads, mostly small farmers' sons, from the local technical school and sent them to Germany for three months' basic training. Then they sent another batch . . . and another. For a while most of the foremen were Germans. Now there is only one left, Joe Hoerhammer, and he has stayed because he has become almost as Irish as the Irish.

What are the earnings like? The works manager told me: 'Our welders are taking home £20 to £25 a week. Basic wage on the night shift is £20, plus bonus, and that could range from twenty to thirty-five per cent. I don't think they could get better jobs in England. We get a lot of applications from England, in fact, and I'm not surprised.

When I worked in Stafford fifteen years ago, I was better off by far than I would have been in Ireland; but you can't compare the conditions there and here now.'

Quite a few of the Steinbock workers have returned from England. They confirmed all that the works manager said; and the chief shop steward provided a further piece of interesting information. 'We have excellent relations with the management,' he said. 'In fact we're a closed shop here.'

Most important of all, however, was the air of enthusiasm. This was something new for me to find; and it was infectious, spreading all over the city.

George Colley had told me: 'For too long it had become an Irish tradition to moan and cry for help to whatever Government was in power. We wanted to encourage people to work, to have confidence in themselves; and we believed they would do so, if they saw what foreigners could do.'

In Galway again I saw the fruits of that theory. Seven young businessmen, seeing what foreigners could do, decided they would start an industry for themselves and for the city in that order—the right order. At that moment they had no idea what they were going to make, though they agreed that it must not only provide jobs and skills for local people, but use a high percentage of Irish materials, too. They discussed and rejected scores of ideas before they settled on crystal glass, because about seventy-five per cent of its value was in the workmanship. At that time all they knew about glass was that it came in shapes which held drink more efficiently than did cupped hands.

So they went to Stourbridge, near Birmingham, the heart of the British glass industry, to pick as many brains as possible; but the Stourbridgians saw them coming and left no brains lying about.

'At last this old man took pity on us,' Séamus Kavanagh, one of the directors, told me. 'He took us into a pub called the Stewponey and gave us all the contacts we needed. Then we advertised for skilled men among the Irish workers in England, offering them more money than they would get there. We had to pay top prices for skill because the customer was going to pay top prices for the result. After that we went to Canada and North America and sorted ourselves out a few markets in Montreal, Los Angeles and New York. Then to London, where we got Harrods interested.

'By that time we had chosen our first design. We had come across this old Galway goblet in wood. It not only looked right, but had a cut which could be reproduced in glass. Now we have seven designs and in a couple of years we will have ten. We have exhibited in Toronto and London and we are exporting to North America, Australia, Iceland, England and Italy. We still pay the highest wages in the business, either here or in Britain, because we have the best men and we want to keep them.'

I feel sure they will, because these seven young men, who continue to run their own businesses, incidentally, have all sniffed that new tang in the Irish air. That I discovered the first morning I met them. It was a Saturday. I telephoned and suggested that we should meet on Monday. Séamus Kavanagh said: 'What are you doing today?'

I was doing nothing. We had lunch together and then I was taken out to the factory, a reconditioned dance-hall. It was in full production at four o'clock in the afternoon with skilled men and young apprentices at work. That was unusual enough. More remarkable still was the fact that three directors took me on my conducted tour, and in the Galway that I knew fifteen years ago, that would have been unbelievable. Directors of any company then would have been playing golf on a Saturday or sailing, or gardening, or at a race meeting, or in Dublin, seeing friends, or swimming, or drinking. To have been working would have been regarded as a mortal sin of such a calibre that only the Bishop himself could have given absolution from it.

When I asked Séamus Kavanagh, for instance, whether there would have been seven men in Galway fifteen years ago with the resources to start such an enterprise, he said: 'Yes. But they wouldn't have done it.'

This line of thought, this new attitude of mind has not just happened, however. It has been created by Seán Lemass, always a shrewd psychologist. 'National apathy was a big problem,' he told me. 'Our first job was to draw up a plan of action, what we called our first programme for economic expansion to cover the years from 1959 to 1963: and we had apathy in mind when we set our targets. We announced that we were striving for an economic growth of two per cent. We knew we could do much better than that, but we knew, too, that public morale would suffer if we set a higher target and failed to keep it.

'In fact we got about four per cent growth. That helped to remove the despondency which existed and convinced people, too, that we could do better. It also convinced quite a few foreign investors that we were offering a sound proposition.'

The Irish, indeed, basically a peasant society, began to behave as if they had been born with silver capstan lathes in their mouths. What matter, they said, if the nearest they had been to a machine was the seat of a tractor? If other human beings could work these factories, so could they—and better.

They meant it; and they did it. One farm labourer, straight from the fields, was hired by an American engineering firm that had opened at Shannon. Within six months his employers flew him to America to show the home team how he had achieved his high rate of production.

That man provided one reason why George Colley, speaking to a group of American businessmen, said: 'The easy-going Irishman of stage and screen is long since dead. We want you to help us lay his ghost.'

Older Irish industries caught the fever, or perhaps I should say that they attended the wake. Irish Ropes sent their salesmen half a million miles round and round the world, and as a result were able to announce that they were exporting ninety-five per cent of one of their major lines—Tintawn, a floor covering. They also exported lariats to California, which adds a nice exotic touch to a firm whose principal customers once were local fishermen.

Guinness, the largest private employer in the country and the biggest brewery in Europe, carried the battle into enemy territory. In 1963 it opened a brewery at Ikeja near Lagos, Nigeria. In 1966 the Prime Minister of Malaysia officially opened another at Sungei Way near Kuala Lumpur. In addition, its product is brewed now under contract in Australia, New Zealand, South Africa, East Africa, Canada, Trinidad and Sierra Leone; and they would love dearly to get into China, for they have discovered from their sales in Hong Kong that the Chinese can shift more Guinness per head than Dublin dockers. Should they succeed in infiltrating, they may have to tone down their famous 'Guinness Means Strength' advertisement in view of the high birth rate there. In many countries, this simple legend is taken to be a hint that the fine, old brew is an aphrodisiac; and the increased sales that have resulted are still baffling the brilliant copy-writer, who never let such a thought sully his mind for a moment.

Waterford Glass, Limited, revitalized in 1950 by the late Joe McGrath, founder of the Irish Sweep, ex-Cabinet Minister and one of Ireland's few millionaires, increased its staff from fifty to 1,100 with an average age of twenty-three, and collected orders for many years to come from all parts of the world.

Waltham Electronics of Long Lane, Dublin, made a cheeky raid into real whizz-kid country and got an order for clocks from Japan, which turns out 20,000,000 of the damn things herself every year.

In Connemara, Lord Mayo was mining for marble and exporting ninety per cent of what he landed, some of it going to Italy, which was another neat piece of market poaching. In the fashion world, Irish designers were busy and in 1968 clothing exports from Ireland were worth nearly £12,000,000, compared with under £1,000,000 ten years earlier. The joint, in fact, was jumping so vigorously that Córas Trachtála, the semi-State body which advises manufacturers and does a polished job promoting exports generally, drew up the following list of strange items which were flowing outwards from Ireland.

Whiskey to Czechoslovakia, biscuits to Iceland, writing paper to Western Samoa, cakes to West Germany, hormones to the U.S.S.R., cookers to Afghanistan, fork-lift trucks to Mexico, metal manufactures to Malawi, skim milk to the Bahamas, tyres and tubes to Guiana, sewing machines to the U.S.A., telecommunication apparatus to Yugoslavia, soap to Australia, pins and needles to Iran, wallets to Nigeria, ropes to Sierra Leone, gloves to Bermuda, paintings to Israel, aluminium to Kenya, seaweed to Italy, nails to India, kettles to Egypt, day-old chicks to Jordan, dog food to Norway, soup to Zambia, glue to New Zealand, dehydrated vegetables to Malaysia, twine to Finland, building materials to Hong Kong, nightwear (nice, coy phrase, that) to Malta, scientific instruments to Kuwait, musical instruments to Venezuela, smoking pipes to Spain, rosaries to the Philippines, pens to South Africa, barytes to Saudi Arabia, peat to the Canary Islands, organic chemicals to Uruguay, ornaments to China, weighing scales to Burma, fencing wire to Ceylon, transformers to South Vietnam, soft drinks to Mauritius, sugar to Sierre Leone, T.V. sets to Uganda, liqueur to Taiwan, butter to Bahrein, cigarettes to Kuwait, locks to Iraq, radios to Switzerland, non-electrical machinery to Bolivia, typewriters to Rumania and veneers to East Germany.

To that I can add that Ireland exported antibiotics to America, wool to the Arabs, books to Thailand, whiskey to the Virgin Islands, sports goods to Japan, Donegal tweed and computers to the Soviet Union and fish to Italy. The first shipment of this last item, I regret to say, went out unrefrigerated. Some exporters were in such a hurry that they had to learn the hard way about the hazards.

The really interesting items, however, were those which went to the Soviet Union, for these represented not only welcome foreign trade, but a major change in thought. For years the Irish were taught that, while all non-green colours were not good, red was positively evil. Communism was mentioned generally in the language of the late Joe McCarthy; and on one unhappy occasion, the Archbishop of Dublin, the Most Reverend Dr McQuaid, forbade Catholics to attend a football match at Dalymount Park, Dublin, between Ireland and Communist Yugoslavia. It was as bad as that, though some encouragement was drawn from the fact that several thousand people ignored the ban.

At the beginning of the industrial resurrection, therefore, it was a hazardous operation to be overheard speaking to the wicked Kremlin men, let alone to be suspected of taking their tainted gold. This I know to be true, because when a journalist friend of mine went to Moscow with a cultural delegation, friends crossed the road to avoid and ostracize his wife, while strangers crossed in the other direction so that they could abuse and threaten her.

Despite this unhappy state of affairs, however, Córas Trachtála decided that its function was to sell Irish goods abroad, and it didn't matter a damn about politics or religion; and with commendable courage they set about doing so in Europe's Eastern bloc. They were not foolhardy about it, of course. They were, after all, a semi-State body, subsidized by the taxpayers. So they decided that their mission to Moscow would have to be secret.

An ex-official told me: 'We sent them winging on their way with a decade of the rosary in Irish. Then we said another in the hope that the Irish newspapers would not pick up their scent.

'They were out of luck. Reuter's man in Moscow picked up the story and sent it back. Immediately the Irish newspapers got onto our head office, demanding to know whether this dreadful news was true; and our hierarchy, I must say, played it very coolly indeed. They made a stiff little announcement, confirming the basic fact that now was known, anyway, and added: "A further statement will be made in due course."

'Then they sat back and did nothing; and for some strange reason, the Press did nothing further, either. It must have been the decade of the rosary in Irish that stayed their hands.'

Unfortunately, the mission, which ran so many risks, did no business. They were lucky, indeed, that they did not end up festooned with unwanted balalaikas, for the Soviets were keen on a bit of barter. Their reception was cordial and they were somewhat shattered to find that their hosts not only knew a great deal about Irish trade, but had provided an Irish interpreter in case any of their guests had little Russian or English.

Apart from the rather important fact that neither side wanted to buy and both wanted to sell, there was one point on which the delegations differed. The Soviets said with supreme politeness: 'We know all about your oil refinery at Whitegate, of course, and know why it is there.'

The Irish delegation raised inquiring eyebrows. They had been under the impression that it was for refining oil, but obviously that view was not shared. So they probed a bit in English and Irish (the interpreter turned out to be excellent in both) and were told: 'That refinery is three times too big for your own needs. Obviously you are going to use it for refuelling the American fleet.'

Ireland, however, was doing all right without setting up fuel stations for passing committed nations, no matter how friendly. Not alone were export orders rolling in, but ideas were busting out all over. The trouble here was that the country was still not geared for the reception of ideas, probably because not many had been hatched in earlier days— at least not in the cause of commerce.

As a result of this flaw in the machinery, she nearly lost business worth one and a half million dollars and, worse still, could have lost the man responsible for this little coup, an industrial chemist called Brian McCarthy.

McCarthy had spent three years, and £4,000 of his own money, working on a revolutionary industrial sealing process in his kitchen-sink laboratory in Dublin. When finally he achieved success, he tried to exploit his invention. Nobody, however, wanted to know about it. Particularly uninterested were the banks, who refused to help him raise the £20,000 he needed for premises and machinery and the further £3,000 that would be necessary to investigate the export market. Finally he was lucky enough to meet Ben Briscoe, a Dublin T.D. (Member of Parliament), who took him straight to George Colley, Minister for Industry and Commerce. Colley, who had been scouring the country for ideas such as this, saw that it worked, though he did not know how, and started yelling for action.

'This man had been given the run around,' he told me. 'British and

American firms tried to break down his formula, but they haven't been able to do it. Now he has signed a ten-year contract, worth a million and a half dollars, with the Phillip Morris Company. Other companies have offered him even more to buy the idea outright, but he has turned it down.'

With all this activity, emigration was bound to slump. Better still, skilled Irishmen began returning from England as the news of the boom began drifting from relatives across the Irish Sea. That, of course, was the one of the ultimate objects of the exercise, but on two occasions it paid dividends which not even Seán Lemass or George Colley had anticipated. The first occasion arose when Jack Mulcahy of Dungarvan, Co. Waterford, returned to Ireland, which he had left in something of a hurry about forty-five years earlier. Like many another man of his era, he had taken the anti-Government side in the civil war which followed the Treaty with Britain; and because of this, he had deemed it wiser to get out of the country fast.

He went to America, where he was immensely successful in business. When he returned to Ireland a few years ago he started a factory in Cork, producing linings for steel furnaces, a process for which he held world patent rights and therefore a very firm grip on the world market. Meanwhile, his main business in America continued to flourish. It grew so big, indeed, that Pfizer, the international drug company, wanted to buy it in a multi-million dollar deal.

Jack Mulcahy agreed to sell, but he made one important condition: he wanted Pfizer to set up a factory in Ireland, he said; and, if they did not do so, he would charge them an extra four and a half million dollars. Pfizer agreed, and the deal could not have come at a better time. Earlier the Arthur D. Little organization of Cambridge, Massachusetts, in a report commissioned by Ireland's Industrial Development Authority, had confirmed in strong words a growing suspicion that Ireland would have to have much larger industries with a high capital and technological content if she were to consolidate her position and expand at a worthwhile rate.

'Pfizer was the first breakthrough in this direction,' Colley told me. 'Others are on the way. One deal like that leads to another, for the word gets around. People talk throughout the world about prospects in Ireland and in that way we get what I suppose could be called unsolicited testimonials.'

The second occasion, which merited a bonfire being lit for a returned emigrant, was the arrival in the Republic of Pat Hughes, a miner. As a youngster he had emigrated to Canada, worked as a labourer and then headed north to the Arctic Circle, where he prospected very successfully for uranium. Profits on this venture he increased substantially on the Canadian Stock Exchange; and, when he returned more or less for a holiday in Ireland in the fifties, he was, like Jack Mulcahy, scarcely short of a crust.

While there, he began to browse over old mineral surveys of Ireland and the country's mining records which went back to prehistoric days. His interest was inspired partly by sentiment, partly by the fact that the subject fascinated him, and partly—to what extent he is not quite sure himself—because he felt that there might be commercial possibilities there. The Government, at any rate, was offering even greater tax concessions to mining interests than it granted to other industry.

His reading, his experience and, perhaps, an instinct developed in the rough, bleak mining areas of northern Canada, told him that he was onto a worthwhile proposition. He contacted three Irishmen with whom he had mined in Saskatchewan—Matt Kilroy from Fermanagh, Michael McCarthy from Skibbereen in Co. Cork and Joe McParland from Newry. Together they formed a company called Irish Base Metals, and began a survey with the most modern equipment and methods ever used in Europe.

It was six years before they found anything worthwhile; and that discovery was due, not to the old documents, not to their joint experience, not to their miners' instincts, but to a legend, the legend of Tynagh in Co. Galway. For as long as anyone could remember, it had been said that once there had been a lead mine there. People pointed vaguely to the spot, but knew no more; and that was unusual, for traditionally stories of old workings are handed down in picturesque detail from father to son.

Pat Hughes and his partners, however, decided to take a chance. They sent their experts to the spot that had been shown to them by the local people; and they found quite abnormal amounts of zinc, copper and silver.

That was in 1961. They drew up a development scheme which was to cost £4,000,000, and borrowed the money from a variety of sources—Belgian, German and French smelters, British metal agents, Toronto investment houses. By spreading the load, they kept a controlling interest themselves. The Tynagh mine, based on a legend, did not go into production until 1965; but in two years it produced enough to enable them to pay back every cent they had borrowed.

Today more silver comes out of Tynagh than from any other mine in Europe; and it sells on the international market at a pound an ounce. About half a dozen groups now operate in the country, some so big that they can plunge ten or fifteen million pounds into a project without feeling pain. Pat Hughes finds their presence satisfying. He had not been able to make up his mind whether sentiment had outweighed knowledge in his case. Now he knows, for green tears do not spring easily to the eyes of the other experts who have joined him in the field.

Other mining centres have sprung up at Gortdrum and Silvermine in Co. Tipperary, Moate in Offaly, Keel in Longford. Exports jumped from £16,000 in 1965 to £4,600,000 in 1967 and by 1970 they will have topped the £10,000,000 mark—more than the combined export earnings of whiskey and stout. That makes the Government happy, for their royalty percentage increases as the profit of the companies increases; and Ireland soon will be the fourth largest producer of lead and the third largest of zinc in Europe.

The employment content of this new industry is important, too. At present over a thousand men work in mining and, indirectly, it provides jobs for another 6,000. The little port of Foynes, a transatlantic flying boat base which saw its dream of prosperity die when land planes took over, is flourishing again now, for the ores are being exported from its harbour to France and Germany.

This boisterous industrial expansion inevitably has reached into virtually every corner of the country, sometimes imposing a heavy strain on local resources, as well as bringing benefits. One large organization which has had to adapt fast to cope with the revolution, is Córas Iompair Éireann, the nationalized transport company which handles all road and rail services. When Foynes was chosen as the port for the mine at Silvermine, for instance, C.I.E. were asked not only to carry the ore, but to build a railway. They did so. Similar requests came from a fertilizer factory in Wicklow and a cement factory in Limerick. They, too, were met.

Rapidly increasing exports, of course, impose a constant strain on C.I.E. resources, but so far they have lived up to their boast that they can move anything, anywhere, any time. This courage under fire must have impressed the new industrial immigrants, particularly if they had preconceived ideas of Irish trains bogged down for days by a cow on a grass-choked track.

The effort is particularly commendable in view of the fact that the rolling stock at the end of the war was just about ready to heave a sigh and die. Neutrality had been rough on it, for Ireland had been cut off from normal fuel supplies and Irish engines staggered from point to point, their firemen keeping steam up by using anything that burned, right down to railwaymen's tool sheds that they passed on the way. Journeys were a nightmare and the misery record was set by one Cork to Dublin 'express', which took forty-eight hours to cover the 161 miles and arrived only with the aid of eighteen separate engines.

After the war, these old warriors were pensioned off and C.I.E. became the first railway in Europe to go completely diesel; and, as if to make amends for the harsh treatment the fuel crisis forced them to deal. out in the bad days, they began operating a service which must be the envy of many a bigger railway, British Rail included. They organized a punctuality control service which conducted an on-the-spot inquiry if a main line train was even a couple of minutes late. As a result, ninety-eight per cent of them are on time, which puts C.I.E. at the top of the World Punctuality League.

Then, to meet the needs of the new, high-speed businessman, they inaugurated fast inter-city services, which enabled him to travel to most important parts of the country, do a day's work and return the same night. It was, however, what began to happen to him while he was on the train, that really set a new standard. First-class passengers could have their meals in their seats. As the train drew out, a public address system gave a brief résumé of the journey ahead, much as an airline hostess does at the beginning of a flight. Whenever a train slowed for signals or any other impediment, the reason was explained to the passengers. All stations, of course, were called out clearly.

These announcements, which soothe many a nerve, are made by another new C.I.E. ornament, their hostesses, attractive girls with nursing experience and usually a foreign language. Their job is to smooth the wrinkles out of the journey and this they achieve with a quiet skill. They get bottles for babies, change their nappies and look after them while mothers go off for a meal. They explain the passing countryside to strangers, pointing out places of interest, and advise about accommodation at the end of the journey. On occasions and in dire emergencies, they sew on buttons.

Tourism is another chore on the long C.I.E. agenda. They take thousands of visitors throughout the country in special trains, equipped with loud-speakers and a studio coach, from which requests are played. Passengers are invited to the studio, if they feel like singing or being interviewed. These trains are used, too, for bingo excursions and for pilgrimages, when the spiritual director goes into the studio and leads his flock in the Rosary.

A fleet of a hundred luxury coaches operates cheap, all-in tours with overnight stops at C.I.E. hotels. These tours have been extended now to Britain, are highly successful and create what I, personally, regard as a uniquely hilarious situation. These Irish coaches do the entire tourist run in Britain, carrying foreigners (with maybe a few Irish among them) from Buckingham Palace to Edinburgh Castle and beyond.

Drivers and couriers have done courses on English history, archaeology and points of interest, which have left them knowing probably more about all three than most Britons. Yet surely the highlight of each of these tours must be the moment when an Irish Republican, voice suitably muted in the shadow of a Royal Palace, is explaining the past glories of imperialist Britain to an American Republican.

When the season is over, the couriers go back to punching tickets as conductors of Dublin buses. They must have some rare old tales to tell, when they reach the towering housing estates of Ballyfermot!

' "Now lookit here, Your Majesty," says I . . .'

3 COMMERCE

'IF there is one vice the Irish really abhor,' Brendan Behan said to me once, 'it is that of success. They think it's a mortal sin the size of a cartwheel.'

He knew what he was saying, this generous, decent man, though as usual, when he was serious, he put a comic coat on it. Sensitive and easily wounded, he could never understand the begrudgers, as he called them, the little people who tried to detract from his talent, who wriggled with thin, mean sneers when his work was acclaimed abroad.

He would not be surprised to know that they still are at it. Whenever I praised him in Dublin recently, all present agreed, of course; and then they stained their anaemic tribute with dark, dreary qualifications.

'I suppose he had talent, or so they say, anyway,' said a writer. 'But what did he ever write?'

'*Borstal Boy*,' I said. 'A fine and tolerant book.'

'That? Sure, that was only an autobiography!'

I did not bother to tell him that an autobiography is, perhaps, the most difficult task a writer can attack. It would have been no use, for here was a typical example of the Irish at work on such subjects.

We love a decent failure and will walk a hundred miles to help him; but God protect from our venom our fellow-countryman who has it made.

It is because of this jaundiced streak in our character that so many thrusting, new factories are condemned with faint praise: 'It's doing fine, I know. I hope it lasts.' It is surprising, therefore, to find that one organization that has proved its worth to the world has been taken without reservation to normally grudging Irish hearts.

That organization is Aer Lingus, which was succeeding quietly for a long time before the others even started trying. Like C.I.E., its burden grows as the new Ireland expands. In industrial freight alone, it carries many thousands of tons; but that is only the ultimate responsibility of the company, the end product of a complex and sophisticated international operation. Aer Lingus, indeed, is not just a national airline, but a unique part of the national fabric. Its officials do more than sell tickets; throughout the world they do a great deal to obliterate the image of the easygoing Irishman of stage and screen, whose ghost George Colley very properly is anxious to lay.

Normally these achievements would be enough to send the Irish in search of the vitriol; not, come to think of it, that we ever have to look much further than our tongues. Instead, most people are not merely proud of their airline, but are glad to say so, perhaps because it was the first major enterprise they could show to the world without a twinge of self-consciousness. They knew it, of course, when it was a baby thirty-two years ago, with one five-seater plane, one route to Bristol, a staff of twelve, a tin hut for the passengers at Baldonnel military airfield, Dublin, and a tin biscuit box to hold spare parts.

They know it now as a major international airline, which carries 1,500,000 passengers a year, has a staff of 5,000, and has made a profit of £1,000,000 in two successive years. It is growing so fast, indeed, that the profit must be boosted soon to £5,000,000 to service loans, which, in the airline business, grow heavier with success and expanding fleets.

How has this extraordinary child grown so big and strong under our very eyes? I believe that it has happened because that first staff, one dozen strong, and all those who have followed them understood a few words spoken many years ago by Dr Jerry Dempsey, the first general manager.

'Never disdain profit,' he said, 'but always remember that it is no more than a by-product of service.'

The Irish are good at service, anyway, provided it means simply making people happy and at ease. Aer Lingus have made a particular study of the theme and that is why they are strongly resisting attempts by other airlines to introduce a bus-service element into flying. They have a slightly higher ratio of hostess to passenger than other airlines, for instance; and they have no stewards. Most people—women included—prefer to have pretty girls looking after them; so let them have pretty girls, say Aer Lingus. I have noticed, incidentally, that the Irish hostess always looks happy in her job, delighted to help, though at times her feet must be killing her. That brave front, in my view, is a priceless asset.

It certainly seems to pay dividends, this emphasis on service. Unlike the airlines of other small countries, Aer Lingus no longer relies on its own ethnic stream. When first it began its transatlantic service, for instance, ninety-five per cent of the customers were either Irish or Irish-American. The remainder flew Aer Lingus merely because they could not find room with one of the big boys. Today, however, only half the transatlantic passengers have an Irish background. The rest come from the sophisticated international jet set and they fly Aer Lingus because they prefer to do so. Somehow the company staff have managed to wind themselves round a large number of hearts, which normally are chromium-plated against such guiles; and this was made very clear recently when an Aer Lingus plane crashed. For weeks Michael Dargan, the General Manager, one of a forceful new breed of Irish executives, was receiving letters of sympathy from all parts of the world.

It is difficult to find any other reason for such a widespread display of concern without going back to Jerry Dempsey's few words about profit and service. I do not imagine, however, that members of the Aer Lingus staff will bother to look any further, anyway. Over the year they have the highest load factor of any airline on the North Atlantic route. In winter, where once they bled to death, to use the words of one of their New York staff, they now make a profit because they hire part of their fleet of Boeings to Trans-Caribbean Airlines, thus ensuring that none of their highly valuable equipment rusts on the ground. Aer Lingus pioneered this type of deal, incidentally, and now others are trying to emulate it.

The full impact of the company, however, probably is not realized even by the Irish. So influential has it become in international circles that on one occasion it was able to borrow money when its own Government had been refused. Jack Lynch, the present Prime Minister, was Minister for Finance at the time. He went to the Export-Import Bank of America for a loan of £5,000,000 and was turned down. Aer Lingus, like most other airlines, borrows from this bank to pay the aircraft manufacturers. It had been loaned £5,000,000 to pay debts which were not quite due. So it handed it over to the Exchequer until it needed it—and in the meantime charged interest on it!

This type of manoeuvre Aer Lingus personnel carry through with an easy charm which other airlines in general and one B.O.A.C. pilot in particular now know hides a lethal efficiency. The B.O.A.C. pilot had taken off from New York about ten minutes after an Aer Lingus International Boeing, piloted by Captain Dick Quinn. Quinn was fairly well known on the route, for not only did he play a ukelele during quiet moments over the Atlantic, but he had a fan club on the weather ships below, for they listened to his music on their radios.

About three-quarters of an hour after take-off, the B.O.A.C. plane overtook the Aer Lingus Boeing at the usual separation of two thousand feet. The Captain called up Quinn on the radio and said: 'You're a bit slow, Paddy. Having trouble?'

'No trouble,' Quinn crackled back, laying down his ukelele for a moment. 'Just a full load.'

Somehow or other, this piece of comedy appeared in a British newspaper. The following day an irate reader, commenting upon it, asked: 'Why must B.O.A.C. lose millions, when little Aer Lingus can make a profit?' That week a similar question was tabled in the House of Commons. The cross-talk about that comic little transatlantic interlude went on in fact, for quite a while. It was reported fairly fully and soon afterwards Aer Lingus made news again, this time by cutting itself a slice of purely British cake. It began operating charter flights from England to New York, carrying, among others, the Bootle Bingo Club, who played all the way over. Whether they chose Aer Lingus because they wanted to listen to Captain Quinn's ukelele-flavoured wit, or whether they had decided that the Irish airline had the edge on others so far as efficiency was concerned, is anybody's guess.

I doubt if even Aer Lingus know the answer to that one, though they can handle most air business questions these days, having successfully married computers to Celtic psychology. Already they are planning well into the late seventies, drafting a programme which will cost millions and which would have appeared out of the question five years ago. By the end of this year, their entire fleet will be jet. By next year, they will have acquired a couple of Boeing Jumbo jets and will be in a position to ferry thousands of passengers a day to and fro across the Atlantic. At present, during the summer, they carry 1,800. With the other end of the decade in mind, they have put a deposit on a couple of Boeing supersonic aircraft, which cost £12,000,000 apiece.

All in all, it seems rather unlikely that they will have to scale down their operations to one five-seater biplane again; and that appears to apply to the country as a whole.

Are there really no problems? Are Irish skies and Irish eyes absolutely clear and smiling? Has not a single, alien (or, for that matter, Irish) cloud had the temerity to creep into the sky? Of course there are squalls ahead; and I think it might be an idea at this stage to take a meteorological check.

When, for instance, the Pope published his encyclical, *Humanae*

Vitae, which most people related to the pill, the Irish Government must have sighed with relief, though not for reasons that had anything to do with morals, ethics or birth control. It was the timing of the publication that was, for the Cabinet, a happy event, if I may use such an inappropriate phrase in this context.

The Potez controversy was at its height. The Great Pill Debate swept it off the front pages of the newspapers and, for a while at any rate, out of the public mind. At first Potez Aerospace, Ltd., had seemed such a happy thought, just the sort of dynamic, forward-looking project to fit the face of the new Ireland. It sprang from the mind of M. Henri Potez, an elderly French industrialist, who announced in January 1962 that he would build executive aircraft in a factory at Baldonnel, Co. Dublin, and that this would give employment to 1,700 Irishmen.

In July 1968, M. Potez telephoned from France to his managing director at Baldonnel, Charles George Erlam, and told him that the factory was being closed. At that time it employed 150, who were informed that they would get one week's notice, two weeks' holiday pay and 'the week's pay now "in the pipeline".'

The workers were worried because they had lost their jobs. The Government was worried because it had invested heavily in Potez Aerospace and stood to lose about £1,500,000. Inevitably the entire question of what was called ponderously 'foreign participation in industry' came under the microscope and the skin-searing lash of Irish tongues. Millions of words were spilt over coffee-cup, pint tumbler and typewriter; but I think they can be paraphrased fairly accurately by quoting the two sentences heard most frequently: 'Are we mad, letting those foreigners run amok in the country? Does that crowd beyond in Merrion Street know what it's at?'*

They were fair questions; already there had been fairly painful body-blows. The Industrial Engineering Company of Dundalk had lost heavily, despite the fact that the State had pumped in £2,815,097; and the St Patrick's Copper Mines, Ltd., Avoca, Co. Wicklow, had gone into liquidation, although it had received State aid to the extent of £2,250,000. In addition, twenty-four smaller enterprises had gone to the wall, taking £1,731,000 worth of State grants with them, though in fairness to the foreign participators, it must be said that nine of the losers were promoted by Irish interests.

* That crowd—the Government. Merrion Street—government buildings.

In the face of those figures, it would seem rather unwise to let some foreigners into the country; nor would 'that crowd' appear to have a clear-cut idea of what they were doing. Statistics, however, are notoriously contrary and losses must be set against assets. According to the Government, the losses amounted to only about ten per cent of the investment in all companies. If the economy was going to expand fast, surely it was inevitable that a bucket of money was going to be kicked over here and there; or, as Lemass had put it some years earlier when questioned in Parliament about losses: 'I can offer deputies a fool-proof alternative, which will ensure that we will lose nothing. We can sit quiet and do nothing.'

He still holds that view. He told me, in fact: 'Potez was not a national disaster. On one or two occasions in the past, when firms came in and folded, we were able to get the factories filled. We were even able to set up industrial regions ... Waterford and Galway, for instance. There is not a single factory in the country, established for an industry which failed, which is not actively used now.'

That would seem to answer the more immediate points. Outsiders, however, particularly those from Britain, still wonder whether the whole, broad idea is sound. Having thrown off one dominating agent, is Ireland not inviting in others, who are perhaps more dangerous—the industrial imperialists? Lemass has no fears there, either. He said: 'It has been suggested that these foreigners could bring political influence to bear on us. I don't think there is any evidence of that happening. In the first place, it would be difficult because there has been so much diversification—British, German, American, Italian capital and so on; and, secondly, I believe that those behind foreign-owned enterprises are well aware that there would be public repercussions if they attempted to exercise political influence.'

Certainly the wide international pattern of investment is not appreciated in Britain. The average Englishman believes that the Germans and Japanese have taken over the country.

The foreign participation league table shows that to be far from true. It is headed, in fact, by the ancient foe, the British, who are behind over forty per cent of the new firms. The Germans, it is true, come second, but they are a long way down the table, with only twenty per cent, and are being chased by the Americans with sixteen per cent. The Dutch have five per cent and the rest are nowhere. What about the Japanese? They came, dallied a while and left. Only one or two individuals remained, but they run no factories. They are teaching judo.

How is the Irish worker getting on with his foreign bosses? What happens, for instance, when there is a clash between Celtic and Teutonic temperaments? It depends on the Celt, of course, and to a much greater extent on the Teuton. There are ways, as the British found out a little too late, of dealing with the Irish. Ask him to run round the world for you and off he is likely to trot, provided you remember to say 'please'. Order him to put one foot in front of the other and immediately he will sit down, folding his arms the while. Indeed, he may go a little further in the opposite direction, as one German found out. He came to Kerry to run an eel farm. His plan was to corral off a little piece of sea, let his eels breed there and, when they were big and fat, whisk them out and export them.

The local fishermen did not like the idea and they sent a deputation to the German to tell him so. He saw them coming and decided without any hesitation precisely the line of action he would take. These were nice enough fellows, he conceded to himself, but they would have to be taught who was master. So, as soon as they came within hearing distance, he bellowed: 'Get off my land! *Raus!*'

The delegates kept on advancing. He made himself clear once again, this time at Gale Force Nine. The spokesmen looked at each other sadly, turned and slowly walked away.

The German closed the door, happy that his approach had been so right. Once one established one's authority, there would be no trouble. Indeed, one would be respected. Liked, probably. Loved, perhaps.

There was only one flaw in his argument. While he might have established his authority, the eels had not. Forty-eight hours later they were all dead, a theory in the neighbourhood being that they must have eaten something that disagreed with them.

That German is back in the Fatherland now, still wondering what blight hit his crop, and telling his friends that the Irish were fine fellows, provided one kept them in their places.

With a little patience, a little compromise, the two nations can get along with each other, though for a while they will drive each other to the brink of murder or suicide, whichever happens to be the faster way out. Steinbock in Galway provided a fair example of this nerve-shredding give-and-take.

The raw early days there were described for me by a man with many qualifications for neutrality, Sona Sevcik, joint managing director, a Czech, who lived in England from the age of seven and has spent the last eight years in Ireland. He runs the factory with amiable authority; and there was tolerance in his voice as he did his best to present both sides of the story fairly.

'The lads we hired had no industrial experience whatsoever,' he said. 'They were expected, however, to keep regular hours and keep the place reasonably tidy and so on. There were five German foremen to see that they did so.

'It was quite difficult at first, but in fairness I must say that we had exactly the same problem in a factory we started in a rural area in Germany. There the workers were farmers, who had their little plots, or farmers' sons. When it was haymaking time, they stayed away from work. Here hay had to be fetched in, too. The fellows just didn't turn up.'

'What happened?' I asked. 'How did the German foremen react to that?'

'How did they react? Normally enough. They beat their heads against the wall and yelled and told all the boys they would be fired and so on. It was difficult, really, because they spoke hardly any English, but I think they made themselves clear. Eventually, however, they realized, hell, this was the ways the boys lived and so they made allowances for it.'

Joe Hoerhammer, sole survivor of the five German foremen, said: 'We had our problems in the beginning, all right. We had very young men—fourteen, fifteen, sixteen years of age. They did not understand about time at first. I had a whistle. Every morning I used to blow it, call them all together and count them before they settled down to work. Then in the evening I would blow my whistle again and count them again before they left work.'

He was quiet for a while, thinking back, perhaps, to the horror of it all. Then he said: 'We used to give them a quarter of an hour tea break. And—you know what?—they used to take half an hour!'

Today those youngsters, who did not know fifteen minutes from thirty and who used to sneak out under Joe's very whistle, are skilled men. From time to time they go fishing with the terrible Teuton who used to yell at them and threaten to fire them. He is a good fisherman, they say, and he likes his jar, too, which is one of the more charming double compliments that can be paid to a person in Galway.

All this, however, is fine-grain stuff. The one question that is seldom asked in Ireland does not concern personal relationships or passports or foreign domination or whether that crowd beyond in Merrion Street knows what it's at. What people like myself, who knew another Ireland, want to know is whether it has changed for better or for worse? It is not an easy question and I am not sure whether I have found the answer.

It is true, as I said in Chapter One, that everything seems fine. There is money around and there is a new freedom, cars and full restaurants, smart clothes, smart talk, holidays abroad and coloured telly without any poverty on the bright, sharp surface. At the back of many an Irish mind, however, is the thought that more money is being spent than is being earned, that any minute now the broker's man will appear. Time and again, I've heard the gloomy forecast: 'There's going to be a crash soon. I can smell it.'

How prosperous, really prosperous is the country? Let us start at the top. There were 119 people earning over £10,000 a year in the year 1965–6, a dozen more than the previous year. Their aggregate earnings were £1,720,000, an average of £280 a week each. There were 58 earning between £9,000 and £10,000; 90 earning £8,000–£9,000; 125 earning £7,000–£8,000; 226 earning £6,000–£7,000; 443 earning £5,000–£6,000; 917 earning £4,000–£5,000; and 1,750 earning £3,000–£4,000.

Altogether there were 3,728 people assessed for surtax, who had earned incomes of over £3,000. Spill them on Dublin on a Saturday night and they would not be noticed. I would guess, therefore, that there are quite a few people who are living at surtax level without the income to meet it. The scampi belt. The bacardi brigade. They own a house in Foxrock and have a Mercedes on the firm. The wife has a mini for shopping and a swimming pool for the garden is on order. There is a cottage in Connemara—'I can really *think* down there'— and an appearance once a week in the Martello Room of the Intercontinental. Wine name-droppers. B.A. (Pass). Top-convent wife with *Ulysses* in her handbag. Oyster festival, but not Galway races. Hard tennis court; yacht in the front garden during the winter. Open-plan architecture and closed-plan minds. Unhappy people with easy laughs and eyes that are always moving, looking for Murphy, wondering whether he is watching and whether he has a mohair suit, too. They are new to Irish life, blurred carbons of English suburbans from the mock-stockbroker belt. They keep up with the Murphys and so they are afraid most of the time. They live high, but that is not prosperity.

Come down a little in the income scale and nearer reality. To the middle-aged ones with children and school or university and about £2,000 a year in a city where the price of butter and meat would shock an English housewife—a very dear little city, indeed. A small car. A small overdraft. A small worry that it will never be paid. A night out occasionally, but with steak not scampi. A few friends in occasionally with a bottle of whiskey and a few dozen stout, bought at the off-licence. They worry about the broker's man, not just for themselves, but for everyone.

That is not prosperity.

Down a little lower. Down to Mr Average Wage. If he lives in Dublin, it is about £17 a week. A wife and three kids. A council house. Bus fares that are always going up. A soccer match at Daly-mount. A few jars with the lads and a bit of a conscience about the wife back at home. Bills and overtime and there goes Saturday.

That is not prosperity, and there are men who earn less. There are single women who must live on half as much. There are old age pensioners with £3 5s. 0d. a week and men on the dole with £1 12s. 6d. a week. There are still housing conditions which make priests speak out in anger. There is the social worker who told me: 'I know a child of three who cannot walk properly because she spends so much time on a bed in one room. There is no space for her to walk properly.' There are new office blocks, reaching for the sky. There are street cleaners, who went on strike this summer because they earned no more than £12 a week. How do they live? I simply do not know.

There is still unemployment, for all the new industry cannot keep up with the flight from the land. There is still emigration with its tragic backlash. Dr Mary P. Spellman of St Patrick's Hospital, Castle-rea, Co. Roscommon, wrote in a medical journal recently: 'The prevalence of mental illness in the county's women would appear to be high ... the factors of emigration and poverty, endemic in the area, might well play a part in the causation of depressive illnesses. All the children of many families in this rural area emigrated to America or England with consequent hardship and loneliness for the parents, who were left to face old age on their small, isolated, uneconomic farms. ... It would seem as though the constant struggle to rear a large family in grinding poverty, added to work in the field and the farmyard, which merely ends in the complete loss of her children, breaks her spirit.'

There are all these things; and yet much progress has been made. There is poverty, but no longer does it shout from every side street now. It is small, quiet. There are bad houses; but they do not stare so much, or maybe there are not so many eyes, and so the guilt diminishes. There are protests, strident and honest; but in a way, they, too, are signs of better times. There is more leisure, more time for social conscience. Life is better, but that is not to say that it is good enough for those who deserve better.

These black marks, however, are no argument against the drive to expand. On the contrary, they should be what the drive is all about, and the fact that conditions have improved so much would seem to indicate that they are just that. After the war, Germany built factories first, then houses. Ireland is trying to do something similar.

It still has a long, dangerous journey ahead. There was a trade gap, when I was there, of well over £100,000,000, which meant that, in spite of those bouncing export figures, the country still was buying more than it was selling. One cynic said recently: 'We're trying to live at imperial standards on a republican income'; and the brokers' men of the world do not like that way of life.*

Yet only more expansion, more exports, more work can bridge the gap and build the houses, can stop mothers in the West from breaking their hearts over children abroad, can give the widows more.

What, then, are the industrial hopes for the future? I put the question to George Colley; and he replied: 'Our exports have been expanding at a terrific rate, despite a shrinkage in the British market. We could have a recession here, but the overall tendency is ahead. I could not have said that ten years ago. In fact we are in orbit. Only a major and prolonged world depression can stop us now.'

---

* As this book went to press a punishing interim budget slapped heavy additional taxes on liquor and tobacco; increased postal charges; restricted hire-purchase dealings; and introduced a wholesale tax to curb inflation, and, no doubt, to keep those brokers' men happy.

4 THE FARMER

AT a public meeting to discuss agricultural policy recently, a stout man from West Cork proclaimed proudly: 'Eighty per cent of Irish farmers are above average.'

A pedant at the back of the hall shouted: 'Above what average?'

Scarcely pausing to draw breath, the farmers' champion replied: 'Above the average of the other twenty per cent.'

It is possible to make a more plausible case for the tillers of Irish soil. They are, for instance, selling to the world and not merely to Britain, which for decades has been their main market.

A quarter of the population of the Caribbean now eats Irish Kerry Gold butter, thanks to some extensive foot-slogging by the salesmen of Bórd Báinne, the Milk Board, which markets it. They report with proper pleasure, too, that wrappers are being printed in Arabic for the Middle East market.

Erin Foods, since it joined hands with that well-known foreign participator, Heinz, has boosted its international sales so high that its payments to farmers have increased from £325,000 in 1966 to something near the million mark this year. This was a unique marriage, incidentally. Erin Foods is a semi-State body, a maiden with nationalization blood in her veins. Heinz is one of the bigger barons of capitalism. Yet there is every sign that they will live happily ever after.

For the first time in the country's agricultural history most of the meat exported is not trotting under its own power onto ships at Dublin's North Wall. More cattle were slaughtered at home last year than emigrated alive, the job being done by new, well-equipped, job-giving Irish factories. The growth rate is two per cent.

That, come to think of it, is not a very impressive list and, in the circumstances, it might have been wiser for me to leave the field to the West Cork orator. In my defence, however, I must say that it is the best I can do for the Irish soil tiller with the material he has provided. The unhappy truth is that Ireland's agricultural produce could be coaxed from field and beast by half the present labour force.

The Government's attitude to that state of affairs seems to be to encourage—some would say force—half the labour force to get themselves urbanized, which is a little rough on those who want to live and work on the land. It becomes even rougher with the realization that industry, despite its spectacular growth, is producing only one job for every two people who leave the farms.

Nations like Denmark or Switzerland would probably approach the problem from the other end. They would say: 'Why halve the labour force? Why not quadruple the output?' They, however, have never gazed deeply into the hearts of Irish farmers. They are not a particularly encouraging cardiacal collection, as the following short burst of statistics shows:

Only forty per cent of Irish farms could be called family farms in the sense that they are run by a married couple with young children.

Sixty per cent are owned by bachelors, widows or widowers.

Between 1926 and 1966, the farm labour force fell from 652,000 to 333,500. In that period, one million people emigrated.

It is the middle-aged or elderly bachelor, I fear, who is lying across the railway that might take Irish agriculture somewhere near to European standards. He could be more efficient; but what is the point of it? His existence is sparse enough, but he wants no more. He has no family to feed, clothe and educate, no son to inherit a going concern.

The Government is badgering him to borrow money for new machinery, fertilizer even. The banks are dying to lend it to him; but he does not trust banks and he does not like debt and the old tractor will do another few years yet. The sociologists say that he should have married years ago and could marry now. Say that to him and he will gaze at the cold, bare house and answer: 'Yerrah, what would a woman be doing in a place like this?' His best friends could tell him, but they never do.

Lack of a wife and lack of an heir are two major agricultural problems than no fertilizer or combine harvester can solve. Almost as big a headache is the married farmer who will not fade away, will not retire and give his son a chance.

According to Professor Robert O'Connell of the Central Statistics Office, Dublin, the average age at which an Irish farmer succeeds to his father's farm is twenty-eight, seven to ten years later than the North European average—and the Irish figure has not increased by even one year in the past forty-two years.

Speaking to what must have been a very depressed rally of young farmers, he went on: 'The almost unbelievable extent (to outsiders) to which the young man's economic, family community and adult sexual roles have to be postponed in Irish rural life—and never taken up in many cases—is the major social problem facing Irish agriculture. It results in frustration, a smothering or total quenching of drive and enthusiasm and a late marriage age, leaving a high proportion of farmers who are very old bachelors or widows.'

The proportion of Irish farmers who never marry is the highest in the world—about thirty per cent, more than twice the average European figure. Two reasons for this are that his father could never save enough to retire and the fact that in the rural areas there are just over 600 girls between twenty and twenty-four years of age to every 1,000 men.

There could be, however, another reason. An Irish farm and the life that surrounds it would not make many women grab for their galoshes. Mrs Ethna Viney, a sociologist, said recently:

'For a large number of Irish rural women, their daily work is sheer drudgery. Leisure time is virtually unknown and they get away from the house and farm once a week for Mass on Sunday. This is not always due to volume of work, but to inefficient, awkward buildings and equipment. . . .

'These women carry every drop of water that they use in the house and it is hard to blame those that cut down on its use. They have no launderettes or laundries and very few washing machines. They rarely get new clothes, apart from shoes. Their voice in the affairs of the parish, county or country is nil. . . .

'The mature, adult woman has a specific place in the community and she knows it and keeps to it. This is, briefly, at home, looking after her husband, house and family. When she makes a public appearance, she is expected to be as self-effacing as possible. On Sundays, if the family walks to Mass, generally she will not walk with her husband. Someone might think that they were fond of each other. He will leave the house either before or after her and join up with some of the neighbours on the road. Generally she will take no part in discussions on politics or social or religious questions, when there are outsiders present. . . .

'She will vote the same way as her husband votes, unless she is particularly strong-willed. Then she will vote the same way as her father voted. . . .

'She will have periodic visits to the nearest town to buy clothes for the children. If the family can afford a car, and very many of them cannot, these outings will be more frequent and may include a visit to the cinema for her husband and herself. On alien territory it is perfectly in order for them to be seen together. It would be unheard of that she should accompany her husband to his local pub at night, as her urban sister does. . . .

'I don't blame the women who have gone under because they have been demoralized by poverty. Who wouldn't, when, for want of alternative accommodation, farmyard, dairy and scullery work is carried on in the kitchen living-room, milk stored, cans scalded, mashes mixed up and buckets of water hauled in and out through an ever-open door?'

Inevitably, Irish farmers came buzzing round the ears of Mrs Viney for painting that grim picture of rural life. Some time later, however, her words were borne out by a survey of 275 Irish farms by Miss Sile O'Neill, a rural economist at the Agricultural Institute. She reported that about half the homes were a hundred years old and a quarter between fifty and ninety-nine years old. Only about half had piped water, fifteen per cent telephones, and eight per cent refrigerators.

Nor were those the last words on the subject. In an address to the national youth rally of the Society of St Vincent de Paul, the Most Reverend Dr Birch said grimly: 'The older people have become so accustomed to what goes on around them that frequently they do not see the evils in our society. They no longer note the fact that in our rural areas, many wives are pure slaves, answering to the whims and wishes of their husbands.'

The debate was on. Mrs Peggy Farrell, President of the 24,000-strong Irish Countrywomen's Association, said: 'The trouble with a large number of marriages in rural areas is the lack of communication between man and wife and the failure of the husband to show his love outwardly to his wife. The men seem ashamed even to express their love in this manner. They feel that giving help to their wives in the home is an unmanly thing. This makes it tough on the wife, who in the rural areas often has to make unbelievable sacrifices to bring up her family. Some years ago, the I.C.A. carried out a survey and we found that one-third of a woman's life was spent carrying water to her home.'

Joseph Rea, President of Macra na Feirme, a young farmers' organization, agreed with the Bishop and said that there was some truth in the old joke about a wife being chosen for her ability to carry two buckets of water up from the yard.

Those interviews make depressing reading; and the story gets even worse, as it goes west. Dr John Scully, who got a Master's degree and a

Ph.D. in agricultural economics in the United States and is now the Department of Agriculture's Regional Officer in the West of Ireland, summed up the situation there as 'dim, but not hopeless'.

'In the next fifteen years,' he said, 'the farm population will be halved. . . . The older generation are reluctant to consolidate their fragmented farms or to borrow money for productive purposes or to adopt modern farm practices.'

Dr Scully's expert views, based on his extensive knowledge and experience, are shared by most people with more than a passing acquaintance with the West of Ireland. The land there is almost empty and dying fast.

Can nothing be done to save it? Certainly present official policies are not setting any turf bogs on fire; and one Government measure seems to be designed to encourage wastage of man power, to applaud idleness. Every farmer whose land is below a certain rateable value, is allowed to draw the dole twelve months of the year. He feeds himself from his bit of land. He gets a remittance from his son in Boston or Chicago or New York. A couple of pounds a month come from his daughter in Birmingham. All this and the dole, too. What is the point of peppering him with jet-set jargon about programming production or planned marketing?

The official argument, of course, is that the man's holding is too small to produce a living and that therefore he must be helped, just as an urban worker can draw assistance when he is out of a job. One answer to that argument has cropped into many minds, only to be left unspoken for reasons of expediency. It is simply this: add all the little, uneconomic holdings together and make them into one big, viable holding.

The reason why this theory is not broadcast too loudly is suggested by John Healy, Parliamentary Correspondent of the *Irish Times*. He wrote a book recently about his home town, Charlestown, in Co. Mayo, which is dying currently, like so many others; in it he said: 'Today there are politicians in Leinster House,* who see, as the solution for the West, the creation of a dozen big communes on the Soviet style. The fear of political reprisals stops them from saying it aloud. But if they had an assurance that the first one would be opened by an Archbishop, sprinkling holy water on it, they would get courage and promote the idea.'

* Where Parliament sits.

There is, however, one man who is not afraid to speak out on this explosive subject though, because of his job, he would seem to be in greater danger from reprisals than any politician. He is a priest, Father James McDyer, one of the most remarkable people I met in all my travels around Ireland. His parish is Glencolumbkille on Glen Bay in Donegal overlooking the Atlantic Ocean. It, like Charlestown, was dying; but Father McDyer has put a stop to all that nonsense in the fourteen years he has been there. By co-operative effort, hard work and vision, he has not only stopped the emigration that had this hamlet down to 250 people, but raised the standard of living higher than it has ever been before.

It has been a big job; but then it was a big man I met in the Presbytery, a heap of a man, who walks tall. His voice has a slice of the north about it, soft, Donegal north; his lapel has a badge in it to say that he does not drink, though a bottle of whiskey is always kept handy for visitors; his eyes are keen with alert bewilderment; and his talk is laced with an irony that never really wounds very much.

I asked him what he had been doing in Glencolumbkille and why he had been doing it. He decided to take the second question first.

'Before I came here,' he said, 'I worked in London. I met a lot of emigrants there, mostly from rural areas, and the sight of them made me feel a sort of shame that we had to depend on a country we had fought to absorb our redundant youth. We seemed to be getting our priorities wrong—talking about the past and doing nothing about the present. Going on about self-discipline and efficiency being the price of freedom, but not paying that price.

'The first thing I did was to build a village hall. It was not the answer, of course, not true progress, but I had to have a basis for financing my plans. It was not a parish hall, incidentally, but a people's hall, to use Maoist language. Every halfpenny we take there goes into the development of the community.

'Then I started on social amenities—getting roads built, rehabilitating the school, chasing up people so that we could have water, electricity, a dispensary. It all took time, though the local authority was very good about the roads and students from seven countries came here through the World University service and helped us channel water to three-quarters of the houses.'

'But why electricity?' I asked. 'I thought everyone could have electricity.'

'So they can,' he said. 'But some local people didn't want it here. They said it would be too dear and too dangerous. I had to sell them the idea and, believe me, it was a hard sell because they're very conservative.'

He paused a while; and then he went on: 'That's one of the troubles about the west. It was the progressive ones who left. Anyway, to get back, I knew roads and water and electric light weren't enough. None of it made sense so long as there still were twenty-five young people leaving Glencolumbkille each year. I knew I had to provide work, an incentive; and that was when I began thinking of co-operatives.

'For years the politicians had been promising us a factory, but we'd never seen sight of it. However, I decided to have one more go and I wrote to Mr de Valéra, who was Taoiseach—Prime Minister—at the time. Then, just in case it got lost in the post, or something, I wrote to Mrs de Valéra.'

Father McDyer, to the amazement of his parishioners, got government help to start a factory. He chose a traditional occupation—weaving. A start had been made on what was to be a remarkable community enterprise.

'But I knew that still wasn't enough,' he said. 'The land alone will never save Glencolumbkille. Neither will a weaving factory. Not even together could they do it. What we needed was four or five pillars on which to build.'

Today he has them. There is his vegetable co-operative, in which they process their own vegetables in their own factory and sell through Erin Foods, who gave them technical help and a guaranteed market.

'Few people up here had heard of celery,' he said. 'The Department of Agriculture had heard of it, all right, but they said that we wouldn't be able to grow it here. They spent a couple of hours pleading with me not to grow vegetables, saying it was too stormy, too dark, too everything. But I started and they grew beautifully. They suit the sort of pocket handkerchiefs of land we have here.'

Father McDyer has built his pillars and is building still. He has introduced progressive methods to sheep and pig-farming. Glencolumbkille now has three modern piggeries and five more are about to start. He is laying down a traditional pattern of farming where no tradition existed.

He has a textile co-operative that pays a dividend of seven and a half per cent to the workers and shareholders who own it. He has a metal-craft co-operative, where a retired silversmith teaches young apprentices an ancient Irish craft. His food-processing factory employs ninety-five people at its busy times, enough to make many a foreign participator envious.

Most significant of all, however, is his building co-operative. It has been a long time since Glencolumbkille needed new houses. 'Youngsters are getting married,' he said. 'There weren't a whole lot of weddings when I came here, and, when they did wed, they were thirty to thirty-five years of age. Now they're coming along to me at the age of twenty-one or twenty-two. The co-op has built two houses already and is working on three more.

'We've other plans, too. We're thinking of going in for mushroom farming. I'm promised a market for it and it could be a very profitable farmyard enterprise. We may have a go at bees, too. They could produce an extra £50 a year.

'We're not a bit interested in an individual's earnings, you see; but we are intensely interested in the family earnings. One family here had a total income of £250 a few years back. Now they are earning together £1,300 and their farm is only six and a half acres. There are five in the family. One of the children emigrated a few years ago and another is studying at the technical school. They rear pigs and the wife is in our knitting co-op, working at home. The other children are working in our factories. Our knitters can earn as much as five pounds a week. I went over to America on a cheap excursion flight and fixed up direct markets, cutting out the middleman and putting thirty per cent more profit into the pockets of the workers.'

All this has happened in the face of a galling apathy. Twenty per cent of the farms are held by ageing couples with emigrant families. Another twenty per cent belong to middle-aged or elderly bachelors. Father McDyer told me: 'I would ten times prefer to face any Government Department in Dublin then to sell any idea locally. Straightaway, I can write off forty per cent of the people here as those who won't co-operate.

'I suppose I could solve the whole problem by a stroke of a pen, by luring one big enterprise to run the lot. But I believe that God gave us land for a purpose; and it's wrong to denude that land.

'In the second place, I'm sufficient of a socialist to feel that it would not be fair to bring a big capitalist here to cream off the profit, pay the serfs and then, perhaps, at the first sign of recession, pull out, leaving everyone high and dry. To my way of thinking, all sources of wealth in

Glencolumbkille belong to the people of Glencolumbkille; and the frontiers of the family are not the four walls of a house any more, but the perimeter of the community in which they live.'

It was at that point that he mentioned something which I thought I never would hear from a priest in Ireland. He said: 'I must tell you about my commune. . . .'

It is true, of course, that the Christian Church operated communes long before Karl Marx was born and that the lives of monks and nuns are based on their community; but that, the conformists say, is different, or, as a rather superior English Jesuit put it: 'It's all right for *us*, but not for *them*!'

Father McDyer, however, is not a conformist. He told me: 'About two years ago, I decided we should have a real go at this commune idea, though I must admit I didn't call it that. I used a nice, wee Irish word: meitheal, which means a group of people working agriculturally together for a common cause.

'First I took some expert advice from the Agricultural Institute to keep me on the right lines. I showed them my plans and they gave them the green light, economically. After that I approached 130 local farmers and said: "Folks, how about knocking those fences down and working as one family? I guarantee the three basics to every house: free turf for your fire; potatoes and milk; and work at standard agricultural rates for every able-bodied man in the community."

'I explained to them that the fences would stay down for ten years to give the idea a chance and that the head man would be a technocrat, who would introduce the most modern farming methods for what would be, in fact a farm of 19,000 acres in mountain and lowland. Beneath him would be a committee of farmers, elected by themselves. After three years, I said, there would be full employment for women, too, under-roof farming around the farmhouse.

'Do you know what? Out of that 130, 112 agreed to come in with me. It took them a bit of time to make up their minds, mind you, but in the end they signed on the dotted line.

'After that I went straight up to Dublin to talk it over with Department of Agriculture and other officials. I wanted to borrow £124,000 —it works out at £6 an acre—to get the most modern equipment available for that farm. I told them that the loan would be repaid in ten years and thought they would be delighted with the idea.

'But not on your life. A whole team of them spent hours trying to pick holes in my plans. When they couldn't do that, they said: "Father, the whole idea is un-Christian; and you are hiding that under the cloak of piety."

' "Gentlemen," I said, "you all are experts in your respective fields; but you will have to admit that at this gathering I am the only expert on Christianity".'

Father McDyer returned to Glencolumbkille deeply disappointed. He told me: 'I'm convinced it could solve the problem of small farms. I believe that the only solution for the West, in fact, is voluntary collectivization, even though some people still insist that it is a dirty word.'

Even without his commune, however, he has transformed the bleak, beautiful hills that surround the hamlet of Glencolumbkille, which has risen again. He has done something which nobody else, so far as I know, has been able to do in Ireland. So before I left, I asked him whether his methods could be applied to other parts of the country.

'If you searched all Ireland,' he told me, 'you couldn't find a tougher nut, geophysically and psychologically, than Glencolumbkille. If we can do it, anyone can do it. The time has come for the priest to become more involved in the worldly needs and aspirations of his people and temporarily fill a vacuum of leadership, even though it meant sacrificing his leisure time. The best way to the soul is through the stomach, for it makes no sense to ask a couple if they've said their prayers, when they're worrying about the grocer's bill and about what is happening to their daughter in Birmingham who has not written.' He smiled suddenly and said: 'I suppose you've heard they call me a Stalin?'

'I'm ahead of you, Father,' I said. 'They've grown tired of that one. Now they're calling you a bit of a Hitler.'

That was true. I had had many talks in Dublin about Father McDyer before I headed for Donegal and too often the air had hung heavy with the cloying smell of faint praise, a poison which the Irish use with excruciating subtlety. I had kept plugging away, however, trying to discover whether there was one positive way in which his work could be faulted; and it was then that they began pinning unpleasant labels on him in the hope that somewhere a seed of doubt might be sown.

'A bit of a Hitler?' he said. 'That's a new one. Well, well . . . what do you know!'

He was still smiling, as he stood in the presbytery door to wave me good-bye. I guessed that he was thinking about his commune; and I made a bet with myself that, next time I passed through Glencolumb-kille, it would be there.

The attitude of the Establishment to co-operatives, let alone collectives, is distinctly cool; and I heard it suggested more than once that official financial assistance for Father McDyer trickled through most reluctantly in the hope that he would fail and that the dangers of his wicked doctrine would be exposed. Nevertheless, co-operatives are busting out all over, particularly in the fishing industry, which all of a sudden has begun to bustle.

It has always seemed quixotic to me that this island people should have ignored for so long the fish that surround them. It could be that in their subconscious they regard it as no more than a Friday penance, a slippery key to a better life; but the fact is that the Irish, surrounded by more water than most, eat less fish than most.

Now, however, fishing fleets are growing round the coast, encouraged by Bórd Iascaig Mhara, the semi-State Fishery Board, whose hire-purchase scheme enables men to buy boats over a ten-year period. As a result, fish worth £2,500,000, is being exported to spots as remote as Australia; and at home it seems to be losing its aura of sacrifice, for consumption is rising. It still is true that five Russian trawlers probably could net as much in a given period as the entire Irish fleet, but that is no reason for scuttling what promises to be a healthy industry. The fishermen of the west, indeed, unlike the farmers, seem to have breathed deeply that tang of enthusiasm which permeates the industrial air elsewhere. In Killybegs, Co. Donegal, for instance, once a hotly tipped candidate for the graveyard, there is a fishing fleet of thirty, a Dutch fish-meal factory and a French factory which processes herrings for export.

The local co-operative, which last year had a turnover of £150,000 and hopes to open its own processing factory, handles the marketing. It has its own fleet of lorries, which operates a refrigerated container service, and they are waiting at the pier to be loaded as the catch is landed. After that they hit the road fast for the cross-channel boat and in this way manage to get fresh fish to British housewives—even to Grimsby housewives—ahead of the local boats. Admittedly the British trawlers are larger, spend longer at sea than the Irish and therefore cannot hope to compete with this service from trawl to dinner plate; nevertheless, it is a considerable accomplishment for an infant outfit.

Other co-operatives have been formed in Kilmore Quay, Co. Wexford, Dingle, Co. Kerry; and at Cleggan, Co. Galway. This last has been organized by Colm McDevitt and I mention him particularly for two reasons. In the first place, he has helped to bring a new spirit to this lonely and lovely area. Secondly, while I was on my way to meet him, I got a little lost and was given the most splendid directions I am ever likely to hear.

I was not quite sure where he lived. So I called at the Pier Bar in Cleggan for advice, only to find it was closed because of the Stations. That is an old Irish custom by which the priest says Mass in various houses throughout the area from time to time. That day it had been the Pier Bar's turn and the proprietress had felt, presumably, that it would not be quite appropriate to open up so soon afterwards. Nevertheless, she was only too pleased to help me. She said: 'To get to Colm McDevitt's house, you'll have to go back the road.'

I thought I had overshot, but I was wrong. 'Back the road' in some parts of Ireland means further on—into the wilderness, I suppose.

'Go back the road,' she said, 'until you come to a crumbling old school. Don't trouble that. Then you'll come to a small lake. Don't trouble that. Then a bigger lake, but don't trouble that, either. But, when you come to the Atlantic Ocean, turn right.'

I have never had such accurate directions in my life. I troubled not the crumbling old school, the little lake or the bigger lake. I rounded a curve in the road and there, blue, dappled and deceptively gentle, was the Atlantic.

Had I carried on, I would have ended up in Brooklyn. The road to the right was there, however, and five minutes later I was knocking on Colm's door. It was opened by his charming wife, surrounded by a tangle of cheerful children. In a voice of woe, for she was sorry for me, she said: 'You've just missed him. He's in Paris!'

Though prospering, the fishing industry is rippled by certain anomalies which are inclined to confuse a visitor. Celtic Fisheries, Ltd., of Rock Island Pond, Co. Cork, for instance, scarcely could sound more Irish. In fact it is owned in the main by Frenchmen, who export prime Irish lobsters to their land of gourmets. That is reasonable enough, I suppose, though it would be better, perhaps, if the Irish did the exporting themselves. What makes it odd is the fact that Erin Foods get their lobsters from Japan or Pakistan.

Another strange situation surrounds the inland fishing rights. Many of them are owned by Englishmen—including, I was informed reliably, a Billingsgate fish merchant—and the natives must pay for the privilege of fishing in Irish waters. These circumstances, I feel, are enough to make even the most reactionary Irishman—and there are quite a few —howl for nationalization.

Oddly enough, there has been no really strong feeling expressed about the influx of foreigners from many lands to Ireland, whether it be for business or for protection from a possible nuclear war. It is true that there have been vague rumblings, half-spoken doubts about the wisdom of the policy; but one of the few men that I met with any worthwhile views on the matter was Father McDyer.

'We're a strange people,' he said. 'For centuries we were prepared to fight to the death over a square yard of land. Then we let it slip from our hands without a murmur. I wonder what the next generation will have to say about it all. Will they say: "You sold our country"?'

Perhaps I exaggerate, however, when I say that there has been no real protest. A very positive stand against foreign participators was taken by one section of the community in Rossaveal, Co. Galway, near where Colm McDevitt has his co-operative. An American company, Galway Bay Fisheries, Ltd., had established itself in Rossaveal to fish for lobster. Local fishermen probably were not over-pleased at the sight of this expensive and efficient equipment coming into their fishing grounds, but they made no really vociferous protest about it.

Then, at two o'clock on an August morning in 1968, the *Marie Catherine,* one of those expensive and efficient pieces of equipment, was blown to bits in Rossaveal harbour. A member of the crew who normally slept on board, was lucky. It happened during Galway race week and he was in town for the night. Soon afterwards, the I.R.A. announced that one of their units had been responsible for the explosion. The statement continued: 'The action was undertaken to protect the Irish shell-fishing industry against exploitation by foreign interests, to protect these natural resources and to preserve them for our own native fishermen.'

It concluded: 'The I.R.A., conscious of its duty as the revolution army of the Irish people, will continue to defend the rights of the Irish people, whenever these rights are attacked by opportunists, either native or foreign.'

For the sake of non-Irish readers, I think I should explain that the I.R.A. today is a small, illegal organization, whose aim is to remove the border by force and establish a republic that will include the entire island. Most citizens of the Republic of Ireland would like to see unity, too, but few support the drastic methods advocated, but not used for some time, by the I.R.A.

The Rossaveal action, indeed, was a complete switch of tactics by the I.R.A. Years earlier, they had been responsible for a series of explosions in Britain, which led, incidentally, to harsh feelings about anyone with an Irish accent. Later they concentrated on Northern Ireland, attacking police stations and customs posts. For them to enter the field of economic warfare was something quite new.

The Irish co-operative movement—the Irish Co-operative Development Trust—quickly dissociated itself from the whole affair, describing it as senseless and retrograde. The statement went on: 'It is a matter of great concern to the members of the Co-operative Development Trust that the military arm of the Republican movement believes it necessary and even possible to remedy the social and economic problems of the people by use of force.'

The Americans moved the *Marie Catherine*'s sister, the *Boston*, to the Aran Islands and stopped using Rossaveal as their home base.

Whether the blast from the explosion was felt inland it is hard to say, but it is a fair guess that some foreigners who had bought plots in the area and had built bungalows, must have paused for a moment to think. Connemara is particularly popular with non-nationals and in Kerry, further south, Dutch and Germans are believed to have bought up over two thousand acres of very beautiful country.

As a result, of course, prices have soared. Land which could not have been given away a few years ago is now fetching £1,000 an acre and this, incidentally, is being put forward as a comforting, if rather shaky, argument to calm anyone who happens to get upset about the situation.

'Sure all the best land is gone,' he is told. 'And them Teuton industrial barons are not mad altogether. They're not going to pay prices like that for a few old lumps of rock.'

The fact that the few old lumps of rock form the basis of some of the country's finest beauty spots is forgotten. Instead what anger there is sings around the head of the Irishmen who were responsible for the sale, which is fair enough. Certainly some people have cashed in on this new invasion and it has not been the small farmer who owned the soil in the first place. Too often he has been approached by an Irish speculator, who has offered to buy a couple of fields that he was not using very much anyway. The price has always been impressive.

Furthermore, the potential buyer has seemed in no hurry to take possession. He has offered to put down a deposit of a couple of hundred pounds and complete the deal at some unspecified date in the future.

The farmer is happy. He has been given money for land which was earning him nothing. The middleman is happy. He can afford to wait for a wealthy foreigner to call and offer him very much more than he had promised to pay the owner. The wealthy foreigner, deprived of a nuclear weapon in his own country and anxious to keep out of the way of those owned by careless strangers, amateurs in the war game, is happy because there is no Berlin Wall in Kerry.

Unhappy are the people who need houses. At a recent meeting of Galway Corporation, Alderman Fintan Coogan said: 'Boys and girls are not going to get married unless we can provide the houses, and we can't do this if there is no land available. Newly-weds cannot be expected to go into rooms. There are already too many of them with young children living in back rooms in Galway.'

The Galway County Manager, Austin Sharkey, replied: 'I have gone to great lengths to try to get land for our housing programme, but was outbid. There has to be a limit to the price a local authority is prepared to pay for land and I have more or less reached the end of my tether. I have now come to the conclusion that the only way to get land is by using our powers to acquire it compulsorily and we are considering this.'

I trust that the contemplation of this action does not take too long. Already there is not all that much land left to acquire, compulsorily or otherwise.

5 TOURISM

IF that noble animal, the tourist, had not been sired by Affluence out of Curiosity (Grand Dam: Status Symbol), the Irish should have invented him. They did not do so, preferring to leave the business to such franc-scrabbling peoples as the Swiss and the French, who, if I may borrow a West of Ireland phrase for a moment, would skin a flea for its hide, and therefore were aesthetically unsuited to the task of rearing this delicate creature.

We had, after all, the most vital quality: a sense of hospitality so deep that at times it frightens colder races, though once they get a taste for it, they cannot leave it alone at all. That desire to make people happy, to help them is, I believe, one of the major differences between the Irish and other nationalities. They genuinely like to help, even without the reward of being liked for their efforts, as anyone who has asked the way in the Irish countryside (or cityside, for that matter) will confirm. Long, tortuous directions are given, even though the guide is a total stranger there himself and just as lost.

As well as this basic ingredient, we had many other natural assets: some of the finest scenery in the world; magnificent, lonely beaches; lakes, rivers and coastal waters, grossly over-populated with fish who, perhaps for religious reasons, had no use at all for family planning; and not only an ability to entertain people with talk, but a genuine fondness for so doing. Until comparatively recently, we wasted all these assets, or, at best, distributed them sporadically and inefficiently. It is only in the last decade, really, that the Irish have got a grip on the business; and the spectacular result must leave them wondering why the hell they were merely messing about with it for so long.

The statistics tell the story dramatically: in 1960 the total revenue from tourism was just over forty-four million pounds. In 1967 it was just over eighty-four million pounds. Say the figures and it sounds easy—just forced growth with the use at last of the proper and incredibly handy fertilizer. The road, however, has been rocky because, by the time the Irish entered the tourist trade seriously, it had grown so complex that it needed attention from both computers and psychiatrists.

The Irish Tourist Board—called Bórd Fáilte at home (literally and very properly that means Welcome Board)—worked incredibly fast, however. Under their Director General, Dr Tim O'Driscoll, who earlier in his career had made a substantial contribution to civil aviation and subsequently improved our national image, as a diplomat, it became a highly sophisticated body. Not only that, but it managed to inject a considerable amount of this sophistication into all those who came into contact with tourists. That alone was a gigantic task. They had to ask the Irish people to be hospitable on a commercial basis; and the frontier between genuine warmth and plastic servility is not as broad as it may appear. For reasons of history and temperament, the Irish were never very strong runners in the servile stakes, and they viewed the prospect with suspicion before deciding that servility was not demanded.

There were other problems—the weather, for instance. God did a fair-to-middling job on the physical construction of Ireland but, maybe because He was so busy with the rest of the world, He left her a bit short on seasons. Spring, summer, autumn and winter blend so gently into each other that there is not a lot of difference between them, a state of affairs which time has taught the Irish to accept with mild philosophy. Thus, when the rain is driving holes in the head, they are inclined to say with a soggy smile: 'Fine, soft day, thank God!'

The Tourist Board, with outrageous skill, grabbed that little problem by its slippery neck and twisted it to the industry's advantage. 'Look!' it cried in wonder to the world. 'Ireland is mild all the year round. You could stay here forever without a twinge of discomfort.' Better still, it had the magnificent, brassy effrontery to advertise its rain in the *New Yorker*; and I make no apologies for quoting this remarkable piece of prose in full. It was written by Adrienne Claiborne, of de Garmo, McCaffrey, Inc., New York, one of the top six advertising copy-writers in the United States, a Polish-Russian-Jewish-New Yorker, who was in Ireland as long as an un-Irish wet day and clamped one slender finger on the secret pulse that normally we keep hidden from foreigners with thick layers of insidious charm and decent guile. For that piece of brilliant detection, she deserves to be made President either of Ireland or the United States; or at least to have conferred upon her honorary membership of the New York Gaelic Football team.

Her heading was: 'You won't mind the rain in Ireland because, for one thing, it's gentle and for another no one around you will be complaining.'

Then she wrote:

We get a terrible lot of rain in Ireland. Measured by inches, we get almost as much as Miami.

It is, however, Irish rain.

So it rains down much more economically than Miami rain. Our annual rainfall of forty inches (seven less than Miami's) suffices to supply all Ireland (an area 500 times Miami's) with a skitter-scattering of mists, dews and rainbow-making showers.

Thus the befuddling Irish weather report. On a day last July when the New York report stated flatly: 'Continuing hot and humid. Current Central Park temperature ninety-nine degrees fahrenheit,' the Irish weatherman forecast: 'Bright and sunny periods, scattered showers in some areas. Average temperature for time of year (sixty-eight degrees fahrenheit).' To clarify, let us suppose that on just such a day, during a 'bright and sunny period,' you go bouncing along in a jaunting car to the Killarney races. You get to the gate. Still sunny, but darkening. And arrive at the stand in a tie—you and the first drops together. Now up go the big, bold umbrellas of the Turf Accountants. Down drifts the rain. Down stream the betters. And, back to the stands again, you pocket your Pac-a-mac (plastic Irish raincoat) dry and warm inside your homespun Irish jacket and watertight Irish handsewn shoes (respectively forty dollars and twenty-nine dollars, carefully made to your measure).

And now they're off! And you peer through the rain (coming down now as hard as it ever does in Ireland). Watch them round the near turn. Lose them at the far turn. And then, (the rain slackening to a falling mist now), see the first horse emerge, still shadowy and ghostly, to float over the first just rainbow-halo'd hurdle.

And all this time no one around you will have said a word about the weather. Unless you've been spotted as an American. In which case—remembering guiltily all that famous sunlight in Florida (or is it California?)—someone will be certain to exclaim: 'Shocking weather, isn't it? Were you here last month? Were you not? It was grand then.'

But perhaps you do not wish to go to Killarney races at all this day, but are instead, when the rain breaks, golfing at one of our 209 rain-greened courses. (Average green fees eighty cents). Without even breaking stride, our Irish golfers continue their fierce pursuit, while their caddies (average fee, forty cents) open great rainbows of Irish golf umbrellas over them. But your caddy, having noticed you are an American, murmurs as he opens your umbrella: 'Shocking weather we're having! Will you be here tomorrow? You will not? They say it will be fine then.'

Or perhaps, and this might be the best perhaps of all, you will this day be in Dublin when it rains and at the very beginning of your Irish visit. Now in fine weather in Dublin—what with the polo matches, the zoo, the flower shows, the Horse Show, the smiling Georgian houses and the walk along St Stephen's Green where the rakes, blades, bloods, bucks and dandies used to walk—there is so much to lure you outdoors, you may miss the pleasure waiting indoors. Unless it rains.

But if it rains, then surely you can dawdle in good conscience, feeding upon cream cakes and raspberries in the light of the stained-glass windows at Bewley's Oriental Café (the café in the film *The Girl with Green Eyes*). And if it rains, then surely you will get to Trinity College for *The Book of Kells* (worth squandering a week of sunny days). And if it rains, then surely you will shop. For that warm, almost moisture-proof homespun jacket. For those watertight, handsewn shoes. And even for that plastic Pac-a-mac (two dollars) which you may very likely need during the rest of your stay in Ireland—although you may equally likely not. (In the latter case, you may use it when you get home to New York. Or even Florida. Or is it California?')

Folly, as I said earlier, that! On second thoughts, indeed, I withdraw my nomination of Claiborne for President of Ireland and/or the United States. I would install her instead behind an enormous bar at Shannon Airport, selling draught water, showers on the rocks (for Americans), Château Deluge and liqueur cloudburst. In a couple of weeks, she would have the country rich enough to bolster up the dollar and would have pushed the sales graph so high that United Irish Distillers and Arthur Guinness, Son and Company, Limited would be screaming for mercy.

Nor was weather the only problem. Every natural asset seemed to be counter-balanced by a disadvantage, every silver lining threatened by a growling thunder.

One of the bigger problems was the fact that we had few places in which to corral our tourists, only a tiny, anaemic hotel tradition. In the bigger cities, admittedly, there were the watering-places of the old Anglo-Saxon ascendancy, the Dublin Castle mob, as they were irreverently called. These were gracious living reservations, with all the trappings of genteel discomfort that the phrase implies.

Elsewhere there were what were known euphemistically as family hotels, some of which were reasonable and some of which were not. This latter, darker lot was divided into two groups: first, there were establishments of immense inefficiency, mild squalor, atrocious food (fossilized brown windsor soup), wall-weeping damp, warmth, friendliness and kindness.

These establishments had some merit. They usually were run by decent, untidy, big-hearted women, who would sew buttons on shirts for their guests and serve drink at all hours of the day and night as an essential service, a way of life, rather than a commercial transaction. They genuinely wanted to make people welcome and their horizons of service were bound only by their gross inefficiency and utter disorganization. To appreciate them demanded a loyalty and understanding far beyond the capacity of any foreigner, let alone any foreign tourist, paying for pleasure.

Without merit were the family hotels in the second section. They were run for masochists by sadists; narrow-eyed women, whose sisters, I believe, were housekeepers to elderly priests,* who accepted them as penances that went with the job. They still exist, incidentally, these pinched, presbytery tyrants, who persecute their masters with boiled fish and wan discomfort and insist upon knowing the most intimate details of every visitor's private life before allowing him to set a sin-sodden foot over the threshold; but they are a dying race, drowned, perhaps, by the wave of liberalism that washed from the Ecumenical Council.

Their sisters, who ran country hotels, were eighth Dan, Black Belt exponents of the esoteric art of inhospitality. They really worked on the job of making their guests miserable. Food was wrecked, not by accident, but by sheer hard graft and cunning. It was served only with the greatest of reluctance and to the accompaniment of whingeing sniffs at the effrontery of those who had the temerity to demand it. Beds were flea-ridden and the fleas, I insist, were bred specially for the purpose—dirty great monsters with jaws like steam shovels. The grinding of their teeth alone would keep you awake. Doors were closed at ten o'clock and battering rams would not budge them thirty seconds after that hour. Once, indeed, I had to sleep on the floor of the Day Room of a Co. Kilkenny police station (or I should say Garda Barracks) because of this curfew and I must say that I got better service there. The Sergeant served me cocoa and ham sandwiches for breakfast and with a smile, too.

Not even the words of Adrienne Claiborne could have magicked away that oppressive cloud, but the combined efforts of the Bórd Fáilte soldiers have made spectacular progress. Standards have been revolutionized.

Between 1960 and 1967 the number of hotel and guest house bedrooms increased from 17,800 to 24,000 and the number of rooms with baths went up from 1,160 to 6,099. This last achievement was particularly praiseworthy because it was achieved in the teeth of a grim, dark suspicion which some Irish hoteliers had in relation to the business of washing. In their hotels there was no running water in the bedrooms,

---

* Some priests had nice housekeepers; but the dragons were more noticeable.

only a huge basin and a jug, half-filled with a tired, yellow liquid that looked as if it could start a typhus epidemic by smell alone. Some manageresses regarded washing as a bit of a weakness, but accepted it; baths, however, they seemed to believe were a new and particularly perverse form of indecent exposure. Bathroom doors were locked; and if a guest managed to browbeat the key-jangling, grumbling custodian into opening them, a penal charge was levied against him.

Now most Irish hotels are clean, bright, happy places. Broadly speaking, the service is good and the food attractive, if not always wildly imaginative. The Tourist Board hope to have 1,500 extra double rooms a year until 1970 and here they are on target. In 1968 alone, eighteen new hotels opened their doors, the capital investment being over £3,000,000.

A fair amount of this capital was foreign—British, American, German—and the investors received a grant of thirty-five per cent from the Tourist Board. In some cases, however, local lads went to work.

Billy Huggard, for instance, is a man with several generations of hotel tradition behind him. He was born in the Butler Arms, Waterville, Co. Kerry, which he now runs, a solid, homely, family hotel, which for many years has given the wealthier fishermen of the world the high, quiet standards they wish. Fish do not exactly grow on trees in the grounds, but they are never very far away, large, vigorous and hungry.

Had he wished, Billy could have confined himself to the tradition he had always known, allowed the wind of tourist trade to pass him by and ended up, in all probability, a wealthy man. He believes, however, that progress is necessary and that it can be grafted successfully onto tradition, if the operation be done with care. This he has achieved with sensitive guile.

The fishermen still stay at the Butler Arms; but so now do a more adventurous section of travelling people, lured not only by such traditional Irish forms of entertainment as a team of well-bred horses, but by sulkies, surfing and sand yachts.

Billy Huggard knows, however, that the modern tourist coming to Ireland demands even more. He knows, too, that he cannot fit them either physically or, perhaps, temperamentally into the Butler Arms. So he has bought a large chunk of land stretching along the coast; and there he plans to build a new hotel. His dream is to combine there the old, warm intimacy of the Butler Arms with the new standards which are being demanded. If he can manage to do so, he will be a genius and I am inclined to think that he is.

He has done much more than dream, however, for dreams this Ireland has discovered somewhat belatedly fill no bellies and empty no emigrant ships. He has spent eight years and a substantial amount of his own money developing this stretch of land, which he has bought bit by bit from local farmers. In that time he has employed sixteen men, who otherwise would have had little work in this barren, neglected, Irish-speaking area; and, though no hotel is there yet, the results already are spectacular. Its boundaries are marked by windsocks, signs of the private planes which have landed there already and of others which, he hopes, will land in the future. The beaches are magnificent and mostly natural; but some he has built himself, grinding the rock away with a bulldozer and letting nature replace it with sand. He has even torn a harbour from the side of a hill that ran into the sea and built a bathing pool. The rocks, dark and craggy, from these operations, have been used for landscaping; and all along the foreshore they stand, hauled into wild, megalithic designs by his sixteen workmen. Complementing this ancient theme are a couple of dozen tiny shelters, built to a traditional design by Dan McCarthy, one of the local workers, stones interlacing in complex symmetary and the result looking at a distance very like the beehive cells of the early Irish monks.

Why were these vast, natural resources not exploited earlier? Because nobody had ever seen them. Because there were no roads to them. Billy Huggard found them by pulling on waders and sluicing through bogs. Since then he and his men have drained the bogs, built the roads, filtered electricity to this barren, forgotten beauty; and now all he needs is the capital to build his dream hotel. Whether he will get it I do not know, but certainly he deserves it.

The trouble is that the tourist industry has outgrown in most cases the resources of any one man, no matter how able, no matter how dedicated. It has moved into the hands of the big combines, the cartels, almost; and therefore, through nobody's fault, really, the humanity of a business, which must be geared to the individual, is at risk.

The Irish individualist, however, is not an easy kitten to drown. Men like Billy Huggard, who fight for a personal tradition, are being joined in the tourist field by others who see tourism as a key to survival, not only for themselves, but for their community. Few areas can live on tourists alone, but some find in it the difference between swimming and going under.

One man who came to that conclusion is Marcus Clements, descendant on the one hand of the Earls of Leitrim and on the other of a couple of well-known Irish squirearchies. I tell his story at the risk of mixing up some branches in a complex family tree because I feel it reflects a spirit which has been missing from the country for too long.

When Marcus was eighteen years old, he inherited from his father the family estate at Ashfield, Cootehill, Co. Cavan. At the time he was a minor and, because the family funds were somewhat anaemic, his elders decided that it would be better to sell.

At this point Marcus (for want of something better to do, he told me) decided that he would punch in some national service in Britain. There, however. he collided with a constitutional problem.

'You can't do national service,' the army told him. 'You're a citizen of the Irish Republic.'

He resolved that by enlisting for three years, and is rather proud of the fact that, despite his education and background, he managed to evade being saddled with the Queen's commission, spending his entire service career in the ranks. When at last he was demobilized, he studied farming for a few years with the intention of buying a small farm somewhere in Ireland. The idea was to get something neat and compact.

Then an elderly cousin offered him another family estate, owned by another branch of the tree . . . Lough Rynn estate, near Mohill, Co. Leitrim. It contained a splendid old house, 400 acres of farmable land, another 400 or 500 acres that could be used for afforestation, 100 acres that were complete waste and 1,000 acres of water.

'It was a most generous gift,' he told me, 'and I accepted immediately. I had a pleasant house with a pleasant view and was sitting, in fact, on a sizeable and, presumably, saleable piece of real estate. I did not want to sell, however, having seen one family estate broken up; and I soon learned that it was a hell of a place to scratch a living. The problem was one of survival.'

He discovered another factor. Those who live in farming areas quickly become a part of the community. Lough Rynn, despite all its water and its unworkable acres, was a big farm which gave a fair amount of employment. If it went down, it would drag many livelihoods with it; and a few score more would take the boat train to Britain.

At that point he decided that he would have to invest more money not merely in the farm, but in the area. It needed something which would attract fresh money, tourist coinage, for instance. If he could acquire a few caravans and rent them to visitors, he felt that the parish would feel new life. Apathy might begin to dwindle in this thoroughly depressed area.

To raise money he decided to sell some family heirlooms; and thus he found himself in the middle of a right old controversy at national level. The heirlooms in question were the Killymoon Hoard, four gold clasps and a gold collar, magnificently worked by craftsmen 3,000 years before the birth of Christ. They had been found in a bog on his ancestors' estates in Co. Tyrone in 1815 and had been in the family's possession ever since.

Marcus Clements took them to Sotheby's in London; and, as soon as the sale was announced, a woeful wail arose. He was selling his national heritage, said the Celtic purists. The Hoard should be handed over to the National Museum to rest forever in the lily-white bosom of Mother Ireland.

Clements replied that there was nothing he would like more than to see such a bosom enhanced by the Hoard. Nevertheless, he felt that the living people of Leitrim (*circa* A.D. 1960) were a more valuable national heritage than inanimate golden ornaments (*circa* 3000 B.C.). If he did not sell, his farm might sink and quite a few people from around Lough Rynn might be forced to decorate the bosom of Birmingham.

The purists, fighting back, demanded to know how this scion of a noble family had taken the Hoard out of the country in face of regulations which prohibited the export of gold worth more than £100. Clements replied (a) that he had put the Hoard in his jacket pocket and (b) that he had not known anything about the regulations, though, naturally, he was extremely sorry if he had broken them.

At that point the situation was complicated further by the Ulster Museum, whose custodians said reasonably enough that they should provide a home for the gold because it was found in Co. Tyrone, which was their territory. The directors of the National Museum in Dublin agreed on that point and announced that they would not bid against Ulster, when the sombre commercial transaction took place at

Sotheby's. Altogether the scene was set for some ripe drama and the production did not disappoint.

At the sale, the bidding rose quickly, with Ulster winking away at the right moments and Dr Liam O'Sullivan of the National Museum in Dublin honouring the promise. Ulster's last bid was £8,500 and after that there was a little pause. It seemed that they had won, which was just as well because they had no more money to spend.

Suddenly, however, there was a fresh bid of £9,500. It came from someone representing Mr X, one of those mysterious, anonymous figures who enliven all the best international auctions from time to time. Ulster sagged to the ropes, beaten by the bank balance. Dr Liam O'Sullivan realized that he was the only person who could keep the Killymoon Hoard in Ireland—but he did not know the strength of the opposition. So he bid £10,000 and sat back, hoping for the best and hoping, too, that Mr X's man did not know that he had flung his final punch, for Dublin's purse was limited, too.

There was, however, no further bid. The Republic owned the Hoard. Dr O'Sullivan went at once to his Ulster rival and told him that his colleagues in the North could have it on loan for exhibition from time to time.

Marcus Clements returned to Lough Rynn with the money and set about investing it. He bought eight caravans and planted them on the shores of the Lough. He advertised pony rides and boat trips amid some of the finest scenery in Ireland. He even went into the Stately Home business, throwing open his house in the hope that visitors might come, see and be drawn back to stay a while in the area with their friends.

'It's not very stately,' he said, 'but the grounds are nice. It can be quite hard work, too, because I've got to keep the drains clear and the lavatories clean and see that I never run out of cigarettes or a nice smile. There are about a dozen of us in the Stately Homes business now, most of them with much grander places than mine, and we're forming a properly organized group—the National Union of Stately Home Operatives and Allied Trades or something—so that we can exchange ideas and discuss common problems.'

Now he is planning to expand, to provide sailing facilities, perhaps, or water skiing on Lough Rynn, which is three miles long. He is hoping to buy more caravans, some static, some mobile for the more adventurous. Yesterday's gold, indeed, seems to have given the area hope for tomorrow; and that, I feel sure, is something which would please the men who worked it so well nearly 5,000 years ago. They would not have liked the thought of emigrating any more than their descendants do today.

BY selling rain—or, more accurately, by down-grading sun in the scale of tourist necessities—the Irish have given themselves an advantage over their rivals. It has enabled them to stretch their season substantially, the ultimate objective, of course, being to keep it rolling for twelve months of the year. In this way they not only keep good staff, but utilize their plant to its fullest extent.

Their next task was, is and will be forever selling Ireland without down-grading the product. This requires guile and subtlety because of the rather fuzzy picture most foreigners have of the country. Take, for example, the problem of the leprechaun. I suppose this horrid little cobbler with his peaky cap and his green, Noddy-type breeches, has some squalid corner in Irish folklore; but I have no intention of seeking it out, for we have a much more valuable folklore to exploit. Unfortunately the non-Irish in general, and the English and Americans in particular, love him. They want him and expect him, and feel cheated when the natives retch at the mention of him.

What can we do about that? If the cash customer insists upon being sold a green pup, must we send him away? Seán White, Press Officer for Bórd Fáilte in New York, gave me one answer: we compromise. He told me: 'The Americans have a cosy, preconceived idea about us. They think Ireland is a misty, backward country, and they are a little disappointed when they find that nobody is starving and that everybody is not drunk all the time, dropping their clay pipes on the floor and singing 'Mother Machree', who, of course, is old, white-haired, rosy-cheeked and bulging with folksy philosophy while she dies of a touch of the famines. You and I know the truth about her and about Ireland. But it is not easy to tell people the truth. They only want to listen to what they want to hear and what they want to hear about Ireland must have its quota of leprechauns and shillelaghs.

'So all we can do is give them an aesthetic leprechaun, a shillelagh which looks good and is made in Ireland rather than Japan. We offer them a great deal more that is genuinely Irish, of course, but you can't shatter old images overnight, if you want to stay in business. You can't say: "This is what you should have in Ireland and this is what you're going to get".'

To erase a false image from the mind, it is necessary to make the genuine article more attractive. This is the Irish aim and a fair example of their tactics in this direction is provided by the medieval banquets provided at Bunratty, Knappogue and Dunguaire Castles, all within an ass's roar of Shannon Airport.

The castles are genuinely ancient and have been restored splendidly. What goes on inside is, of necessity, plastic to a degree, but the tourists love it. They sit down in baronial halls. Very attractive waitresses tie bibs round their necks. The food—chicken, salmon, roast beef, spare ribs of pork—could be ancient or modern, but the whole atmosphere is sered yellow and, whether guests wish to eat with their fingers or not, they polish massive plates to the accompaniment of traditional Irish songs, beautifully sung by professionals. The whole affair is drenched with mead, of course, which helps the night along like a following wind. Whether the traditional ancient Irish peasant ever had much traditional ancient Irish mead as a meal-time gargle, or whether, for that matter, he had many spare ribs of pork to toss to the wolfhound is a matter of opinion; but what the hell? We never were much of a people for the strict letter of the law and the whole gravy-stained carnival is a whack over the ear for Larry, the lousy leprechaun.

Aer Lingus, the Irish airline, incidentally, give a gentle tweak to the same ear in one of their advertisements. They show a sketch of an American tourist holding up a thoroughly disgruntled Larry to a doubting customs officer. Underneath they say: 'Find one and we'll fly him home with you. Free!' Splendid, doubt-planting stuff, that. Every tourist knows that what is free is false.

The traditional Irish music offered at the Castle is watered down to some extent to make it palatable to international palates. It would be too much to expect them to swallow it neat, for only a few Irish can do that. This watered-down melody is served up in liberal enough doses in many parts of the country, for most Irish hotels offer cabaret now, which is something new; and, though the purists may squeak with outrage, the general effect is pleasant enough and the interest aroused in genuine Irish traditional music quite substantial.

Other audience-participation programmes provided for tourists are gaily-painted gypsy-type caravans, in which they meander around the country in any direction they or the horse chooses; and horse-drawn cabs, which ply for hire in Dublin. Again purists or cynics get uppity about the sight of these anachronisms, but with little cause. It is true that there are no gypsies in Ireland, only tinkers, a different breed altogether. It is equally true that the caravans have most mod. cons.

But what is so great about suffering? And what better way to see a bit of the country than slowly?

Certainly no Dubliner would be seen dead in a horse-drawn cab, unless extraordinarily drunk (a condition in which he is seen less frequently these days); but he should be the last person to destroy the tourist's fun. We are not alone in this last, harmless, lucrative little foible anyway. Surreys with fringes on top amble about New York. I was dying to have a go in one myself when I was there, but I was afraid somebody might think I was a tourist, which, of course, I was and obviously at that. Every stranger in a strange land should be a tourist, no matter how hard he is working there.

The disadvantage of the castles and the caravans and cabs, is that they separate the visitor from the native to some extent. This cuts across Tourist Board policy, which is that the visitor should get to know the host and learn to enjoy his way of life. In this way leprechauns and shillelaghs should wither in the light of reality and everyone would be happy. To counteract this touristic apartheid—which exists in every country—the 'festival' has been invented. The Irish have discovered in their artistic souls a genius for creating festivals for the most unlikely subjects and now they are producing them as fast as the Japanese build ships.

They have beer festivals, film festivals, theatre festivals, opera festivals, dancing festivals, choral festivals, angling festivals, oyster festivals, lobster festivals, and festivals for anything else that happens to trip someone with a glimmer of imagination. The latest offering was a Steam Traction festival and a wild, gay affair it was, too, with mobile steam barrel organs oompahing their way around city and country. In 1968 alone there were 156 of these organized junketings and they were so successful that the Tourist Board subsidized them to the extent of £32,000.

It could be argued—and probably is—that these appeal to sectional interests only. That certainly could be true of other countries, but not of Ireland. In the first place, we are rolling them off the assembly belt at a terrible rate of speed and their sheer volume, therefore, must ultimately envelop everybody. Secondly, a genuine interest in the subject matter can be a positive disadvantage because usually, as soon as the affair comes under starter's orders, its theme is drowned in a garish welter of other activities—drinking, singing, dancing, laughing and seducing, all of which go on round the clock, breaking out without warning, but with great intensity.

My own baptism took place at the Kerry Festival, which probably is unique because its purpose is quite unashamedly to bring money into Kerry. I stuck the six-day course for three days; and I can say that, if other Irish festivals are one quarter as good, Córas Trachtála, the Irish Export Board, should start bottling them and scattering them around the world in the interests of international amity. Never have I known a wilder time with less discord. Never before have I seen the inhibited Irish dancing in the streets at three o'clock in the morning and not giving a damn who saw them. Never did I believe that I would sing 'God Save The Queen' in the streets of republican Tralee at midnight without being lynched; but that I did, not in a wave of nostalgia for my home in England, but as an act of faith to prove to myself and the world that anything could happen at the Kerry Festival without a bit of bother. My faith was justified, too, for my hymn was cheered, and those who knew the words—a drunken trio of mixed parentage—joined in.

It all began, according to official legend, in Roger Harty's pub in Tralee in 1958. Dan Nolan, Chairman of the Race Week Carnival committee, was there with his brother, Ned, Joe Grace, Florence O'Connor and, of course, Roger himself. They were conducting post-race-week mopping-up operations, when one of them said: 'How about a festival instead of a carnival next year?'

Please do not ask me what is the difference. It would be better not to ask them, either. It is enough to say that the thought triggered off a wild sequence of other thoughts, one of the worst of which was that they should have a 'Miss Rose of Tralee' beauty contest. I say 'worst' because it looks that way when put down on paper. The song itself, in my view, is no more than a rush of cloying sentimentality to the teeth, perpetuated only by the fact that every adenoidal tenor in Ireland seems to have the words drilled into his skull at birth. To build a festival around it seemed like placing Tralee's neck on a shamrock-spangled guillotine.

Yet somehow it worked. That first year there were Roses from New York, London, Birmingham, Dublin and Tralee. The year I was there, there were twenty-three of them, a bundle each from Ireland, England and the United States, with Australia, New Zealand, Canada and France—yes, France!—joining in.

For me even the launching was bizarre. There I was on an Aer Lingus Boeing (which was bound for New York, but due, we hoped, to stop at Shannon) with Miss Georgina Maureen Gerassi, the Paris Rose, who assured me that her mother was of Irish descent, which made everything above board and decent and anyway, hadn't she a middle name to prove it? I said that it did, indeed, and that she had, indeed, before realizing that we were not alone. A team from *Paris Match* was there. A team from French television was there. A man from *Figaro—Figaro,* more sombre than *The Times*!—was there. A screed of journalists capable of covering Britain's entry into the Common Market with a seven-day war thrown in and all on their way to record the dream that was dreamed in Roger Harty's pub!

If it was colour they were after, they soon got it, even though they may not have been able to understand much of it. Waiting at Shannon to greet Miss Rose of Paris were all the other Roses together with a girls' pipe band from London. 'But London,' said a French journalist, 'is in England.'

'London is in England,' I said. 'But there are probably more Irish there than there are in Ireland.'

'But the Irish don't like the English.'

'The Irish have a fondness for English money. Or French money, for that matter. And they don't really mind the English.'

'But you fought. . . .'

'We fought. . . .'

One of Adrienne Claiborne's skitter-scatters of rain came down, extinguishing that little flame of conversation. The Roses piled into a cavalcade of cars and we were off to Tralee, eighty miles away.

The French journalist said: 'Where is the next stop?'

I told him: 'Feale Bridge.'

'Is it a big town?'

'It's not really a town at all.'

'A veelage?'

'No . . . not a veelage. A bridge, really.'

'But why do we stop?'

Taking a deep breath, I said: 'It's the frontier between Limerick and Kerry. The girls have to collect their passports to enter Kerry. And all their relatives come down from the mountains to meet them there.'

'But Kerry is in Ireland.'

'Yes.'

'And Limerick is in Ireland.'

'Yes. It's . . . it's part of the Festival. A bit of fun. A . . . a . . . gimmick.'

But he was not listening. He was flicking the pages of his passport to see whether it was valid for Limerick. And for Kerry.

I was not exaggerating when I said it was a gimmick; but again the aura of Roger Harty's porter hung over us all. We stopped at the border. The passports were handed out. The relatives came down from the hills. The people cheered, men, women and children. The guards smiled; and, as an objective observer, I have to report that the whole damn ridiculous nonsense was quite moving. Those cheers were real. Those greetings, shouted into every slow-moving, Rose-laden car were real, a gorgeous opportunity for the Irish to pour out a few buckets of humanity without inhibitions; and they have buckets to spare.

That, I believe, is the secret of this festival's success. Inhibitions are shed like fading rose petals and, contrary to popular belief, the Irish carry quite a few of them around in their hearts and their minds. One reason, I think, why as a race we drink is so that we can forget them for a while and do what we would not do otherwise. A skin of puritanism, perhaps, has been laid on the Irish, by Cromwell, by the Famine, which killed laughter as well as people, by Queen Victoria, whose matriarchal robe stretched far. Perhaps we are only just getting over all three of these troubles.

On, anyway, into the night to Tralee, where the girls, skitter-scatter rain and all, transferred to floral floats. Up through the town, ablaze with lights hired from Blackpool, the procession headed by boys and girls on horseback. For some strange reason, or maybe for no reason, I had transferred from the car of Carl O'Sugrue, the Aer Lingus Press Officer in New York, a Kerryman who was chaperoning the American Roses, and now I was in a police car on the receiving end of the most friendly catcalls I have ever heard in my life.

A civic reception. A scattering of Roses into the arms of relatives, friends and the warm, damp, summer night. Another cavalcade, this time to the Festival Club, where there were quite a heap of happenings because its bar stayed open until three o'clock in the morning. Most Irish festivals, incidentally, have clubs which stay open until three o'clock in the morning; after that you drink in your hotel or in some-body's hotel.

It was in the Festival Club that the first crisis erupted. One of the French journalists said to me: 'Miss Paris . . . her luggage is missing.'

Now I have never entered a beauty contest; but I know that, if ever I do, I shall need a change of clothes, particularly after a journey from Dublin to Shannon to Feale Bridge to Tralee. I sought out Bart Cronin, another Aer Lingus Kerryman, who was inextricably entangled in the whole Festival fabric, and told him about it.

'I'm working on it,' he said. 'Not to worry.'

Working on it he was. So were Aer Lingus men in Dublin and Shannon. So was the telephone operator at Tralee, who felt as sorry as the rest of us for poor Georgina Maureen and was tearing the wires into flitters in his efforts to contact all who had touched her luggage in the past three or four days. Here was teamwork at its finest, under the captaincy of Cronin, who somehow managed to direct operations and simultaneously take part in a triangular debate about the future of the Irish language, Ireland's chances in the Common Market and whether or not Kerry would win the All-Ireland Gaelic football final.

By four o'clock in the morning, the battle of the baggage (though not the language, the market or the match), was over and Bart Cronin had won. Miss Paris's baggage had been found at Shannon and we all sang the *Marseillaise* with relief. It had been abandoned in its hour of need by the French team, overcome by the sound of London-Irish pipes. It was at that moment that I discovered that I had mislaid my hotel. I had been under the impression that it was about a mile out of town—in a dormitory suburb of Tralee, so to speak. It was, instead, in the village of Fenit, eight miles away, and I had no car. Not even a Boeing.

By five o'clock I was still pondering the imponderable, at which stage in stepped Bart Cronin, who seemed to be chewing problems instead of pep pills. From the double room he had booked for himself and his wife, Máire, who, like myself, had managed to weather the marathon so far on tomato juice, he borrowed a couple of blankets and a pillow. He took them into the upstairs lounge of the hotel, made a mattress out of the biscuit cushions of half a dozen easy chairs and manufactured a bed fit for a Texan oil magnate. I slept there until a quarter to eight; and at that hour, as I was groping my way to the bathroom, I came face to face with another slice of the spirit this Festival breeds.

A couple of Roses, looking as fresh as tomorrow morning's mushrooms, came up to me at full gallop. Together they panted: 'Did the French girl's luggage turn up?'

'It did,' I said. 'A couple of hours ago.'

Together they turned their lovely eyes to heaven and whispered: 'Thanks be to God!'

They meant it. They were genuinely delighted. I am willing to bet my membership card for next year's Kerry Festival Club (a valuable document, God wot!) that in any other beauty contest, most contestants would be secretly pleased if one of their competitors were to lose her trappings; and in a few contests they would have been glad to organize the loss.

I would like to make it clear that Kerry is an affair with wide interests. For those uninterested in beauty and black porter, there are the races at Ballybeggan Park, a veteran car display, football matches, a canal swim, a polka exhibition, a folk theatre, a donkey derby, a golf tournament, judo and wrestling exhibitions and races for tricycles and roller skates. Name it, and, if Kerry has not got it this year, it certainly will programme it for next. These festivals certainly bring in the specialists and the semi-specialists, who learn more, probably, about Ireland than they do about their favourite subject; but what about those who come merely to eat, drink and be merry? How do they fare?

About two million people a year spend over twenty-four hours in Ireland. If they all were dumped down together, they would almost double the population and blow hotel gaskets all over the place. Because of this shortage of space, the Tourist Board—though they would not like to admit as much publicly—would prefer one hundred millionaires to one thousand middle-income-groupers for the simple reason that they spend more money, while taking up much less room. The authorities do not put it quite so bluntly, of course. They say with splendid Irish tact: 'The country is not geared for the mass holiday.'

Because of that, more and more of the new hotel accommodation being built is fourteen carat stuff—Grade A Star, which generally provides fairly high international standards.

That policy certainly gets in a lot of money from the few, rather than a little from each of the many; but it cuts across the Board's expressed desire for their guests to get to know the people. It is possible for Americans to cross the Atlantic, stay in a hotel in a state of suspended, centrally heated animation and return, scarcely having scratched the loose topsoil of the Irish.

This lonely, pointless operation costs a great deal of money. It can also pack a long-term backlash for the tourist industry. Staff trained in these hotels will become pale cosmopolitans, denationalized reception machines; no longer will they be capable of offering anything different and their guests, having been given bread, wine and clean linen alone, will seek their tourist kicks elsewhere the following year, which is sad because Ireland's most valuable asset in this field is its difference from other countries.

Some of the bigger groups realize this danger and are taking evasive action. Córas Iompair Éireann, the Irish nationalized transport company, which owns three hotels in Kerry, one in Galway, one in Sligo and one in Donegal, has its own training scheme, where staff are taught that a welcome is not enough. Only an Irish welcome will do. In this way they have managed to keep an identity, a personality.

This has taken careful planning, for there is always the risk of over-doing the Irish bit, of subconsciously slipping on the stage-Irish jacket, which foreign guests think fits so well. So far, however, they have stoutly resisted this temptation. In the Galway Great Southern, for instance, local visitors may wince at the sight of a sign reading 'Traditional Irish Bar', with its twin phrase in Irish 'Cois Fharraige'. (I shall not attempt to give the phonetics of that because if I did, somewhere a true Gael would burst a green bloodvessel.) When they enter it, however, their fears of finding plastic Celtic (or, worse, still, that frightful leprechaun) vanish. One wall is made of perforated limestone, found in Lough Corrib and about 250 million years old. The floor of Liscannor flags is not a whole lot younger; and the white flashes on the polished limestone bar counter are the fossilized remains of shells and corals. On another wall what looks like a piece of weird and impressive art is, in fact, a five thousand-year-old chunk of yew tree, dug up from a bog in Letterfrack.

It is difficult to get anything more traditional than that collection, but the Great Southern, Galway, have managed it. Dispensing drink from behind the bar are charming young girls from the Gaeltacht (Irish-speaking) area. Not only are both their Irish and English beautiful, but they sing well in both languages and from time to time do so for the entertainment of the customers.

These C.I.E. Great Southern hotels, indeed, are setting a fair yardstick for the rest of the country. Fifteen years ago they were trundling along quite happily, catering for wealthy, elderly English visitors, who wanted to relax in peace. Since then the quantity, quality and nationality of the guests has drastically changed, as a cosmopolitan wave has hit Ireland. New needs had to be met without chipping the old-world charm. They had to expand, for instance. This the Great Southern managed by building on an entire new storey, which was no mean achievement in view of the fact that the building is over a hundred years old. The penthouse now provides a fine restaurant overlooking Galway Bay; a heated swimming pool; and—a thought to make some of the now extinct, Black Widow-type manageresses twirl in their graves—a sauna bath.

With all this building and extending, together with the consequent rise in standards, prices are moving high, a sad fact of life which gives the Irish pessimist, of which there are still many, the chance to knock his largest single industry.

'We're pricing ourselves out of the market,' he moans. 'It took us seven hundred years to get rid of the British, but, aren't we shifting this new bunch of invaders overnight? If we'd only shoved hotel bills instead of guns in the face of the Saxon, he'd have gone centuries ago.'

This, like all Irish laments, has its element of dark blue truth. Prices are high in some places, staggering in others. Bed and breakfast at Dromoland Castle, Co. Clare, for instance, can cost £11 3s 0d at the height of the season. A bottle of Guinness there costs 4s. 6d. and other drinks can cripple a pound note even more quickly. All spirits cost 14s. a double, more than twice usual hotel prices.

It is true that there is no compulsion to enter Dromoland Castle and that its owner, American millionaire Bernard McDonough, can offer less frightening tariffs at two other places he owns, the Shannon International Hotel and the Clare Inn, which is in the grounds of the Castle. Nevertheless the scale of charges in his mother house would make many a European hôtelier grow pale with either terror or envy. Perhaps because we have become such devils for millionaires, there is a gap between the boarding-house and the Grade A Star hotel in the accommodation we have to offer. The Tourist Board claims that it is helping to fill this gap by encouraging the owners of farmhouses to take in guests. There, tourists certainly get a unique holiday. In one Wexford farmhouse, for instance, guests were taught to make rugs by curing sheepskins; and the entertainment is a two-way traffic. An elderly farmer's wife, asked whether the guests caused her much trouble, said: 'Not at all. In the summer they give me someone to talk to. And in the winter they give me someone to talk about!' Only the

Irish can appreciate the full flavour of that remark. Talking about people is a popular blood sport in both city and country.

Motels are popping up here and there to help the less well-heeled move around Ireland without pawning the car. The Irish, however, call them motor inns, which may confuse American tourists somewhat. The reason offered for this rather cumbersome name is that some contemporary paperback literature in general, and *Lolita* in particular, have given the word 'motel' a connotation which has little to do with rest. Come to think of it, some Americans and other nationalities, too, will be more than confused. They will be downright angry. Motels or motor inns, however, it is quite clear that the Irish have plunged deeply into the tourist business and expect to see it expand to un-precedented dimensions in the next few years; and some find this dedicated professionalism a little frightening. Could too much of it change the national character? One airline executive to whom I put this question, said: 'In five years' time I'm afraid you will find Ireland a very different country.'

It is certainly true that a few European countries, once renowned for their lazy charm, have bred a new generation of sharp scavengers. Could the Irish become similar pirates, lying in wait for the tourists, their knives at the ready to sink into the soft underbellies of the wallets?

Personally, I have faith; but there are tiny danger signs, floating in the wind. In the Great Southern Hotel, Galway, for instance, a large gin and tonic costs 6s. 11d., which is not an exorbitant price in a house of this calibre. Unfortunately, some pubs in Galway and Salthill, which do not offer either the service or the comfort of the Great Southern, charge a similar price; and this practice is spreading to places where no tourist rests his head. In one village pub, for instance, the proprietor chatted happily to my wife and me, telling us, as he served a large gin and tonic and a tomato juice, that he had been in the business for twenty-five years. We kicked this little conversational ball around amiably for a while; and, when the time came for me to pay for the drinks, he gazed at the glasses, as if seeing them for the first time. Then softly he said: 'How much is a large gin and tonic? You know I do forget the prices.'

I said nothing. Screwing his face into an agony of concentration, he said: 'I think it's six and eleven.'

A West of Ireland man, who has been a publican for a quarter of a century, would know the price of a large gin and tonic, even if he had been beaten unconscious with the bottle. Here was a clumsy carelessness and that hurt more deeply than the minor robbery. This wisp of contempt for the customer is being revealed in another way by a few hotels and snazzier bars, whose managers seem to think that regulations should be made for the convenience of the staff, rather than the guest.

In one plush establishment in O'Connell Street, Dublin, I ordered two gins and a coffee. I was told: 'You'll have to go into the other bar, if you want coffee.'

I said that I would buy my coffee in the other bar, carry it in and drink it with my friends. The young barman shook his head and said: 'You can't do that. It's against regulations. If you had coffee in here, twenty other people might order it.'

The fact that the profit on coffee was higher than that on drink cut no ice with him. He was concerned only with the trouble of serving it; and I got it only after I had called for the manager.

In some hotels I have found rules which lay down where coffee must be drunk—'not in that lounge, sir, in this one.' Whenever I asked why I could not sit where I wanted to sit, I got no reasonable explanation, only a muttered grumble.

I must say, however, that throughout my ten-thousand-mile tour of Ireland, I was treated generally with courtesy and kindness. The watering-places, which have collared the above black marks, were a very small minority. I still remember with warmth, for instance, the small hotel in Co. Donegal, which forced good value on me.

I asked for a pot of coffee. A charming little girl said: 'Coffee and biscuits, sir?'

'No, thank you. Just coffee.'

There was a long silence. Then, with reddening face, she said: 'I'm sorry, sir. We don't serve just coffee.'

'Why not?'

'We only serve coffee and biscuits.'

She brought me a pot, which contained three cups of excellent coffee, and a plate, piled high with fig rolls. The bill was 1s. 6d.

7　POLITICS

ANY elderly Irish politician, able to take a few minutes off from nursing his hypochrondriacal constituents to view the scene dispassionately, must wonder whether the shadow of anarchy be darkening the constant, constitutional sun.

For the first time since the country won its independence in 1922, party allegiances are not being handed down from father to son, as ballads used to be before they went commercial. This hereditary system, which so many believed was what Irish democracy was all about, is dying. Until this strange sickness of independent political thought struck, it had all been so easy and predictable. There were, after all, only two doctors available to keep the nation healthy.

On one side of the bed was Éamon de Valéra's Fíanna Fáil party. The name is pronounced Fee-anna Foy-el and means 'Soldiers of Destiny', or something equally embarrassing in this self-conscious age. It was made up of men who had opposed the treaty with Britain in 1922 because it gave freedom to only twenty-six of Ireland's thirty-two counties, leaving six in the ancient Province of Ulster beneath the Union Jack.

On the other side was William Cosgrave's Fine Gael party. The name is pronounced Finuh Gay-el and means, roughly, United Irishman. The men who formed it had accepted the treaty as a reasonable compromise in view of the fact that the British were holding a very big gun to the nation's head at the time it was signed.

Since 1932, with the exception of two reasonably brief periods after the war, Dev's party has been in power and Fine Gael has been the main opposition. The two breaks in the sequence were provided by shaky and unlikely coalitions between Fine Gael; Labour; an extreme Republican party (since dead); and a Farmers' party (since dead).

It may seem quaint to outside observers that the main political features should be fashioned by an event which took place nearly half a century ago, that the two major parties do not represent respectively the Right and the Left in Ireland; but it is understandable. The treaty was followed by an ugly civil war between the architects of the two main parties. Families and friends fought each other and killed each other. Worse still, men were executed by those who had been their comrades in the battle against the British. That civil war left a deep wound in the Irish mind. I have always maintained that it would have healed much more quickly if we had not kept on probing it open; but then I was born in 1922, when it broke out, and I did not smell the blood.

Now, however, the whole political scene is beginning to shift. A new generation, just about to get the vote, has cried halt. It is sick of yesterday's acid and is much more interested in tomorrow's job.

The old generation is dying or retiring. Mr de Valéra is eighty-six and President now, above politics. Only one of his civil war colleagues, Frank Aiken, Minister for External Affairs, is in the cabinet. Cosgrave is dead and his son, Líam, now heads the party.

Yet the changes in the political line-up are not yet visible to the naked eye. Fíanna Fáil is still in power, with seventy-three seats in parliament (the Dáil, pronounced Daw-il). Fine Gael is still the main opposition with forty-seven seats; and, if you want to confuse yourself still further on the Irish political scene, ask any local politician what is the major difference between their policies. He may not mention the civil war; he, too, is sick of it, like the young, anxious to forget it, to get on with the job; but it will be there, clinging to the back of his mind, like the old man of the sea.

Young men and women may no longer vote as their fathers and fathers' fathers voted; yet still those fathers react traditionally at election time, their vote being little more than a nervous tic, where once there was that old wound. Garret FitzGerald, a youngish Fine Gael Senator, summed it up well when he said to me: 'Politicians have to choose between the length of old memories and the impatience of young minds.'

Another politician told me: 'The differences are not so much between the parties, as within them.' He is right, I believe. Euthanasia must take place quietly; and that old man of the sea is a long time dying.

It is true that some brave politicians did their best to define for me the difference between Fíanna Fáil and Fine Gael; and their answers show at least how difficult the task is.

Séan Lemass, Prime Minister (Taoiseach, pronounced Taeshauch and that is so rough it will make some Gaels grind their teeth) until he resigned in 1966, told me: 'We in Fíanna Fáil have always been thinking of what to do and Fine Gael has been thinking of what not to do. In Fíanna Fáil there is this constant inquiry about existing procedure.'

George Colley, Minister for Industry and Commerce, said: 'The average voter believes that Fíanna Fáil is doing the job and is doing it better than anyone else could. Fine Gael is just promising to do it. Fíanna Fáil is radical, whereas Fine Gael is somewhat conservative.'

Senator Garret FitzGerald of Fine Gael: 'Fíanna Fáil tends to be concerned with making it easy to get things done. They devise laws to enable the Government to achieve quick results, neglecting the impact of those laws on the freedom of the individual. Fine Gael is more concerned with the liberty of the subject. In the thirties, Fíanna Fáil was a party of the Left and we were to the Right. Now it has moved Right and we have moved Left.'

Brendan Halligan, thirty-three-year-old Secretary of the Labour Party: 'Fíanna Fáil and Fine Gael don't really relate to anything except the historical differences. Fíanna Fáil is a conservative-type government. Fine Gael are caught in a cleft stick. They are seeking a philosophy, having a crisis of identity. There are those who want to develop the party by pushing it to the Left; and there are the rest, who have no other interest than being in opposition to Fíanna Fáil.'

This political schizophrenia is more marked in Irish political parties, I think, than it is in those of any other country. The left wings of Fíanna Fáil and Fine Gael, for instance, are probably more socialist in their thinking than the right wing of the Labour Party. Fíanna Fáil was a radical party in the thirties, as Senator FitzGerald said. Now, however, it is accused of being the tool of big business. Yet it has introduced a significant amount of socialist legislation, including that which nationalized transport; and it has established sixty-one semi-State boards, which handle not only such obvious matters as land, sea and air transport, but are concerned with such diverse affairs as greyhounds, salmon, blood transfusions and seaweed processing.

Fine Gael claims to have moved to the Left and produces its new policy, 'Towards a Just Society', as evidence of the shift. This document certainly outlines the need for major social reforms and tells how Fine Gael would bring them about; but few voters seem to believe it. It was the basis of the party's campaign in the last general election. It did not win a single extra seat; and Michael McInerney, Political Correspondent of the *Irish Times*, commented afterwards: 'The party had wandered much too far from its traditional line of conservatism and private enterprise and . . . the electorate saw a divorce between party and policy.' The old memories beat the young enthusiasms, which must have left many politicians wondering whether old soldiers ever fade away, let alone die.

I have always maintained that Irish memories ('that oul' church was burned by that oul' louser, Cromwell') are laughably long, while

English memories ('don't let's be beastly to the Germans') are dangerously short. I did not realize, however, just how vivid and alive yesterday is to many of my fellow-countrymen until Senator FitzGerald told me about his experience, canvassing in Waterford with some young members of his party. On a number of occasions they were greeted by elderly householders, who said: 'You're for Johnny Redmond, aren't you? We still have his picture on the wall!'

The Redmondite Party represented Ireland at Westminster before and during the First World War. It died with the 1916 Rising and the independence which followed it. Some of its members transferred their allegiance to the newly established Irish Free State Government, manned by those who subsequently founded Fine Gael. The youngsters with Senator FitzGerald were amazed to find history erupting so naturally on the contemporary political scene; but who can blame the old folks, who had been brought up to believe that politics are inherited, even though it is not always easy to understand just what is being handed down and to whom and by whom? Am I not having the same trouble myself, indeed, trying to untangle the tenuous thread for the benefit of poor, ignorant foreigners, so simple that at times they do not even know their political left hand from their right?

The rejection of Fine Gael's progressive policy was due probably to two reasons: the old folk did not want it and the young Left did not believe it would ever be put into force, even if Fine Gael won an overall majority. Credibility gaps in Ireland are splendid open spaces, much wider than those in America, where they first were named, if not invented.

Fine Gael, nevertheless, are not downhearted. In a recent television debate with Jack Lynch, the present Taoiseach, Líam Cosgrave, the party leader, said calmly and confidently: 'We shall form the next Government.'

Senator FitzGerald told me: 'We are making ground, though not as much as we should. The Labour Party may be recruiting more young people than we are, but we are getting a better quality academically, youngsters who are not happy with the right-wing image of the Labour Party. They have come to us in search of the Left.' This confidence is shared by the other two parties, which is unusual only because the immediate future in Irish politics is clouded by the new revolution in thought and by an expanding social conscience.

Fíanna Fáil is confident because it cannot see the electorate turfing out the architects of affluence while the money is still flowing. Labour is confident because the Left is surging and because at last it has set its own house in order; and this despite the fact that it lost two seats in recent by-elections, dragging its total number down to twenty. It, too, is bedevilled by a yawning credibility gap. It is also true that it declared recently for the first time that it is a truly socialist party, mirroring the thoughts of James Connolly, the only Marxist among the leaders of the 1916 Rising who were executed by the British. Again, like Fine Gael, it has produced a policy to prove it; and certainly it is an extremely radical document.

It calls for public control of industry, banking and credit; workers' representation on boards; community control over all building land; and the compulsory acquisition (with compensation) of land owned by big farmers, old widowers, widows and the lazy. This last thought is brave indeed, for history has taught the Irish to treasure land to a degree that is almost obsessive.

Indeed, there is nothing fuzzy about this policy statement, no compromise, no hiding of intent behind a heavy veil of words, an art which we Irish practise with skill and dedication. On foreign policy, for instance, it demands that Ireland stay really neutral and not be merely a 'kept' neutral. It criticizes Aiken for 'speaking with the voice of Dean Rusk' and for failing to back U Thant's request for a stop to the bombing of North Vietnam. Finally it states that diplomatic relations should be established with the Soviet Union. Ireland, admittedly, has moved far from its McCarthy days, when most politicians thought it advisable to give a little spiel about the dangers of atheistic communism, even while talking about drainage in Ballyslapgattery; but not all of the country has moved that far yet and the Labour policy-framers, therefore, are to be admired for their courage, whether or not one agrees with their views.

The trouble is that admiration of the Irish by the Irish is a rare commodity. The past generally transcends the present and the promise of a future, as a result of which one of the more overburdened clichés in Ireland is: 'He's a nice fellow, but . . .'

So it has been with that foreign policy statement, which contrasts strongly, incidentally, with that of Fine Gael. Despite its loudly acclaimed love of the Left, it proclaims in 'Towards a Just Society': 'The foreign policy of a Fine Gael Government will be based upon the defence of freedom at home and abroad against the imperialist aggression of atheistic international communism.' That stems from the dark ages, to which I referred a few paragraphs back. They all talked that way then, even the Labour Party; some would say, indeed, particularly the Labour Party, because it had a more difficult task in persuading the people that it was not roaring, rampaging red. Thus its leaders spent a fair amount of time trying to get themselves photographed with bishops and standing well back from any foreign socialist who happened to be passing through with fraternal greetings. Those old days are remembered. The fresh, new policy is a nice fellow, but . . .

In fact some of the reaction remains; and it is powerful because its main support comes from those within the Parliamentary Labour Party itself. Brendan Corish, the Labour Party leader, has denied that there is anything like a split between the Parliamentary Party and the rank and file; but few Irish political commentators pay much attention to that. It is well accepted that the men in Parliament are nervous of the vigorous new members who have joined the party. Just how nervous they are is difficult to gauge accurately, though Senator Jack McQuillan from Roscommon gave his own assessment when he resigned from the Party recently because of its inactivity. 'Mention socialism at a meeting of the Parliamentary Labour Party,' he said, 'and they sprinkle you with holy water!'

When I suggested to him that the new policy statement contained a fair share of socialism, he said: 'It's a pity the fellows who drew it up wasted so much energy. They won't get anywhere because the Parliamentary Labour Party does not believe in them. When I was a member of it, I used to try and get them to discuss stated Party policies —matters like public ownership of the flour-milling industry, for instance. But all they would talk about was who had paid his sub and who hadn't.'

There we go, back to the credibility gap again. Cannot even the Labour Party beat it, at a time when a social conscience is thrusting its way to the surface throughout the country and so many are genuinely anxious to get done precisely what Labour says it will do in the fields of housing, health and full employment? Again I can but report confidence, though in this case it is supported by figures reasonable enough to water down the taste of two lost by-elections.

Brendan Halligan, who, as Secretary, is one of the newer and brighter young men in the organization, told me: 'We have fifty per cent more party branches than we had two years ago. This year we expect eight hundred delegates to our annual conference, compared with eighty ten years ago. It costs a lot of money, remember, to come up from the country for a conference.

'We have increased the number of Labour Councillors in the Dublin Corporation from five to thirteen and now are the second largest party there, only two seats behind Fíanna Fáil. The party is growing quickly and most of the new members are young—under thirty. In the last three years we have formed branches at University College, Dublin, University College, Cork, University College, Galway, at Trinity and at Kevin Street College of Technology. Nor are they just talking-shops. The students are hard workers for the party, not only doing essential research for our policy-makers, but the dirty chores, too, like sticking up posters at election time.'

The most significant development, however, is the recent affiliation of the Irish Transport and General Workers' Union, the largest and most powerful in the country. It may seem odd to non-Irish socialists that such a vast voice of the worker should not have shouted early and loud in favour of the Labour Party, but the relations between unions and Labour Party are so complex that they deserve another book, which I have promised myself I shall never write. The arrival of the I.T. and G.W.U. on the political scene, however, means not only a fair degree of financial security for the party, but a new element of persuasion, too. Irish trade unionists, remember, were also martyrs to the political hereditary system, too often voting as their fathers voted, the strong ties of blood blinding them to principles, or even interests. Now a number of the bigger unions are actually asking their members to vote Labour and this could well have been reflected by the Dublin Corporation election results.

Brendan Halligan told me, indeed: 'My own aunt always voted Fíanna Fáil. Then her union sent out a circular, asking her to vote Labour. And she did.' He hopes, naturally, that many others have aunts like he has, but he is not blind to the credibility gap. 'We can do our sums as well as anyone else,' he said. 'We know we need fifty-five more seats, if we are going to become the Government. Until recently it has been argued that it would have been almost impossible for us to think of gaining power because we had no policy, no organization, no money. Now we have all three. We must give ourselves about five years' room for development and expansion. In that time we have got to make people believe that we can form a government, that it's socialism for the seventies; and for that reason we are contesting every constituency at the next general election for the first time in the party's history.' Whether or not it will be socialism for the seventies in Ireland, it is safe to say that there will be the more orthodox political balance of Left and Right by then; and that will be progress, particularly in view of the fact that Ireland is becoming industrialized so rapidly.

Two factors which have led to more liberal thought in Ireland are, as I have said, television and cheap holidays abroad. Two more were suggested to me by a man who has as much chance of leading an Irish Government as has Edward Heath of England and George Wallace of America. He is Mick O'Riordan of the Irish Workers' Party, the country's Communist party. The fact that he is still there after the violent attacks against him in the bad old days is a sign, not only of progress in the field of tolerance, but of his own cheerful optimism and resilience.

In New Books, a left-wing bookshop which he runs in Pearse Street, Dublin, he said: 'Pope John and the first sputnik set a lot of people thinking, and that is always a healthy exercise. The Vatican revolution opened their eyes to a new world. The sputnik, buzzing round that world—even over Ireland!—made them wonder whether all the propaganda about the Russians starving under the wicked communist yoke could be a little exaggerated. The next thing they knew was that Kruschev's son-in-law and daughter were being received by Pope John, and they could hardly be called daily communicants. It was a bit bewildering at first, I suppose, but things began to change soon ' afterwards and they have been really moving for the past eighteen months. People have taken a good look at their country, you see. They have realized that, so many years after the treaty, the basic problems remain. Now they are searching for a new social philosophy, and, as they search, so the old taboos disappear.'

For Mick, the changes certainly have been welcome, for he had more than his share of the old orthodoxy. When he ran as a candidate for the Dáil in 1951, for instance, a letter from the Archbishop of Dublin was read from city altars, warning people not to vote for him.

'I didn't hear it myself,' said Mick, 'but he said it would be a mortal sin to support me. I wasn't elected, of course, but I got four hundred votes and it's not many men that can say they had four hundred mortal sins committed for them all in one day. I got one poor fellow into terrible trouble with his wife. He had to confess that he had voted for me and the priest kept him so long in the box, bawling him out, that the wife was convinced that he must have been out with a woman. She wouldn't listen to his nonsense about voting for Mick O'Riordan.'

He was a conductor on the Dublin buses at the time and it is good to be able to report that, despite the propaganda against him and his brand of politics, none of his fellow-workers ever turned against him. 'On the contrary,' he told me, 'when I resigned, they gave me a presentation. I was the only man who ever got one. It was a huge chiming clock, but I had to take the chimes out because they were keeping the whole neighbourhood awake. The boys were a bit puzzled, of course, the night I appeared on television with Father Sweetman, the Jesuit. The pair of us were obviously getting on well together. Next day this driver I know stops his bus in the middle of O'Connell Street during the rush hour, hauls back the window and roars at me: 'Hey, Mick . . . when are you hearing confessions next?'

It will be a long time before Ireland becomes a People's Republic. In the meantime, Mick is an ornament to the cause. He may never get himself elected to the Dáil, but that is no harm. Being a member of parliament in Ireland is a rough old station, according to a pamphlet produced recently by Tuairim, a society which seeks to encourage Irish people to participate in public affairs.

Tuairim—the word means 'opinion'—circularized 141 deputies out of a full strength of 144. They would have done the lot, but for the fact that two seats were vacant at the time and they had decided not to ask the Speaker, who in the Dáil, incidentally, is always addressed in Irish as Ceann Comhairle (Kyown Co-er-leh). The object of the exercise was to find out about their lives and hard times; and the completed questionnaires would have driven the average British Member of Parliament or American Congressman into a monastery at the thought of the life.

The society received eighty-seven replies on the question of particular burdens carried by deputies, and constituency problems easily topped the list. Of the eighty-seven, forty-five complained of the following chores: doing errands for constituents; having them call at inconvenient times; being unable to help them when help was needed; trying to persuade them that they have no grievance; writing letters.

Letter-writing must be a greater chore to Irish deputies than it is to any other parliamentary representatives in the world. One deputy for a rural constituency told Tuairim that he spent two-thirds of his political working time on his correspondence. Another said that he wrote a hundred and fifty letters a week and a third gave the figure of thirty a day. An independent survey by the *Irish Times* came to the conclusion that Dáil deputies between them write over one million letters a year. This costs the Post Office approximately £25,000, a sum which is debited to Parliamentary expenses, for the law-makers do not have to buy their own stamps for these letters.

The demands made by Irish constituents reveal not only a great faith in their representative, but a certain amount of cynicism about law, order and fair play, as the following extract from the Tuairim report shows:

Several deputies stressed the unreasonable nature of some constituents' demands. A Fine Gael deputy described his greatest burden as 'trying to persuade constituents that they are wrong and have no grievance', and another described his as 'trying to convince a small number that the law works on the whole fairly'. Another Fine Gael deputy complained of being 'needlessly harassed by members of the public who groundlessly believe that a deputy's intervention is essential to obtain a right or advantage'.

Fíanna Fáil deputies expressed much the same sentiments. One complained of 'being asked to do impossibilities by constituents and trying to explain why they cannot be done.' Another stated that his greatest burden was 'interviewing, in particular those who make unreasonable demands or are suffering from some imaginary grievances or who think things can be got by 'pull'.

Tuairim suggests, however, that deputies are exaggerating their burdens a little. The pamphlet, splendidly compiled by John Whyte, lecturer in politics at University College, Dublin, states: 'Another possible explanation of why deputies spend so much time dealing with the individual problems of constituents is that they like it that way; that they actually prefer the electorate to believe that they hold the keys to public benefits. Such suspicions are probably fairly widespread among the general public and, indeed, the replies to our questionnaire show that they are not unknown among deputies themselves. One Minister, in putting the case for abolishing multi-member constituencies, had this to say:

The present system of a number of deputies competing for votes in the same constituency leads to a certain degree of corruption of the public mind since there is sure to be at least one who will try to convince his constituents that services, grants, etc, provided by the State or the Local Authority can only be obtained through the intervention of a deputy.

If the burdens of correspondence and constituents are so heavy, why do not deputies deal only with those which really merit their attention? The answer was given simply by a Fine Gael deputy, who wrote: 'Letters must be answered or the deputy will eventually lose his seat. Country deputies are "Penny Boys" and *have* to do messages.'

American readers, who have heard whispers of a place called Tammany, will understand readily much of the above. The thought that a public representative can fix things is not new; it is traditional, springing from the mother country, where it has been known this many a century—even in the days when the straight-batting British were there!

An item which should please Irish voters concerns the advance in education among their representatives. In 1944, according to another survey, forty-eight per cent of them left school at the age of fourteen, having no more than a primary school education. Only twenty-two per cent had university or professional training and forty-one per cent a secondary education up to the age of seventeen or eighteen. In 1965, only twenty per cent had no more than a primary education; thirty per cent had university or professional training and fifty per cent a secondary education.

The report goes on:

A further break-down of the Fíanna Fáil party, distinguishing office-holders from back-benchers, produces an interesting result. Of the twenty Fíanna Fáil deputies who, after the last general election, were given posts as Ministers or Parliamentary Secretaries, sixty per cent, had had a professional or university education. Of the remaining fifty-two members of the party, only seventeen per cent. had had a university or professional education. Though a high level of formal education does not seem important to enter the Dáil, it seems to matter when it comes to Ministerial promotion.

How does a deputy enter the Dáil? Once more the hereditary system pokes its nose into politics. Tuairim reports: 'The general election of 1961 resulted in the return of no fewer than thirty-three deputies, who were connected with former or already sitting representatives of their own or other constituencies. In the general election of 1965, the total rose to the remarkable figure of forty-one, or twenty-eight per cent of the Dáil. (The figures include two deputies in 1961 and one in 1965, who were sons, not of Dáil deputies, but of Members of Parliament in the old Redmondite party.) Of the forty-one relatives returned in 1965, four were widows of former deputies, twenty-seven were sons and one a daughter; six were nephews, one a brother and one a son-in-law. The remaining one, Mr P. Lenihan of Longford-Westmeath, created an interesting precedent by being probably the first father to follow his son into the Dáil.'

A new road to Leinster House, where the Irish Parliament sits, has developed only over the past fifteen years. It is the road from the playing fields. Tuairim records: 'Nineteen of the deputies elected in 1961 (thirteen per cent of the Dáil) and twenty-one of those elected in 1965 (fifteen per cent of the Dáil) could be described in this way (prominent in sport). The twenty-one elected in 1965 included thirteen prominent in Gaelic football, four in hurling,* three in rugby and one each in swimming, association football and long-distance running. We do not suppose that all these sports are equal in electoral drawing power, but, to put it at its mildest, it seems to do a candidate no harm to be a star in football or hurling.'

It certainly does not. Jack Lynch, the present Taoiseach, played hurling for Cork and won five All-Ireland medals, though I had better add quickly and sincerely that he has many other excellent qualities besides his skill on the field. Another sportsman is Alderman Robert Molloy, a Fíanna Fáil deputy who became the youngest-ever Irish Lord Mayor when he took the chain in Galway. I mention him because his sports are rowing, swimming and hockey.

That may not have much significance outside Ireland, but in fact it is a commentary on the changing times. Twenty years ago, Fíanna Fáil would never have dreamed of adopting a candidate who played such a wicked, foreign, un-Irish, English game as hockey; and if he had slipped into the lists by accident, the electorate in Galway would have shunned him completely. If the pendulum should swing any further, they will be playing cricket soon on the lawn at Leinster House.

Before I leave the subject of politics, it might be reasonable to take a quick look at Ireland's impact on the international scene. Considering her size, it has been quite considerable over the years.

---

* A Gaelic game, played with something like a hockey stick. It is said to be the fastest ball game in the world and ice hockey players who disagree should remember that they wear skates.

In 1932, de Valéra was President of the Council of the League of Nations. During the time he represented Ireland there, he strongly condemned Fascist aggression in both Abyssinia and in the Spanish civil war.

In another era and another place, Frederick Boland, an Irish diplomat, made his mark. He became President of the General Assembly of the United Nations; and Tony Gray in his book *The Irish Answer* recalls that on one occasion he broke his gavel trying to restore order to a meeting which included Khruschev, Eisenhower, Nehru, Macmillan, Tito, Nasser, Sukarno, Nkrumah and Castro.

Ireland, indeed, has played a more than active part in the United Nations. She has sent troops to the Congo, to Cyprus, to the Middle East and to various other parts of the world, where a good, neutralist police force was needed. Until some years ago, too, her voice at the United Nations was admirably free from influence by the giants. For four years, for instance, Frank Aiken, Ireland's Minister for External Affairs, worked hard to get a resolution accepted to limit the spread of nuclear arms. Ireland was the first country to propose such a resolution and at the time—1958—Aiken said: 'If we ever get this through, I'll go to Moscow to sign the Treaty.'

Ten years later, he went to Moscow to sign the Treaty of the Non-Proliferation of Nuclear Weapons, yet another sign that we were growing up. Ten years earlier, when the witch-hunts were on, no Irish Minister would have dared to make such a journey for fear of the attacks which would have been made on him at home.

It is interesting to note, incidentally, that Britain, America and France abstained from voting, while the Soviet Union backed the Irish proposal; clear evidence, surely, that Ireland was taking an independent stand.

Further proof of this unbiased and uninfluenced attitude came when Ireland, through Frank Aiken again, showed herself in favour of the entry of China to the United Nations. According to Dr Conor Cruise O'Brien, who was with Frank Aiken at that time and later joined the United Nations staff, that, however, marked the end of an era. He said recently:

In recent years Ireland has become aligned with the United States in the United Nations. That is regrettable and unnecessary, for we are not trying to borrow money from them or anything; and until then we had played a useful part in helping to relax international tension.

When Mr Aiken supported China's entry, however, the Republican Government in the United States called on Cardinal Spellman and his diocesan Press promptly began denouncing Ireland as Red. The Irish Government took fright and today they are still running. Now it is being said that the Pope is to the left of Mr Aiken, but I suppose that, once a people get scared, they stay scared.

Later he told me: 'Ireland now votes against the seating of a Peking delegation to represent China, a vote universally regarded in the United Nations as one expressing subservience to U.S. policy, not merely in relation to China, but to all matters on which the Americans find it necessary to issue their "whip".

'The situation has been somewhat disguised by the fact that initiatives taken by Mr Aiken during his progressive period early in 1961 sometimes have yielded fruit years later. His "nuclear spread" initiative, for instance, dates from 1958, when it was unpopular not only with the U.S., but with the U.S.S.R. too.'

It is sad to see our Minister for External Affairs—or those who move him—back-pedalling at a time when the rest of the country is moving forward so fast. But there it is. We can't win 'em all!

ONE of the more ludicrous myths about the Irish is that we are gay, laughing, happy-go-lucky folk, who froth swiftly to anger and then sponge it away a couple of seconds later with a pint or two. Much as we hate this piece of folklore, we are inclined to foster it because we would prefer foreigners not to know the truth. In fact the Irishman disciplines his temper shrewdly, exposing it for tactical purposes rather than on impulse. This ploy is particularly effective with innocent Englishmen, who are choked with the myth and will give way at the first flare of tantrum, rather than risk death at the hands of the prancing lunatic before them.

When the Irishman displays his real anger, it is an ugly sight. He is cursed with a wealth of words and he uses them like rusty razor blades, leaving scars that frequently are permanent. Normally he does not draw these weapons on foreigners, perhaps because he believes they are not in the same league and that it would be unfair to take advantage of them. Unfortunately this skilful, hurtful word-play is based frequently on a half-truth; and it is the half-lie part of the dangerous composite that lives on. Thus a considerable amount of damage was done when some cynic said: 'By teaching school subjects through the medium of the Irish language, we are becoming rapidly the only nation in the world that is illiterate bilingually.'

That, of course, was nonsense; but it was a hell of a good phrase and so it lived on. Unfortunately it bit deep and dangerously into an undoubtedly damaging controversy that has been bedevilling education in Ireland for over thirty years. When the State was young, it was decreed that the Irish language would be a compulsory subject in all schools; that students who failed in Irish in their State examinations would fail the whole issue; and that those who completed papers through the medium of Irish would qualify for ten per cent extra marks. This privilege meant, presumably, that a clever Irish-speaking student could get 110 marks out of 100. In addition, schools were encouraged to teach all subjects through the medium of Irish, though very few of them did so; and there, of course, rests the half-lie in the comment of the cynic above.

Are many Irish illiterate, bilingually or otherwise? Does our educational system lag far behind those of other English-speaking nations? Both questions are complex, entangled in the Irish language controversy and difficult to answer in one-syllable words. Let me say, however, that until comparatively recently Irish education was worse than that in England, but since then it has leapfrogged into the lead. Here there has been yet another bloodless revolution, which makes me wonder whether the Irish can absorb any more upheaval without reaching for the gelignite, if only to relieve the monotony.

Until the recent industrial revolution, education was split, but by no means down the middle. The majority of youngsters left primary school at the age of fourteen, got themselves jobs as messenger boys and, when they had grown out of their bicycles, turned their eyes towards Liverpool or Birmingham, Camden Town or Kilburn, Boston or New York. They had to work because their parents needed the money. They could have gone at night to vocational schools, but how many do in any country after a hard day's work?

The minority, the children of the middle classes, went to secondary schools, for which their parents paid, though at times they could ill afford it. They left school at the age of seventeen or eighteen and queued for badly paid but thoroughly respectable white-collar jobs. Drapery stores, advertising for staff, made it clear that only those with honours in their leaving certificate, the highest State examination for schools, need apply. Universities were more or less luxuries, for not many parents could afford to support their children into their middle twenties.

All that linked the minority with the majority was a mutual fear and consequent dislike of the Irish language, which threatened to brand them as failures in the State examinations, no matter how brilliant they were at other subjects. All that linked most of their parents was this same mutual fear and dislike. Many told their children: 'What's the good of that old Irish? Where will you use it when you leave school? Where will you get a job without your certificate?' Nobody bothered to tell them that less than one per cent of pupils failed their Irish examination. Plenty of people, however, trotted out that crack about bilingual illiteracy, which went down well with parents worried to distraction about their children's future.

Apart from the jaundiced views they shared on the language question, there was little communication between primary and secondary school children. An effective and unspoken apartheid operated. Children from the secondary schools regarded those from the primary schools as 'no class at all'. They spoke of them as 'gutties', an attentuation which made the implication of the word 'guttersnipe' even more objectionable.

This class distinction, bred by the educational system, was almost indestructible between the sexes. A secondary school boy might lust after a primary school girl—or, more usually, after one who had left at the age of fourteen and since had reached the age of consent. If he let his feelings be known to his fellow-pupils, they would jeer at him by saying: 'Wait till she opens her mouth! Wait till you hear her speak! What would your parents say?' His parents, in fact, would have been horrified, for this barrier was as strong as the colour bar in Britain today. The whole attitude, indeed, was purely Victorian, despite the fact that that particular Queen was not very much loved in Ireland.

Then came the revolution. Down went the barricades. Education until the age of eighteen was made free in 1967. Moreover, shrewd psychological steps were taken to minimize the drop-out, to break the old habit of sending children out to work as soon as they reached the age of fourteen. The age of what now was called 'transfer' was lowered from fourteen years to twelve or twelve plus. In that way it was ensured that all children would get at least two years of post-primary education and it was hoped that many more would stay on to sit for their intermediate certificate at the age of fifteen. By that time the family might have become so acclimatized to secondary education that the pupil would remain until he was seventeen to take his leaving certificate. No secondary school was forced to take part in the new scheme, but ninety per cent of them agreed to co-operate. That still left plenty of headaches for the Department of Education, however. Its officials had to provide new schools, extended schools, more teachers, transport.

There already had been a quiet revolution in the teaching profession. The ban on married women had been removed. Ireland became one of the few countries in Western Europe to stop recruiting untrained teachers. Two new training colleges—one for Catholics, the other for Protestants—were in hand at an estimated cost of £2,000,000. Over ten years, a thousand extra teachers were recruited and classes were cut well below the fifty level, at which they had stood for too long in the cities; and this was done by building about a hundred and fifty prefabricated classrooms in Dublin and Cork. The school building programme was given a boost and in one year 130 new primary schools and 121 major extensions were built, an Irish record. Every primary school was provided with a library; and the drive was intensified to eliminate the small one and two-teacher schools. In the budget for the year in which the scheme was announced, £4,000,000 was made available to secondary schools to build accommodation for the new pupils they would be receiving.

It was all done with a speed and efficiency which not even the Irish themselves believed they possessed and which the rest of the world thought had been drowned centuries before in all that lovely, soft Celtic rain. Even the transport problem was solved ahead of schedule. The Department of Education handed it over to Córas Iompair Éireann, the national transport company which runs all buses and trains, and said: 'We want you to carry 65,000 school children to and from school. We would like whatever scheme you draft to be fully operational in three years' time.'

C.I.E. had their scheme in full operation eighteen months later, halving the estimated time for what amounted to a major military operation. Today they are carrying 80,000 school children in bright yellow buses that not only look well, but warn motorists about the dangerous cargo they carry.

The whole complex manœuvre, indeed, could not have taken place without unparalleled co-operation among all the many interests involved. Certainly it would have fallen flat on its scholastic face if the civil servants in the Department of Education, many of them men just about to get their pensions, had not tossed themselves into the battle with all the enthusiasm of newly promoted junior executives. For years, it seemed, they had been waiting for just this moment; and they grabbed it. They showed that education meant much more than a safe job to them. Not only did they provide new plant and extra staff to man it so that thousands of children would have new opportunities, but they give a brisk spring-cleaning to the whole time-worn approach to education. They boosted the morale of the vocational schools, making them an integral part of the scheme, erasing still further the line between a skilled man with a white collar and one whose collar was blue. They stressed that education was more than a matter of academy, but must provide sound, practical knowledge, too. The curriculum in the post-primary schools was extended to take in subjects such as woodwork and metalwork; and the programme of the vocational schools was widened, too, to include modern languages and all that would be needed for the leaving certificate and later the university. A psychological service was made available to guide students into the most suitable channels; and that move alone was enough to make the older, more conservative teachers eat the strap, which they always had regarded as the only worthwhile guiding missile.

Teaching methods in a variety of countries were studied and their better points were incorporated in a comprehensive Irish scheme. Visual and audio aids were introduced. The expansion of co-education was encouraged where possible, and many post-primary schools are now going co-ed. There is even a convent school which takes boys up to the age of eighteen. Best of all, it was decided that the old iron discipline, which could never be questioned, would have to be relaxed. In future Irish children would be encouraged to ask why, not to accept blindly.

It was an immensely successful revolution, more far-reaching in its effects than many a bloodier affair in Irish history. The early leader was George Colley, but when he was transferred from the Department of Education to become Minister for Industry and Commerce, Donogh O'Malley took over. He was a handsome, strangely glamorous character. He had been educated at Clongowes Wood College, Ireland's Eton and scarcely an incubator of social reformers; and he had a quirkish humour which needled a few of his cabinet colleagues.

Always a sharp dresser, he would turn up at meetings of the Government wearing clothes which were just a nose ahead of current fashions. Other members were inclined to raise a disparaging eyebrow, but a week later some of them would sneak off quietly to their tailors and order something similar. Generally speaking, they were too late. O'Malley, too, would have been to his tailor and would turn up at the next meeting one jump ahead again, smiling, bland, charming.

Here was no sophisticated clown, however. When it came to his job, O'Malley was unyielding and dedicated, his words chunky with truth. When he spoke of the poorer children to whom he was offering new opportunity, it was as if he was sitting in the desk with them in a crumbling, damp-dreary rural school, or walking the long walk home with them, rain oozing through his shoes. Once, for instance, he was asked why he did not have a means test, why this scheme of his should be free, even for those who could afford to pay. He replied: 'Don't think that we did not consider one. We decided, however, that the psychological effect on a child could be damaging. If some of the pupils were paying fees and more of them were not, the pupil who was free could get it into his head that he was in some way inferior to the others.

'The same line of thinking decided us not to have a means test for the free transport. Can you imagine a bus pulling up on a cold winter's morning and the conductor shouting to a group of children: "You five are free. You three are not."? This trend would be equally upsetting to the young mind.'

Asked what he had seen wrong with Irish education, he replied: 'The major defect, when I became Minister, was lack of equality of opportunity. Many of our children were denied the opportunity of climbing the educational ladder because their parents could not afford to send them to post-primary schools. Ability to pay school fees and in many rural areas ability to pay transport costs governed participation in post-primary schools. My scheme for free education, which provides for free tuition, free transport and free books, takes care of this problem. At present I am considering the possibility of extending the opportunities of university education for students who have the necessary ability.'

He died in March 1968, at the age of forty-seven, at a political meeting in Limerick City, where he had his constituency. School-children lined the streets in spontaneous tribute as the coffin passed by; and, when a stranger remarked on the size of the funeral, one of Donogh O'Malley's fellow-Limerickmen said: 'Wasn't he the biggest man in Ireland?'

The following day, writing in the *Irish Times*, Liam McGabhann asked a question which was by no means rhetorical: 'Which will outlive the other in his countrymen's minds—the legend or the loss?'

O'Malley's monuments are the fresh, new schools and new class-rooms that hold new hope; and, not least, the gay yellow buses I saw wherever I went in Ireland, the buses on which everybody rides free.

Inevitably, the Irish language was caught up in the revolution; and here again substantial progress was made. For too long this pond had been stagnant and the movement to stir it was helped along by public opinion, which was becoming more vocal. In Ballinasloe, Co. Galway, where children in one school were taught through the medium of Irish, parents organized a referendum and voted in favour of teaching through English, despite the fact that some of them received threatening letters and phone calls.

The Gaelic League, oldest of all the societies for the promotion of the language, protested that, out of 4,700 primary schools in the country, only 250 taught through the medium of Irish; and of those 250, 230 were in Irish-speaking areas. It pointed out, too, that the Ballinasloe school had won more scholarships and academic distinctions than any other school in Ireland, which should have nailed forever the lie about bilingual illiteracy.

The parents' decision was accepted, however; and in Dublin pressure was being applied from a different direction. A number of people formed a group called the Language Freedom Movement to press for the abolition of Irish as a compulsory subject. One of its meetings in Dublin was so boisterous that police cars and Black Marias were drawn up outside, which some visitors regarded as a piece of international one-upmanship.

'All over the world the students are protesting,' one tourist said to me. 'In Ireland their parents man the barricades.'

The L.F.M. represented the extremists. If Irish had not been a compulsory subject, the language probably would have died, which would have been sad. Today, however, though few speak it fluently, most people—myself included, despite over-exposure to Anglo-Saxon influences—can muster a few words. What had been wrong for years was the grim-faced approach to the subject and this the Department of Education decided to change. Its senior officials were inclined to agree that they had tried to achieve too much too soon. So they formed a team to carry out a scientific study into methods of teaching a second language. They were impressed particularly by the American and French approach; and now at last modern courses, incorporating the use of tape recorders, films and other audio and visual aids, are being prepared for schools. More emphasis is being placed on oral Irish; and pupils who fail only in Irish in their Leaving certificate, are allowed to have a second run at it.

The most dramatic move, however, was the publication of a new Irish phrase book, called *Buntús Cainte* (Basic Speech) and containing conversations far more meaningful than the usual 'pen of my aunt' variety. It was presented on television by mini-skirted girls, which was a major break-through because the older Gaels had emphasized constantly that Irish and modesty were synonymous.

Some have dismissed this departure from the old puritanical line as a rather heavy-handed gimmick, like a bishop trying to do the frug. Generally, however, the programme has been accepted with more smiles than frowns and it probably has done a good deal to change parents' attitudes. Some see their children enjoying *Buntús* and feel that Irish cannot be so bad after all. A few even join in the lessons, being helped by their own youngsters as they scrabble in their minds for long-forgotten phrases.

All in all, Irish education is in a healthier condition today than it has been for decades; and, having said that, it might be an idea if I had a look at the end product: Irish youth. I found them very much like youth all over the world today, except, perhaps, less so; and that surprised me, knowing how partial the Irish are to extremes.

They can quote you the first five in the Top Twenty, but would not tear down a hotel lounge to catch a glimpse of the Beatles or the Rolling Stones. In fact Number One Stone Mick Jagger spent some weeks in Ireland recently with his girl friend, Marianne Faithfull, and nobody bothered them at all. They are, in the main, critical fans with an instinctive liking for ballads and a good, broad knowledge of them. They also have invented a pop phenomenon all of their own—the Show Band, which is about twice the size of a British group and a good deal more versatile than most, though it plays the same kind of music.

They have more money than had the previous generation because the previous generation (now their parents, if you follow me!) allow them to go out and work for it during the holidays. Their grandparents would have been horrified at the idea and would have forbidden it because of what the neighbours might think. When I was staying in the Rio Hotel, Salthill, Co. Galway, many of the waitresses were secondary school girls, and a very good job they did, too.

They probably are as genuinely religious as their parents are, but more inquiring, less ready to accept as a Divine ruling what their clerical elders say. One group of vocational students told me, for instance, that they had walked out of class the previous day because their priest teacher had cancelled their normal break without explanation. 'If he'd had a reason, it would have been different,' they said. 'But he wouldn't give us a reason. He's a man who keeps telling us to ask him any question we like, but when we do, he won't give us an answer.'

They demonstrated this independence of mind again, when we were discussing the contraceptive pill. They had voted narrowly in favour of it on a split decision and for reasons of humanity. Then a young priest present said: 'Would you not obey a ruling of the Pope?'

I must stress that he was seeking knowledge genuinely, not expressing horror, for he was one of the new progressives. The answer was: 'No . . . not if we believed he was wrong.'

Neither of those statements would have been made, or even considered fifteen years ago. Nor would they have discussed such matters as contraception with a Martian from another generation, like me. They were well aware of this new state of affairs, too, for one girl said to me with a grin: 'If my grannie heard me talking like this to you, she'd have my ears.'

It is interesting that she should have said that to me and not to the priest. They found it perfectly natural to be talking freely in front of him because he was nearer their age and they knew him. Fifteen years ago, however, no matter what his age, they would have said no more than: 'Yes, Father . . . No, Father.' The slightest rebellious thought would have been cloaked in their minds.

A few teenagers use drugs in Ireland, but they are very few. They drink, but not, I would say, as much as their predecessors. Quite a number of girls told me: 'Our fathers drink too much. Much more than our boy friends.'

Unlike the girls in Britain, who blatantly do the chasing, the Irish girls still keep up the pretence that they are the hunted and rather shocked at the idea. The only difference is that fewer and fewer of the boys believe them, perhaps because in Dublin at any rate, young women considerably outnumber young men. One teenage girl told me, in fact: 'A lot of the fellows are after only one thing now. No beddies and it's bye-bye.' That thought was expressed to me many times; but never quite so well. Do many go to beddies? Again I would say that the Irish girls are not nearly so promiscuous as those in Britain. There are, of course, the exceptions, as a recent newspaper report from Cork made very clear. It read:

Cork Corporation at its meeting tomorrow will consider a motion from Mr T. P. Leahy, calling for an immediate conference between the Corporation, Harbour Board and other bodies to arrange for the closing of Cork quays and wharfs to unauthorized persons.

The Cork port chaplain, the Rev. Leo Lennon, O.P., has called for greater awareness among the people of Cork to the extent to which girls in their early teens frequent the Cork quays and board ships.

A glance at the Mrs Wyse columns of the women's magazines also leads one to believe that here and there an Irish girl wanders from the road of purity. The following letters appeared over a period of a couple of months:

'I am sixteen and had intercourse about two months ago . . . Could I be pregnant?'

"I am fifteen and a half and have been with a boy on two occasions. Could I be pregnant?'

'I am fourteen and a half and I have had one intercourse with my boy friend, whom I love very much. Could I be pregnant?'

'I am a girl of fifteen and Mum allows me to go to some socials and parties during the school holidays. Am I very immoral, if I French kiss?'

'I am sixteen years and last summer I worked in a hotel and as a result I despise married men. One offered me a roll of notes, if I would do wrong with him. Others, even one with a wife and young child in Dublin, kept after me and said I had sex appeal. I then met a lovely English boy and he told me all about sex and said that we were made for one another. We had sexual intercourse, but he said I wouldn't become pregnant. I was thrilled and we are going to get married in the summer and can have a nicer honeymoon because I know about sex, but do tell the married men to mind their wives and keep away from girls . . .'

I do not believe that the average girl writes to women's magazines, only the lonely and bewildered. Certainly in all the talks I had with priests, teachers, doctors, social workers and young people, I found little evidence that the writers of those sad, naïve letters were typical Irish adolescents. The letters reveal, of course, a lack of sex education and that still is a problem. Now at last, however, something is being done about it, even in a few of the convents, where once the nuns would have punished a girl who so much as mentioned sex.

One middle-aged Sister in a teaching Order told me: 'We have great hope for young people getting married now. The system of education was partly to blame for failures in the past. I went to school in the forties and we were not allowed to socialize at all. It was not just a question of no sex education, but no boy friends. The pattern was monastic.

'Now the attitude is much healthier. When the new programme of education was introduced, we nuns had to go back to college ourselves. That, incidentally, was the first time I had set foot on a bus for years and the first time I had faced four or five knives and forks at lunch. I felt very gauche. I learned, however, to create a new relationship with the children. If we failed to achieve communication, we were the failures, not the pupils. That was the new policy and it was all very exciting. Young people today are not accepting so much. They are asking questions—good questions. They are more expressive, where we were more . . . passive. I was never taught about sex, for instance, either at home or at school. I was expected never to discuss it and, had I attempted to do so, my mother would not only have been furious, but shocked and embarrassed.

'Now it is different. We do not have special lessons on the subject, setting it aside, putting it under a microscope. We landscape it into the programme. Yesterday, as a matter of fact, it came up during the English lesson.' She thought for a while before adding with a smile: 'Times have certainly changed. It was a case of change or perish in Ireland.'

Her pupils are fortunate, for not all nuns are so progressive. One girl told me: 'I discuss sex with my mother, though I think she is still a little shy about it. She told me once that she had six children before she knew as much as I know. But I'd never discuss it with a nun. They're not like people at all.'

Those with little sexual knowledge obviously are at risk. Those who have been educated in the subject seem to retain an attitude of sensible caution, either because of their religion or because of the more immediate physical consequences. They are tolerant about those who become pregnant and angry with those who condemn them. Most young girls to whom I spoke said without hesitation that they would help any school friend who was going to have a baby. One group spoke strongly against the parents of a girl because they would not allow her to associate with the sister of a girl who had had an illegitimate child.

'Why should they hold it against the sister?' they asked. 'And why wouldn't they give the poor girl who had a baby a chance to live it down?'

One added: 'My parents would have helped her. I asked them and they said so.'

This loyalty between girls is a strong feature of Irish life. There is little bitchiness. In England, where the sex war is total, most girls are rivals in the battle to get a boy. Irish girls presumably want boy friends just as much, but they stick to a more humane set of rules.

The conversations recorded above were with those of school-going age and from different backgrounds. The university scene differs slightly perhaps because most students in Ireland are middle-class and rather self-conscious. When the first batch of students comes out of Donogh O'Malley's free education oven, the situation may change.

When student protests were flaring in other centres throughout the world, Ireland was reasonably peaceful. There were some demonstrations against the war in Vietnam, but nothing big enough to merit a water cannon.

Father Fergal O'Connor, a Dominican priest who lectures in politics at University College, Dublin, told me: 'The students have an immense interest in politics, in social theory and in any attempt to try to describe a society which would be more humane, more fulfilling; but basically they are potential Establishment types.'

Compared with students elsewhere, too, they protest only mildly and, perhaps, because they feel it is expected of them, about the way their universities are run. Father O'Connor explained: 'We have relatively small universities here. There are only 8,000 at U.C.D., for instance. Facilities are reasonable. They have been protesting, of course, but so far they have been using the formal channels and, by and large, the authorities have been making adjustments. They are generally sympathetic towards the students and personal relationships are good.'

Throughout the summer, indeed, staff committees met at U.C.D. to consider how students could be given a stronger voice in university affairs. As a result, students will now play a part in running departments and even faculties.

The morals of university students seem fairly stable. Father O'Connor said: 'Most of the men seem to prefer an evening in the pub to a night with a girl. There is a vast gap between the sexes. Most of the girls have been given very high standards by the nuns.'

A psychiatrist who in three years has interviewed 1,500 Irish students a year told me that in one year he would deal with only about five cases of pregnancy, a far lower rate than that in British universities where, according to the British Students Health Association, between two and three per cent became pregnant annually. Girls who do become pregnant at Irish universities are not sent down, however, as they still are in some British universities. They are simply put down as sick and excused, a remarkably civilized system in a country with a reputation for narrowness.

The psychiatrist told me: 'Both male and female students are remarkably innocent about sexual matters compared with their British counterparts. Often I have to give them a complete sex lecture. I have to explain to them that there is no such thing as a dirty thought or a bad thought, just a thought that is not good. Quite a few of them are worried about their sex impulses and I have to tell them that it merely means they are well. They are martyrs, of course, to the old Irish theory that sex is wrong. There is a repression of emotional spontaneity with a consequent stifling of sexual spontaneity. They often find it difficult to verbalize—to chat up a bird.

'When students ask me about sexual problems, I try to tell them how certain forms of behaviour would affect them emotionally. When they ask about the moral aspect of the matter, I have insisted that it is a matter for themselves, their conscience and their religion.'

About twenty per cent of the students he sees have some sort of psychological upset, even if it is only insomnia, brought on by worrying about examinations. Very few, however, have serious breakdowns.

'Where they do, however,' he told me, 'I get a very bad response from the parents. The mother will come to see me occasionally, but seldom the father. The absentee father is a familiar figure in Irish life. He is there physically, but he opts out.'

Allowing for a natural exaggeration, the students more or less bore out what the priest and the psychiatrist said about moral standards at university. The following conversation which I had with one young man may not be typical, but it reveals how at least one section thinks.

'To put it bluntly, is there much fornication in your university?'

'Not a lot.'

'Why? Is it because the girls are modest, strictly brought up, have religious scruples?'

'Not really. I think it is the men. They talk a lot, but, when the chips are down, they're scared.'

'Why? Religious principles? Fear of the consequences?'

'I'm not sure. I think they're just scared. . . .'

The psychiatrist would and did say that emotional spontaneity was stifled and sexual spontaneity, too. How now about the romantic, passionate Irish?

After all that, it may seem a little quaint to drag the thought back to the Irish language. It plays a part in the lives of those students, however, if only for the sake of their examinations; and it will play a part in their future, too, if only because they will have children who will be learning it at school. Also—in some small way, I gallop to add—the subject of the revival of the language is not without a tiny sexual undertone.

Not so long ago the language was in the hands of well-meaning, dedicated men, who somehow managed to dehydrate it. They seemed to believe that Irish symbolized all that was pure, noble and sober, which was strange because it is a language rich in expletive. They accepted only with reluctance that among the Irish people were lechers, after-hours drinkers, blasphemers, wife-beaters and sundry other sinners, who from time to time backed horses, told lies and collected parking tickets.

They tried to be purists themselves, particularly about the language, and that was a grave mistake. Those who spoke it inadequately were greeted with the sort of anaemic smile with which an English country vicar receives the local divorcee. Those who made chronic grammatical mistakes and did not give a damn were lectured on their national heritage or ostracized.

Here was a closed shop; and a few of the stewards, I suspect, wanted to keep it that way, a cosy, select, little union to which they paid their dues in the only currency they possessed—an ability to speak Irish. If they had achieved their aim, which was to have the whole country speaking the native tongue, their only purpose would have disappeared and they would have been penniless. Luckily for the language, people like Dónall Ó Moráin of Gael Linn, have passed the picket. They realized that Irish must be made attractive if it was going to make any impact on the average home. People would have to be encouraged to want it, not to regard it as a duty, for the duty gave them a guilt-complex rather than fluency.

So Gael Linn was formed and immediately set about breaking all the unwritten laws cherished by the older Gaels, riddled as they were with thoroughly British Victorianism. First, they encouraged people to gamble, organizing pools based on Gaelic games. Then they began producing newsreels with an Irish commentary and later magazine feature films of high international standard.

Next came recordings of equally high professional quality; and here Gael Linn had a stroke of luck. Folk music suddenly began to sweep the world, and heaven knows, if the Irish had nothing else, they had enough folk music to keep the world singing and dancing for centuries.

Better still, they had experts to spare, people like Seán MacRéammoinn, Séamus Ennis and Ciarán MacMathúna, who were not narrow-gauge Gaels, but a gregarious mob of many talents who loved the language, but refused to view the world through green-tinted spectacles.

The recordings not only sold well, but worked their way into the Irish charts. Youngsters who spoke no more than the shattered phrases of Irish from their schooldays, bought them and played them and discovered to their amazement that the world of the Gael had a living art to offer.

Gael Linn pressed home its advantage. It organized bingo with the numbers being called in Irish, which most of the customers found to their surprise that they remembered. They encouraged hotels to put on Irish cabarets and—a major step—they went into industry. Dónall Ó Moráin told me: 'We have a furniture factory and, in the Gaeltacht area, where Irish is the mother tongue, a fishing industry. This provides not only money for the language, but work for those who speak it. Without work, they must emigrate and that would be yet another nail in the coffin of the language. We're in the hotel business, too, with a road house on the Naas Road and plans for a hotel in the Gaeltacht.

'The scene has changed dramatically in the last few years. Those of us who joined the Gaelic Society in U.C.D. in the forties, for instance, were regarded as a small peasant minority. Now it reflects a much wider and hippier spectrum and that goes for the other universities, too.'

The degree of change could be measured this summer of 1968, when the Merriman Summer School met for a week in and around Ennis, Co. Clare. Bryan Merriman was a bawdy, wild, eighteenth-century poet who held a brilliant, hilarious mirror to the life and loves and hates of the people at that time. The reflection may not have been ideal convent reading, but it was accurate.

The older Gael with the ingrowing mind was shocked. Some Irish people, he was prepared to admit, had become decadent, commercial, a disgrace to the heroes of the past. Their forebears, however, had never been like that. They had been pure and saintly, men and women without blemish. Merriman, if ever he had existed, was no more than a renegade. Accordingly, when Frank O'Connor translated the work, it was banned. When Merriman devotees tried to raise a memorial to him in Feakle in the hills of East Clare, where he wrote his poetry, there was opposition, fierce enough to postpone the project for a couple of years.

Today, however, the plaque is there near the shores of Loch Greine, where he taught in school. It was unveiled by the Minister of Education, Dr Patrick Hillery; and, to ensure the new respectability of this

once-respected man, President de Valéra turned up at the summer
school. Also present was Luke Kelly of the Dubliners, whose recordings of Irish ballads, ribald and otherwise, have been highly successful
internationally. The fact that he and the President were sharing common ground demonstrated that the Irish language, Irish song and Irish
story now had a catholic appeal, indeed.

It is true that there are, still, pockets of austere resistance. Irish
dancing remains in the starch of rules that have no bearing that I can
see upon the Irish character. The feet may fly, but above the navel
there must be no movement. No smile. No waving of the arms. No
decadent emotion or sign of sinful gaiety. I asked some of the new
Gaels about it. One agreed that it was divorced completely from the
national temperament and added: 'It looks as if it was invented by a
computer.'

Another became more lyrical. He told me: 'It represents nothing
more than an obsession with death. The dancer is the corpse on the
hangman's rope, body heavy, but feet tinkling in the wind.'

Those who still support this dismal image are fighting back, of
course. After the Merriman Summer School (at which there was a
festival-type bar, which stayed open until three o'clock in the morning,
causing one well-known Gaelic scholar to mislay his dentures), a letter
appeared in an Irish evening newspaper, stating: 'Let any man, possess-
ing even a mediocre literary talent, introduce into his work a sour
criticism of the Irish clergy or of the dirt, ignorance and superstitition
of the Irish people and his fortune is made. Instances of men who have
achieved fame and fortune by this manœuvre are James Joyce, Seán
O'Casey and Brendan Behan.'*

The heading, inevitably, was: THE MERRIMAN CULT!

I doubt if that will damage the cause very much. More dangerous,
perhaps, are the faint-hearted commercials of Salthill, Co. Galway, a
seaside holiday resort.

On the doors of the six public lavatories, the local Council put the
signs 'Fir' and 'Mná', erasing the old scars of Saxon domination,
'Gentlemen' and 'Ladies'.

There was confusion, particularly with regard to the 'Mná' sign.
English gentlemen tourists thought that the sign writer had transposed
the last two letters of the word and that his intention had been to write
'Man'.

* I have no fortune and therefore must be pure.

It seems that they learned the fallacy of this interesting theory the hard way. The Council chickened out, Councillor Michael Smyth commenting: 'The experiment was a mistake . . . The toilet signs were causing great confusion, particularly to English-speaking visitors, and as a matter of courtesy they need to be changed.'

Note the significance of the name. Smyth, if you don't mind!

Nevertheless, despite that dangling, dancing corpse, despite the frenetic collisions in the lavatories of Salthill, the Irish language is in with a big chance. The hair-shirt has been ripped off, to be replaced, not so much by a gimmicky mini, but by comfortable, casual clothes that anyone can wear.

The thing that has taken and torn me in twain
find has pricked me with pangs and has plagued me with pain
Is the number of women, old and young,
For whom no wedding bells have rung . . .

> Cúirt an Mheadhon Oidhche (The
> Midnight Court) by Bryan Merriman,
> circa 1750, translated by David
> Marcus

ABOUT two hundred years after Merriman, fine sensationalist that he was, had savaged the men of Ireland for their timidity and lack of virility, Michele Soupplet, a young teacher from France living in Dublin, wrote in similar vein: 'When the History of Great Irish Lovers is written, it will be the thinnest book in the library.' In between the two of them and since, that thought has been expressed many times, usually by Irish women.

Let us first take a look at marriage in Ireland, for therein lie most of the clues. Immediately I must state that the average Irish married couple are not all that much different from those elsewhere. They are reasonably content, if not deliriously happy, twenty-four hours of the day. They get bored with each other and angry with each other, frequently take each other for granted, but would be rudderless if separated for any length of time.

When an Irish marriage goes wrong, however, I believe that the reasons are frequently different from those responsible for matrimonial misery in any other nation. They are complicated and devious and they create a cycle of inter-related problems that are almost insoluble. Consider, for instance, the following composite case: Maureen is twenty-eight and has been courting for five years. She does not know much about sex because nobody has told her much about it. Seán knows little more, though he would not let on about his ignorance to anyone, let alone to Maureen. On the contrary, with flickering winks and castaway words, he implies heavily that he is something of a Kinsey from the Celtic twilights.

The wedding takes place. It is embarrassing because it has compulsory sexual undertones, with which men and women present, married and single, make much arch play. This is rather daring, for everyone knows that sex is sinful, basically wrong, a dirty word.

The honeymoon takes place. Maureen and Seán blunder through its physical aspects ineptly and often unhappily, the shadow of their ignorance clouding the bedroom. If only they would admit ignorance at that time, tell each other frankly that they are not quite sure of their facts or fancies, they would face the future with a fair chance. That, however, they do not do, for their minds have been branded by parent and Church, by time and tradition, with the axiom that sex is sin, sex is wrong, sex is dirty.

That brand is not erased by the marriage vows and remains a part of their lives together. Always there is an element of furtiveness about their love-making and therefore it creates no bond between them. They do not talk much, for they have little to say to each other, having been brought up apart in hermetically sealed compartments. Seán spends more and more time with the boys—boys of forty by this time, remember!—and, worse still, his absence is not just physical. He shelves his responsibilities, imposed unfairly to make life difficult. He refuses to face them, discuss them, or do anything about them. 'Don't bother me with that now. Can't you see I'm tired? I'll do something about it tomorrow.'

For Seán it is always tomorrow. Somehow the children come along, but he remains outside them, never gets to know them. Maureen, on the other hand, deprived of a husband, of a father figure, immerses herself in their lives, particularly in the life of a boy. She cossets him and slaves for him, seeing him as the husband and father missing from the home. Then suddenly she realizes that he may marry, leave her. From that moment on, she protects him with frightening ferocity. This she rationalizes by telling herself that she wants to see him married, cannot wait for it, in fact; but it must be to the right girl, someone who will understand him, make him really happy. Yet basically she is thinking of herself and she sees all girls as rivals, to be beaten away, vanquished; and, when they have departed, crushed, she says to the unhappy lad: 'Sure, you're better off without her, love. She wasn't right for you. Your old Mammy knows best, you'll see.'

Eventually, of course, he breaks free from this suffocating feather mattress of love. He marries and, because of his upbringing, he treats his wife precisely as his father treated his mother. The cycle continues.

Lack of education and this sad sense of sin, perhaps, are the main causes of unhappy Irish marriages—and here I must stress again that I am not writing about the average marriage because I do not know enough about it. Unfortunately nobody does.

I have a feeling, however, that there are, perhaps, more unhappy marriages in in Ireland because the country is racked with inhibitions which prevent discussion, destroy communications. Many Irish wives have never undressed in front of their husbands. Many enter marriage knowing that 'babies are made in Mammy's tummy', but with only the flimsiest knowledge of how they escape from it. They learn the hard way, of course, in labour, though occasionally even that lesson escapes them. A hospital Sister told me of one woman who learned the full facts only when she woke up too soon from the anaesthetic while having her third child. An English girl, living in Dublin, told me that she was shocked by the number of Irish girls who believed that babies came out via the navel. A few girls thought that another exit was used, though this unhappy admission, hampered by natural modesty, was made only reluctantly in many stumbling words.

This lack of knowledge may be erased by the new, more liberal educational system, by the new wave of progressive nuns who just now are beginning to appear. Their numbers still are few, however, and normally no girl would even mention a boy to a nun, for to do so would mean a torrent of hell-fire talk. Parents, too, are to blame, of course, for in the main they simply duck the issue when questioned about sex by their children.

As a result the new, liberal women's magazines in Ireland carry an unusually high quota of letters which begin: 'Can you tell me where I can get a good book on the facts of life?' They can and they do, I am glad to say; but some pathetic letters from those who were born too soon show that for many there is little hope.

Nellie, who wrote to one magazine, for instance, is thirty-seven. She was married recently to a fifty-two-year-old farmer, the wedding taking place in another town, on neutral ground, so to speak, 'to avoid publicity'. By that, of course, she means: to stop people sniggering at the thought of all that sort of foolishness between people of their age.

She wrote: 'I knew I had to submit myself, but I did not think it would be so often. I made a terrible mistake and I think often of doing away with myself. I am very fond of him in every other way.'

Submit! With a scarcely controlled anger, leavened with deep sympathy, the magazine's marriage counsellor wrote:

The trouble is that Nellie has been trained from childhood, more by implication than by actual word, to regard everything concerning the difference between men and women and the mystery of procreation as something sinful and obscene, which God permits in marriage because there is no other way of keeping the human race going.

The intimate side of Nellie's marriage (and there have been quite a few Nellies in my postbag) is a crude, unsavoury and bewildering failure. Her husband is one of the thousands of inexperienced, middle-aged, lonely country-men, who have only a rudimentary knowledge of the facts of life and with their natural capacity for love and tenderness totally underdeveloped, or ironed out altogether by the hardship of their upbringing and the strictures against young love, sex and normal courtship, drummed into them at home and in school. . . .

When Nellie has learnt to live in marital harmony, she will be able to train her husband to gentleness. The only danger is that many ignorant men regard any response in a woman as evidence that she is promiscuous and he will be watching her for signs that she is being unfaithful.

I know that letters to women's magazines do not give necessarily a cross-section of a nation. Nevertheless, they are a sign in society and cannot be ignored. As the marriage counsellor suggested, there are many Nellies.

Father Fergal O'Connor, a Dominican priest, who spent ten years advising on pre-marital and post-marital problems, told me: 'Very few men in Ireland see a woman as a friend. They still believe that her place is either in the bed or in the kitchen. They still want her to be housekeeper, mistress and brood mare—nothing else. Women in Britain would not tolerate that. As a result, too many Irish women have no companionship with their men. A lot of the romance is lost. Boys should be given a solid, personal education—not just sex education, but something which will give them an understanding of themselves as men and girls as people. They have not been getting that in Ireland.'

Back we go to the old, high hurdles: lack of education; lack of understanding; lack of communications; shame; guilt. Monica McEnroy, ex-nurse, wife of a doctor in Wicklow town, mother of three children, local Councillor, and writer of articles, splendid with exasperation in *Woman's Way,* told me: 'I know a girl whose marriage was ended by one thoughtless, guilt-sodden, immature remark by the husband. She was expecting her first baby and was delighted. Then her husband said: "The neighbours will be guessing, when they see you going to early Mass."

'She said to him: "Why should we go to early Mass? We always go to twelve." Her husband stared at her in disbelief and said: "Surely you're not going to twelve o'clock Mass, pregnant!"

'At that moment, the girl told me, her marriage was finished. He never knew, of course, never realized the damage he had done, and she never told him. A permanent adolescent—that's what he was.'

Mary Maher, Woman's Editor of the *Irish Times,* is from Chicago and has been living in Ireland for three years—long enough to have well-balanced thoughts on this tortuous problem. She told me: 'The only recognized status for women in Ireland is motherhood. It is not considered feminine to be interested in politics, trade unionism, anything controversial.

'Some of the letters we've had in response to articles—on the pill, for instance—indicate that the writers neither understand nor like sex. I have never met a girl in Ireland who has ever had sex education at school and the vast majority have never had it from their parents, either.

'The doctors could help, but few do. One woman, who had been married only five years, told her doctor that she only had intercourse with her husband twelve times a year. He said: "That's not uncommon".'

Is there no hope? I can offer one tiny glimmer. One correspondent wrote to the medical adviser of a magazine: 'I am sixty and have been treated for raised blood pressure, which was not very high. Occasionally during intercourse, I feel that my blood pressure might be increased. Is this dangerous?'

That woman and her husband should be elected Irish Married Couple of the Year, but I doubt if it will happen. I have told the story to quite a few people and one reply sums up their views on it. A girl in her thirties said: 'The dirty disgust!'

If sex is so unsatisfactory in these unhappy marriages, what about extra-marital activities? I would say that, compared with her British sister, the Irish wife is a non-starter in these stakes. Men certainly stray much more frequently than women, though immediately after they have made love, they are whipped with guilt. To get out from under the lash, they turn a fierce resentment on the unfortunate women, who have taken them illicitly to bed. 'It was all her fault . . . the dirty disgust.' This attitude is not surprising, when it is remembered that husbands have this subconscious guilt even about their wives.

There is no real problem finding the third corner of the triangle in Dublin, though in the rural areas it would be much more difficult and happens less frequently because of the all-seeing eyes that are always on duty. In Dublin, however, there are far more single girls than boys; and sheer frustration can force some of them to seek relationships inside somebody else's marriage vows.

Mary Maher said: 'Put it this way: there are 24,000 single women in Dublin. The Civil Service, alone, employs 10,000 of them. A girl up from the country, living in a bed-sitter, probably gives in after a year through sheer boredom because even the best-looking girls find a hard time getting any kind of active social life.'

One intelligent and attractive twenty-six-year-old girl told me that in six months she had been invited out by married men five times. Each time she had gone. Dublin, indeed, is becoming much more tolerant about affairs and mistresses. In more sophisticated circles, a girl friend is almost a status symbol for a married man. Everyone— even a fair percentage of women—in this bracket knows about it, smiles indulgently, but never tells the wife. The smarter restaurants, which stay open late at night, are often liaison bases, with the men in their thirties and the girls more and more frequently from the dolly brigade.

This section of society is small, of course. The less sophisticated are more discreet; and sometimes, because of that old hag, guilt, they seek their sex very surreptitiously indeed. Girls to whom I spoke, talked of the kerb-crawlers, and I heard about them so often I can only conclude that they are becoming a more significant part of Dublin life than they are in other cities. One sixteen-year-old said: 'Whenever I walk along the street at night alone, a car is likely to stop. It even happens to my mother; and some of these fellows are quite old. You know—the married type.'

A single girl wrote in bewilderment and irritation to a magazine recently: 'In Dublin, if a married man wants an affair, he grabs the nearest willing typist and spends time and money extricating himself afterwards. If he is the sexy type, he picks up something in the car, but, God above, could any man of intelligence be reduced to that kind of kerbside relieve-io?'

A young woman teacher writes to the same magazine about 'randy business and professional men, kerb-crawling around Harcourt Street, Fitzwilliam Square, certain areas in Cork and other places, too.'

Dublin has prostitutes for those who prefer sex on a commercial basis to grabbing a willing typist or coasting round the square. Most of them are Irish, Mass-going Catholics; and some even go to confession. The following fascinating interview I borrow from *Scene* magazine, an Irish glossy. It is with Concepta, a twenty-year-old Dublin girl, who worked in an office until she got fed up. Now she has from eight to eleven transactions a night, spending, at the most, twenty minutes with a customer, and on average ten minutes. She said: 'I go to confession. I hadn't been for about eighteen months and this Legion of Mary girl said to me: "Well . . . would you like to go to confession?"

' "Put it this way," I said. "You tell me to go to confession tonight and it is Saturday night and it is a good night. I go to confession and tomorrow I go to the Chapel and the same night I am out doing business. What good is it doing me?"

'She said to me: "You're still making an effort, an attempt. It is still in you." So I say all right then and I go.'

'Do you confess everything?'

'Oh, yes, I do. I say: "Bless me, Father, for I have sinned. I've been out on the town." He'll say: "Ah!" and he goes into all your family and parents and all that jazz. I say: "I get used to the money and I can't stop, Father." He says: "Your own will-power can make you stop." And so on . . . a big, long lecture. But the majority of times I go to confession, I don't confess it. I go to Communion and I am out that night. The Legion of Mary girls tell me that I can be forgiven, but I don't understand that sort of thing.'

In Cork, prostitution in some quarters is even more blatant. Father Leo Lennon, the port chaplain, had this to say about it from the pulpit of St Mary's Dominican Church, Pope's Quay: 'Though we naturally deplore it, we are not shocked by the flagrant prostitution practised on the quays of Cork; but we priests, gardai and social welfare workers are shocked and appalled at our utter helplessness to cope with what is happening there. Anyone of any age and at any time of the day or night can go aboard a foreign ship and cannot be prevented from doing so. On the quays of Cork, the maritime law supersedes the law of the land.'

He added that fourteen and fifteen-year-old girls had been seen being carried, helplessly drunk, from the ships. Conscientious fathers had to fight their way on board to take their daughters away from seamen's cabins.

I think that it can be assumed with safety that not all the customers of all the girls in Dublin and Cork are sailors and single men. Many married women in Ireland—once more must I say 'not all'?—have a fairly rough time, though, in fairness, I should state that a large proportion of them increase their unhappiness by their reaction to their husbands' inadequacies, by their possessive jealousy, where their sons are concerned, for instance.

In 1964, however, there was a new development, which brought a glimmer of light to many a sombre domestic scene. The contraceptive pill arrived, not, perhaps, as an answer to a maiden's prayer, but certainly as a solution to a serious problem. Until then the sale of contraceptives was banned in the Republic. It was possible for enthusiasts to cross the border and bring back supplies for their own personal use or the convenience of their friends, and quite a few did so; but to sell was a crime.

Just before I left Ireland, indeed, a seventy-year-old chemist was trying to persuade the authorities that he had a hundred gross of contraceptives 'for his own personal use'. He had not appeared in court by the time I left and it was only many years later in New York that I caught up on the verdict. An old friend from Dublin told me that he had been acquitted, which shows, I think, how conscientiously we Irish emigrants keep up with local affairs.

Before the arrival of the pill, Catholic women were forbidden by law and conscience from buying anything which would 'unnaturally prevent conception'. Only a minute percentage broke that rule, approved, as it was, by State and Church. Most couples who wished to limit their families, abstained, used the rhythm method (with spectacular lack of success in many cases because the Irish are very bad on dates) or practised *coitus interruptus*. Many of those, unable to manage any one of these three unsatisfactory methods, suffered deeply because they had more children than they wanted or than they could afford. In some cases, health was endangered and too often misery was the total result.

There seemed, however, to be little objection to the pill; and what doubts there were could be swept aside easily by amateur theologians. Certainly many doctors began to prescribe it, some calming any flutter of conscience by telling themselves and their patients that it was to 'regulate the cycles'. Later, indeed, Dr Raymond Cross, a well-known and brilliant Dublin gynaecologist, stated with a hint of satire, I suspect: 'If a woman has heavy or irregular periods, or painful periods, or sometimes none, or if she has pre-menstrual tension or endometriosis, bleeding between periods, excessive hairiness or pimples (caused by an excess of androgenic hormones) or is excessively fat or is approaching the change of life, her doctor is morally justified in prescribing any treatment he likes.' His colleagues pointed out that his list was sufficiently comprehensive to cover half the women in the world.

Certainly consciences seemed to have had plenty of elbow room and by 1968 it was reckoned that five Irish women in every hundred were using the pill, compared with ten—a minimal figure, this—in every hundred in Britain. In most cases, the husbands approved, though in some cases the wives omitted to tell their spouses what was going on. One husband, who learned too late, was so enraged that he gathered up the pills and flung them in the fire.

Then, however, came the Papal bombshell. In his encyclical, *Humanae Vitae*, Pope Paul came out against the pill and the Irish hierarchy supported him to the hook of their croziers. Immediately there was uproar all over Ireland. Newspapers were overwhelmed with letters and, as the great debate gathered momentum, published entire pages of them. Most of the writers, oddly enough, were men, though one woman dipped her pen in ammonia and wrote: 'Sir . . . Pil desperandum'.

Nor was Telefís Éireann, the Irish television station, standing aloof. It brought doctors to the screen and a majority of them—particularly those who worked in Dublin's vast housing estates—said that they would continue to prescribe the pill whenever they felt it was necessary to prevent suffering.

Women who were actually using the pill when the encyclical was published, kept quiet. They were thinking. I spoke to a cross-section of medical representatives—the men who actually sold the pill to doctors—and they told me about the post-encyclical reaction. Almost immediately, they said, sales went down all over Ireland by twenty-five per cent. Then gradually, as the debate died, they began to rise again and now are back where they were in the days before the Vatican announcement.

'It's like a penny on the pint in the budget,' said one representative with a handy turn of phrase. 'Fellows cut down for a while, but in a few days they are back to the old quota.' It certainly seems that any woman in Ireland who wants to use the pill, can find herself a doctor who will prescribe it. Some of the older men will have nothing to do with it, but many of the younger, more liberal doctors are putting their calling first and their religion second.

An opinion poll, conducted in the *Irish Medical Times* by its Editor, Dr John O'Connell, a Labour Member of Parliament, recorded that over sixty-seven per cent of those questioned disagreed with the encyclical. Of these, ninety-one per cent said that it would not lead to any major changes in their family planning advice to their patients.

Another survey, carried out by two doctors among Catholic final year medical students at University College, Dublin, revealed that forty per cent of them said they would prescribe the pill, when qualified, to any patient who requested it. Nearly eighty per cent of them wanted the Church to change its position on birth control.

A few doctors felt so strongly on the issue that they made their views public; and prominent among them was Dr P. J. Leahy, District Medical Officer at Ballyfermot Health Centre in the heart of one of Dublin's largest housing estates. He scarcely could have been in a better position to study the problem, for many women with large families came to him and said that they could cope with no more.

When Joseph Foyle, President of the Lausanne Group, which claims to be the voice of right-wing Catholics, wrote to the *Irish Times* about the sin of contraception, Dr Leahy felt that it was his duty to reply in fairly strong terms. He wrote:

Sir—I refer to Mr Foyle's letter, wherein he informs us that the 'gravity of the sin of contraception may be affected by compassionate considerations'. I personally prescribe 'the pill' to many mothers out of such considerations. I do not consider that I am committing sin by doing so. I would be guilty of criminal negligence as a doctor, were I to do otherwise.

May I now ask Mr Foyle if it is in order for me to reassure Catholic mothers who accept my advice and treatment that in their very special circumstances their sin is at its worst but venial? This reassurance would be some comfort and would help them to continue to practise their religion.

Mr Foyle must tell me on what authority he speaks. He will, I hope, understand that many of my patients would not be satisfied, were I to say to them: 'The President of the Lausanne Group told me so.'

Finally, I would point out to Mr Foyle that he makes his greatest mistake, if he thinks that the 'disputing is virtually over'. The encyclical may well cease to be news. But the dispute will go on as long as it is customary for married couples to go to bed together. I personally would like to think that this custom has come to stay. . . .

Occasionally a chemist refuses to dispense the pill, but on that front there has been very little trouble. A chemist is not to know why a particular prescription has been written; and those who have any agonizing doubts about the matter can seek comfort in Dr Cross's encyclopedia of gynaecological hazards.

The advent of the contraceptive pill only barely rippled the lives of single girls. Few doctors would have prescribed it for them and few girls, for that matter, would have had the courage to ask for it. Indeed, the only unmarried women who might seek it would be those openly living with a man, who, for one reason or another, they would not or could not marry.

What is life like for single men and women in Dublin? One girl I asked summed up for me fairly well, when she said: 'Half the fellows spend most of their time in the pub. The other half have a ball!'

Considering the ratio of men to girls in Dublin and the opting out of half the men, that is not surprising. A single man said: 'If I want female company, I get it. I was the only boy and had three sisters. My mother always told me that girls were only out to trap me and how right she was! I've beaten them off like flies for years. They go mad for rides in a big car and a free lap of the social circuit.'

He beat them off, like flies! And Mammy right behind him, urging him on, 'give it to them good, boy, the dirty, thieving hussies,' a righteous, glowering, glaring, protecting, avenging angel, riddled with purity and a fear that she might lose him.

I wonder was 'City Girl, Cork' one of those who felt his fly swat. She wrote to an advice column recently: 'I am a forty-year-old virgin and, after much deliberate consideration, have decided to have a love affair. Please don't moralize. I have the man, but know nothing about birth control. Please let me have the benefit of your experience.'

An American girl told me: 'Irish men are such unsophisticated philanderers, incredibly casual with women. Back home I had been used to a social system in which a fellow rang up a girl for a date three nights in advance, called for her and brought her home at the end of the night. He would never suggest bed until the third or fourth date at least and then it was up to the girl. Here in Dublin it's: "I'll meet you for a drink around half ten." There is very rarely a meal, just a few jars and then a clumsy-coy proposition. If the girl does go to bed with him, of course, he runs like hell afterwards.

'He's a trainee-smoothie. Adolescence lasts longer in Ireland, I think, than it does in any other country because the sexes are segregated so rigidly.' Certainly it sounds like sexual apartheid, the nibbling of forbidden fruit that tastes so sour so soon. The nibbles, too, must be taken when nobody is looking; what would the boys say, if they saw a fellow trotting around after women? It was a priest who gave me the definition of an Irish homosexual. He said: 'It's a fellow who prefers women to drink.'

I am not quite sure whether to be surprised or otherwise that, out of this twisted jungle, with its lust-hate relationships, come so few pregnant girls. The illegitimacy rate in Ireland is one of the lowest in Europe. The figure, however, is not accurate. So many girls who find they are going to have a baby go to England that social workers and almoners automatically jot down on their papers: 'P.F.I.' It signifies 'Pregnant From Ireland.'

This forced emigration is understandable for a number of reasons. English girls, too, seek to get as far away from home as possible, hiding their heads in the sands of London or, during the summer, in one of the big holiday resorts.

The Irish girl can find anonymity more easily still, though an abrupt departure from town, or, worse still, village, can give rise to gossip, even when it is not justified. In England, too, she can have the baby free on the National Health Service. She has another reason for taking herself out of Ireland and it is a pity that she does not know how false it is. It is accepted fairly widely that a pregnant girl who has her baby in Ireland will go to a home, where she will have to work until the labour pains start, while nuns thrust her sin into her ears.

A Catholic social worker in England said, for instance: 'The fear in these girls has to be seen to be believed. It is only by endless gentleness that we can persuade them that going back to have their baby wouldn't be so awful. What sort of society do you have in Ireland that puts the girls into this state?'

I suppose that Ireland once had a system which was cruel enough, but so had many other countries, England included. Today, however, the homes, run by nuns for unmarried mothers, are humane, cheerful places. The only pity is that there are not enough of them.

The Irish attitude generally to the unmarried mother is softening, indeed, though there still are pockets of grim, matriarchal resistance, as this awesome letter, published in the *Irish Times,* reveals:

Sir . . . I infer from Miss Scott's letter that she wishes to extol the 'virtues' of the unmarried mother. May I point out that the great majority of unmarried mothers are not just 'unfortunate'. They are indulgent, selfish, spoiled examples of womanhood. Christ has clearly shown all girls what womanhood should be. First—the Blessed Virgin. Very well, we dare not hope to attain her standard. What of the other two Marys? Surely we dare hope to live to their level—at least to learn to love the good and forget the bad.

Does the girl who 'falls' ever stop to think she has also debased some man? Girls! Girls! Listen to me. There is no such thing as a 'bad man'—only bad girls. What may be considered a 'bad man' will not be bad in the company of a good woman.

Again, am I right in thinking Miss Scott suggests we populate our beautiful little country with a hoard of nameless and, perhaps, diseased (VD) children. I would like to remind her, we in Ireland still respect the 'married state' with its privilege of parenthood and, of course, its responsibilities. May our country long continue to do so . . . yours, etc., (Mrs) Frances Swanwick, Ballinasloe, Co. Galway.

At the beginning of this chapter, I quoted an excerpt from Bryan Merriman's poem, 'The Midnight Court'. The mind totters at the thought of the stanzas he would have scribbled about (Mrs) Frances Swanwick of Ballinasloe.

THE scene was not without a sense of theatre. On the one hand there was the Cardinal, Dr William Conway, Archbishop of Armagh, head of the Catholic Church in Ireland, just arrived at Dublin Airport after long, gruelling sessions at Ecumenical Council meetings in the Vatican. On the other were the representatives of Irish newspapers, sound radio and television, questioning him with appropriate solemnity and deference about the meaning of it all. Then suddenly there came a flash of Seán O'Casey, verging, indeed, on the Behan. With Kerry innocence—always a dangerous commodity, to be handled carefully—Líam MacGabhann of the *Irish Times* asked: 'Your Eminence, what the hell happened to Limbo?'

To Catholics over the centuries, Limbo had been a place of rest, where the souls of the unbaptized could relax, but would be denied, for technical reasons, presumably, the sight of God. Most modern clerics had been embarrassed by the whole idea for some time; and so they were relieved when the Council seemed to consign Limbo to Limbo. The Cardinal, however, was much too astute to be drawn into public debate on the subject and, side-stepping adroitly, he answered simply with a grin, which showed, perhaps, his knowledge of the Kerry language with all its diverse subtleties.

MacGabhann, of course, was joking. In the darker recesses of the joke, however, there were other questions which he did not ask: would the spirit of the Council be adopted by the Catholic Church in Ireland? Would it move with the times and the Vatican, or would it argue that the removal of certain religious practices from the obligatory list did not make them any less beneficial to the soul, if they were carried out?

Fish on Friday is one minor example. The Vatican had decided that it need be compulsory no longer to forgo meat on that day and it left the lifting of the ban to the bishops. In most dioceses in Britain, Vatican guidance has been accepted. In Ireland it remains fish by order. Mass, it is true, is said now in English, or Irish,* rather than Latin, in Irish churches, in accordance with another Vatican ruling. There is, however, a reluctance in many fields to accept the new look.

Nevertheless, there have been spectacular changes in the Church in Ireland, initiated mainly by the example of the splendid Pope John, who grabbed the whole organization by the scruff of the cassock, shook hard and removed not only the suffocating dust of centuries, but many

* In most parishes one of the Masses is said in Irish on Sunday morning.

of the parasitical moths, too. Because of this lead, many priests in Ireland have accepted wholeheartedly the spirit of the Vatican Council, even though many members of the Hierarchy have shuffled their feet over its findings.

Not so very long ago the parish priest, particularly in rural areas, exercised powerful influence over his flock. His wishes carried the weight of orders. His private life in the vast majority of cases was at least comfortable, no matter what degree of poverty existed in other houses. His power, bolstered, it is true, by the people themselves, was seldom questioned. Some may have thought that his shadow lay too heavily over their lives, disturbing their privacy, obstructing their freedom of decision; but it would have been a strong and determined person who would have told him so. Such independent action could have earned not only pastoral frowns, but social snubs, too. It has been suggested, indeed, that some emigrants might not have deviated so sharply from their religion once they moved away, had the influence of the parish priest been less oppressive at home.

Today the shadow is lifting. More and more priests are more and more concerned about social problems—decent housing for their parishioners for instance—than they are about counting the heads of children. The five-day-a-week-golf-priests are diminishing slowly in number and in a number of cases their successors are expressing embarrassment at the comfort of their own existences. One said the other day: 'I am well aware of the miserable homes of many in my parish; but how can I say a word, living, as I do, in this huge mansion and my curates each with a house of his own?'

That new attitude, that desire to help remove hardship, if not necessarily to share it, is a major change in Ireland. There have been others, less important, but significant all the same. Until about ten years ago, for instance, the hierarchy was extremely strict about giving dispensation for marriages between Catholic and non-Catholic Christians. The Archbishop of Dublin, the Most Reverend Dr John McQuaid, was particularly unyielding; and my own case is a fair example of the general attitude.

My wife—or should I say my wife-elect?—had been refused a dispensation in Dublin to marry me, a nominal Protestant. Because she was resident temporarily in Britain at the time, she was given one by a British bishop, without any hesitation. Despite that, however, we were told in Ireland that we could not marry in either of our own parishes, but would have to take our custom to neutral ground. The ceremony would have to take place before eight o'clock in the morning; only a limited number of people could attend (three or four, I think); it would have to be held in the sacristy, not before the altar; and there was to be no publicity of any kind. These quaint conditions were enough to drive many a couple to a wicked civil ceremony, of course; but we accepted them for the sake of her parents, who would have been deeply unhappy had we done otherwise.

Today the attitude is much more reasonable. Understandably each case is considered on its merits, but dispensations are granted liberally and without many strings. I know, because I attended a mixed marriage while I was in Ireland recently, and it took place before the altar with all the trimmings.

Until comparatively recently, too, Catholic students found it difficult to get a dispensation to go to Trinity College, Dublin. The need for a dispensation at all was just about as anachronistic as the need for a Gaelic Athletic Association ban on foreign games: Trinity in the past had been violently anti-Catholic. Those days however, are gone. Today most students who particularly wish to go to Trinity may do so, which shows, I think that the Church in Ireland is developing a refreshing faith in the strength of her children and no longer believes that their religion will be shattered by the first tiny patter of proselytizing feet.

There are other trends in the right direction. The whole approach to the teaching of religion is changing. The catechism, the words of which once were calculated to dislocate the jaw of any child, is being revised so that children will be able to understand what they are reading. Even cremation—permitted since 1964—is being considered without much disfavour, though I suggest with respect that some more traditional minds may be influenced here by the shortage of land. Many Irish graveyards soon will have to put up 'House Full' notices; ashes take up much less space. Those who wish to be cremated, however, must be shipped across the border to Belfast because so far there is no crematorium in Dublin, though Mammon is responsible for that state of affairs, rather than God. Dublin undertakers who have investigated the possibilities, have discovered that it could cost £250,000 to build one in the Republic, a sombre fact which led one of them to say with that knockabout humour peculiar to the profession: 'You won't see it in your lifetime!'

A North of Ireland extremist—and some, who are not so extreme, too—would dismiss all these elements of progress as being of no consequence. He would say—and many did say to me while I was there: 'The Roman Catholic Church is still the boss in the Republic. It does not allow contraception. It does not allow divorce. It will crush social progress, as it did when Dr Noel Browne tried to bring in free medicine for mothers and children.'

These are three solid points which deserve contemplation. It is true, for instance, that the Republic's Constitution states that 'no law shall be enacted providing for the grant of a dissolution of a marriage'.

It is possible, of course, to get a legal separation, which is not very satisfying, if one or both of the partners want to marry again, particularly if the reason for wanting a divorce is a wish to marry someone else. Those with money can get round the Constitution by going to England, establishing residence there and seeking their decree in the British courts. Those without money—or with religious scruples—presumably continue their empty, miserable lives together, or separate unofficially so that they can live with whomever they like, a course which automatically puts them beyond the arms of the Church.

Many non-Catholics and a few Catholics, too, have argued over the years that it is wrong to have such a clause in the Constitution, that the rule of the Church should not be made the law of the State, that the rights of the minority should not be sacrificed to the beliefs of the majority. They have pointed out, too, that the Constitution was drafted to cover the whole island, in anticipation of partition ending and that the million or more Protestants in the North were going to fight like mad, rather than be dragged in beneath that particular wing of it.

All these points were taken into consideration when a Dáil committee was set up to consider possible changes in the Constitution. In its report just before Christmas, 1967, the Committee recommended that this clause and another which gave 'a special position' to the Roman Catholic Church should be removed. On the question of divorce, it suggested an amending clause, reading: 'In the case of a person, who was married in accordance with the rites of a religion, no law shall be enacted providing for the grant of a dissolution of that marriage, other than those acceptable to that religion'. It further recommended that a clause which prohibited the recognition of foreign divorces should be dropped altogether.

Inevitably, and understandably, perhaps, there were strong protests from the bishops. In his Lenten Pastoral of February 1968, the Archbishop of Dublin, Dr McQuaid, wrote for instance: 'Recently a proposal has been put forward by an informal committee to allow certain facilities for civil divorce in some instances.

'Civil divorce, as a measure which purports to dissolve a valid marriage, is contrary to the law of God. The experience of other countries has proved that civil divorce produces the greatest evils in society. The effort, even if well-intentioned, to solve hardships within marriage by civil divorce has invariably resulted in a series of greater sufferings and even deeper evils.'

Since then, nothing has been done to implement either the recommendation with regard to divorce or that concerning the 'special position' of the Catholic Church. The argument that constitutional changes would involve a referendum are not very strong in view of the fact that a third mild suggestion by the committee—that it might be thought worthwhile to consider abandoning the proportional representation system of voting in favour of a straight vote—was put to the people. (It was rejected, incidentally, by an overwhelming majority, a major set-back for the Government.)

Government supporters, of course, will say that the voice of the Church has not influenced them in any way on this issue. One even said to me: 'In the same Pastoral Letter, Dr McQuaid gave out about dirty books and magazines and said that they provoked all sorts of sensual thoughts and actions. But they're still there, provoking away. The Government didn't sweep them into the sea, did it?' Nevertheless, the impression remains, rightly or wrongly, that someone somewhere along the line chickened out and that it will be a long time before the people of Ireland will be asked to vote in a referendum on the divorce clauses of the Constitution.

The question of contraception, of course, has been complicated hugely by the pill, and the Hierarchy's reaction to it is not calculated to have their Northern Protestant brethren tearing down the customs posts with their bare hands in a frenetic attempt to embrace the rule of Dublin.

As soon as the Pope announced in his encyclical, *Humanae Vitae*, what was, in effect, a ban on the pill, the Irish Hierarchy pledged their support. This was reiterated on a number of occasions in the weeks that passed by various individual members. Unlike members of some other hierarchies, they seemed to have no reservations. The immediate public reaction, however, was quite different. I had expected to find, certainly among the older people, disappointment, but acceptance. On the contrary, the first person with whom I discussed the announcement, an elderly lady from a most orthodox background, condemned the encyclical completely and said: 'The Pope has split the Catholic Church right down the middle.'

Everywhere I went, I heard this view. It was more than concern. It was anger; and the more I listened in those early days, the more I felt that the Hierarchy and the people were veering towards a collision course.

Significantly, however, from the clergy themselves, there was only one voice of public dissent. The Reverend Dr James Good, Professor of Theology and Lecturer in Philosophy at University College, Cork, announced: 'Assuming that the accounts so far received are substantially correct, I think that Pope Paul's statement on birth control is a major tragedy in the Church.

'The understanding of problems put forward by the Pope in this document appears to be out of date and inadequate and, in my view, the conclusion drawn about birth control is unrealistic and incorrect.

'I have no doubt that the document will be rejected by the majority of Catholic theologians and by Catholic lay people. For my own part, as a teacher of theology, philosophy and medical ethics, I cannot see my way to accepting the teaching on contraception put forward in this document.'

The Bishop of Cork, the Most Reverend Dr Lucey, was on holiday when Dr Good made this very clear statement of his belief. When he returned a week later, he withdrew the Professor's faculties for hearing confession and preaching; and in the circumstances there was little else he could do. He did not make his decision public, but informed Dr Good, leaving it to him to make any announcement that he thought proper.

Public controversy continued at gale force and most of those taking part seemed to mirror the views of the Professor of Theology. Grille, an organization formed to represent the Christian Left, announced that it would hold a Pray-In in St Andrew's Church, Westland Row, Dublin, to demonstrate its opposition to the Pope's findings.

I was in Dublin at that time and I felt that here was the opportunity for which the protesters had been waiting. Here was their chance to stand up and be counted, to let it be known that the people of Dublin at least were against the Pope's ruling; I expected scenes of excitement such as St Andrew's Church had not known since the moving moment many years earlier, when Jack Doyle married Movita there.

I was wrong. About twenty people joined the protest. Another group turned up to protest against Grille. When the Grille leader began reading excerpts from the Bible, the rival establishment knocked the book out of his hand and shouted abuse at him. Some minutes later the pro-Grillists transferred to a more peaceful church and concluded their little service, interrupted only by the crying of a baby, who was being baptized at the time.

If the Pray-In can be taken as a measure of public wrath, the people of Ireland are solidly behind the Pope, a verdict unlikely to be cheered vociferously in Belfast. It is argued that they stayed away because they regarded Grille as a group of ivory-tower intellectuals, divorced from the real problem of rearing ten children in two damp rooms; but that I cannot accept. I doubt if the ordinary people had ever heard of Grille. If they were sufficiently angry, however, they would have turned up to be counted, no matter who was carrying the banner.

The debate certainly seemed to have moved into a fairly high intellectual sphere. One week-end in late September, a group of about fifty met to discuss the issues in Bargy Castle, Co. Wexford. They included specialists in medicine, gynaecology, biology, psychiatry, pathology, sociology, history, communications, law, philosophy and dogmatic, moral and pastoral theology. Among them were many married couples. Their findings they sent to the Hierarchy, whose members must have drawn little comfort from them.

The medical specialists at Bargy Castle stated, for instance, that the biological premise upon which the encyclical's recommendations of the rhythm method was based was scientifically untenable. The reference to natural laws and rhythms was incorrect and could not provide the basis for a sufficiently effective method of regulating birth. They added that the use of these methods frequently disrupted the harmony of married life and stressed that the contraceptive methods condemned in the encyclical had been found to foster conjugal love, helping towards the attainment of maturity in marriage relationships. The tensions and fears brought about by total abstention or by the use of the rhythm method, they said, frequently led to a deterioration in the quality of family life as a whole, especially in cases where further pregnancy was absolutely contra-indicated. These views were endorsed by the married couples present.

The group concluded by stating that the sections of the encyclical, condemning contraception as intrinsically evil, were felt by many to be unconvincing.

About ten days later the Hierarchy met at Maynooth and issued a short statement, confirming their full support of the Pope's teachings. It did not mention the Bargy statement.

It would seem that deadlock has been reached between the Hierarchy and the specialists, including Dr Good. Will this radical difference of opinion cause a drift from the Church in a country that for so long has been so completely loyal? I doubt it very much.

Certainly the Cardinal does not regard the advent of the pill and the Papal encyclical as issues which face the Church in Ireland with a major crisis, though he agrees that they are of very profound significance everywhere, including Ireland.

'I have made very deep inquiries about this,' he told me. 'I don't really live on the moon here and have, in fact, a fairly good monitoring service. I think that the great bulk of the ordinary people simply accept what the Pope has said.

'Among some classes there has undoubtedly been much disappointment and some criticism, although not as much as is sometimes thought. For example, I was surprised that a limited spot-check which I had taken by a layman among professional classes indicated that six out of seven of the men felt that the Pope could not have come to any other decision, though with the women it was different. I'm not suggesting that this was the general pattern, but it is interesting to note that a National Opinion Poll survey among young people in the fifteen to twenty-four age group, where you would naturally expect to find revolt, indicated that a substantial majority approved of the encyclical.'

My own monitoring service suggested acceptance, but not always approval. From many interviews throughout the country, I gained the impression that most women will accept the Papal teachings, albeit with grumbles and much tossing of the head. Many of those who were using the pill before the encyclical, however, are likely to continue doing so. One married woman told me: 'There is no question of them leaving the Church. I believe that they will probably stay away a bit longer than they normally would from confession. For a while they may stop using the pill and return to the sacraments. Then they may weaken again and so on. Non-Catholics may dismiss that as hypocrisy or double-think, but it is what happens and has been happening for quite some time with regard to other sins and it seems to work fairly well. The Church, remember, is for sinners, not for saints.'

The intellectuals hope that their strongly held beliefs will filter down to the people through study groups, discussions and so on. Perhaps that will happen, though the subsequent reaction is anybody's guess.

Broadly speaking, however, they back the Pope on this particular issue. The decision, even more controversial, to ban other contraceptives would appear, therefore, to be something which the people uphold, rather than an imposition foisted on them by a harsh, relentless Church, meddling in affairs of State.

Visitors, who meet the Irish casually, of course, are inclined to overlook the fact that fundamentally they are a pious people in spite of all their carry-on. Their pilgrimages to Croach Patrick, where they climb a mountain, sometimes in their bare feet, and to Lough Derg, where they spend two days and a night, fasting and without sleep, must be two of the most rigorous in any religious calendar.

Nor is it only the quiet, daily communicants who make these harsh journeys. The dolly girls, with their bejeaned boy friends, go too; and, though they swear they will never go again, many of them return year after year.

It is significant, too, that, of the Irish who go abroad each year, more choose Lourdes than any other centre.

The sombre case of Dr Noel Browne and the Bishops was quite different. Here the Hierarchy and a Cabinet Minister clashed. The Minister was forced to resign; the Government fell; and it was defeated in the subsequent general election.

Dr Browne entered politics in the late 1940s with one major driving force: he was determined to do something about tuberculosis, which for years had gripped Ireland. He knew more than enough about the subject, because not only had he been Assistant Medical Superintendent in Newcastle sanatorium, Co. Wicklow, but he had suffered from the disease himself. He was elected to the Dáil and found himself Minister for Health in a coalition Government. His record in the field of tuberculosis was spectacular. Between the years 1948 and 1965, the death rate was reduced from 125 per 1,000 to 15 per thousand. In the meantime he had turned to a new project—a scheme to provide a comprehensive free medical scheme for mothers, and children up to the age of sixteen years.

First the Irish Medical Association fought him on the grounds that the scheme represented a dangerous advance towards complete State control of medicine. Browne fought back, despite the fact that his tuberculosis had reappeared. From his bed, he carried on his Ministerial duties and his campaign to make his mother and child plan law. He was able to handle the opposition from his colleagues in the medical profession. He did not know, however, that far heavier guns were being primed. The Hierarchy suddenly announced its opposition to the scheme, a major complaint being that the right to provide for the health of children belonged to parents, not to the State. Exactly one month to the day later, Noel Browne resigned, abandoned by all his Cabinet colleagues. His defeat on this issue was complete. He had maintained throughout that from the spiritual viewpoint he was not at fault, and he told me later, indeed, that throughout the crisis he had been advised constantly by an eminent Catholic theologian priest on doctrinal matters and on moral and social teaching. He refused to reveal the man's name to me or to anybody else—not even to his wife. Such was the atmosphere of the time, however, that they used to meet secretly, often discussing the battle in country lanes.

Here was a blatant example of the Church intervening in a matter of State and winning. Could it happen in Ireland now?

During my interview with the Cardinal, I raised this question, though admittedly with some diffidence, for I had no wish to stir these murky waters with this considerate and thoughtful man, who had not been involved directly with them. I think, however, that he appreciated my motive, which was to measure change; and his reply was simple: 'I don't know the details, as I was not a bishop at the time, but I have the impression that there was a good deal of misunderstanding resulting from faulty lines of communication.'

Speaking of the relations between Church and State today, he said: 'The relations in the Republic are the perfectly normal relations which exist in most countries. There is no more coming and going there than there is between the Catholic Hierarchy and the Government in Britain, for example; and there is very much less than there is in the Republic between the Government and the Trade Unions or the Farmers' organizations and similar bodies. The idea that the Church exercises any kind of political control in the Republic behind the scenes is one of the great myths of the twentieth century; but someone has said that myths are indestructible.'

He seemed genuinely amazed by the suggestion, and, as if to sponge away old memories, he turned to more positive developments, to the new face being shown to Ireland by the younger priests.

I had quoted to him—without mentioning names, naturally, for I had no desire to trigger off thunderbolts!—a young cleric whose views I had found particularly narrow and reactionary. Quickly the Cardinal said: 'I don't think you will find him typical.'

'On the contrary,' I said. 'I was surprised only because I found him so untypical of all the young Churchmen I have met.'

He smiled and said: 'I'm glad. Younger priests are breaking through whatever barrier there was. It was something which grew up naturally in previous generations largely as a result of the tremendous respect which the people had for their priests through the difficult years of oppression.'

That barrier has been partly responsible for the popular view that Ireland is a priest-ridden country. It is true that many priests enjoy the fence, which sets them slightly apart from the people, so long as it is sufficiently low for them to vault when they want a game of golf or poker. It is equally true that the number of priests is high. In fact a cleric, back in Ireland after a considerable time in South America, said recently: 'The population of most of our small towns and villages has decreased by fifty per cent; but the number of priests in these remains the same. The work done formerly by one is now divided between two.'

On the other hand, that barrier has kept others in lonely frustrated isolation. They wanted to be among the people, to be part of their lives; but that was denied them. Priests were for baptisms and weddings and funerals, for Mass on Sunday, for saluting in the street as a mark of respect, for sickness. Priests were different, not quite men, not quite friends, though never enemies. The tone of the voice changed, when they appeared, and the subject changed, too. The act was on, though few realized they were playing. The façade slid into place and remained there a moment after this man in black had gone, while everyone said what a grand mixer he was, an honest-to-God fellow, no nonsense, right down to earth. They believed it, but it was not true. He tried to mix, but they would not let him.

That is the barrier which, as the Cardinal said, the younger priests are trying to destroy. They are having remarkable success, for it is a very difficult, almost a dangerous, job. Failure can be absolute and will be followed by an even emptier isolation. If they try too hard, they can be misunderstood, given the 'swinging priest' tag, or some similar kiss of death.

Father Peter Canning, one of the Radharc group, currently making excellent documentaries for Telefís Éireann and world distribution, is a man who made this hazardous journey. One of his earlier appointments was to a curacy at Roundwood, Co. Wicklow, the highest village in Ireland. It could have been a soft posting, for Peter Canning likes life in the country. He likes shooting and fishing, though not stage-English style, with the 'g' dropped. He decided, however, that his first job was to understand the people around him for, until he managed that, he could not help them fully. He had one advantage. He is an accomplished musician, a good guitar player; but that he left aside for a while. He began dropping down to Seán Kavanagh's, with the legend on its walls 'The Highest Pub in Ireland'. He took off his clerical collar and wore an Aran sweater, not because he thought that clothes would change minds much, but more as a symbol.

It took time. He had his fair share of awkward silences, broken quickly by a welcome that too often was too enthusiastic. Gradually, however, he got to know his parishioners as people and they got to know him as a man. Soon he was taking his guitar with him, playing and singing. He was part of the community.

That I know because I went back with him to Roundwood, to Seán Kavanagh's, the highest pub in Ireland. The welcome he received was warm, sincere and utterly uninhibited. He sang for them and with them. We all sang. It was quite a night, in fact, with only one problem for Peter Canning. Somehow he had to stop everyone from buying him a drink; and that is very difficult for a man who is back among old friends again.

I was the stranger. People were polite to me, hospitable to me, thoroughly considerate in every way, but they did not know me. They would not have known Peter, either, had he not stepped off that pedestal and waded through tradition to meet them.

More and more priests are identifying with the people, where once they were doomed—or glad—to be members of the Establishment. For years their privileged position had been protected, encouraged by the Hierarchy, by all hierarchies, let us face it, for no group has cherished the status quo so diligently throughout history.

Father Austin Flannery and Father Michael Sweetman, who have

smelt the decay of slums, campaign ruthlessly on behalf of those
forced to live in them, and draw pompous, slightly frightened rebukes
from Cabinet Ministers who think that these priests really should
know their place, which is apart.

Father Peter Lemass preaches in Bray in support of Dublin's street
cleaners, on strike because they earn only £12 a week, and tells his
congregation: 'We have a moral right to back these men who remove
garbage from houses which have Mercedes cars in the garages, and are
owned by people who can afford to take holidays on the Continent.'

Father Michael Cleary, curate at Marino, Dublin, attacks the Government for neglecting the emigrants, among whom he worked in
Britain, castigates Irish employment agencies for their irresponsi-
bility, quotes the case of young girls being sent to jobs in cafés which
were no more than brothels.

Father James McDyer mobilizes his co-operative army in Donegal,
shaming the men who live in power houses and wait for the wake of
the West.

Father Tom Fehily champions the cause of the itinerants: the
tinkers, the travelling people, who are bulldozed off camping sites
and embarrass those with houses, as the West Indians embarrass the
British. 'But they really smell, my dear . . . and would you let your
sister marry one . . . and aren't some of the children sweet?'

Dr Birch, Bishop of Ossory, shares his care, befriends his own
tinkers on their caravan sites in Kilkenny and condemns a tradition
which the Irish always deny they possess: the tradition of snobbery.
In a speech to young people in Naas, Co. Kildare, he says: 'We tolerate a system in which half the population of this country is excluded,
for what reason I do not know, from the priesthood or the ministry.
I believe we will have progress here when I see an itinerant ordained a
priest, or a tinker girl taking her final vows in a convent. You young
people have the power and the energy to dissolve the stains in our
society, which is riddled with class distinction.'

The Church in Ireland is changing, all right, matter a damn who
eats fish and who eats meat on Friday. The air is fresh at the very top,
too. Cardinal Conway said to me: 'This consumer society is trying to
brainwash young people into thinking that happiness consists of a
refrigerator and a colour television set; but it is failing. The youngsters
have discovered how unsatisfying such a society can be. They have
learned that not on bread alone does man live. The spring of this year

saw the first signs of that spirit. I think it must have been one of the most exciting springs ever.'

I wonder whether there are any other members of the College of Cardinals who would applaud the happenings that spring in the world's universities—and understand so well why they took place. No wonder he was not all that worried about what happened to Limbo.

WE Irish, as most people know, are devils for our culture. Be there, I mean, a Dublin docker, who, after his nineteenth pint of nourishing stout, does not open the sandwich tin, take out the egg-stained copy of James Joyce's *Ulysses* and start quoting Molly Bloom's moving message to his damp-eyed fellow-workers in a suddenly silent Ringsend pub on a Saturday night?*

It is particularly sad, therefore, to see the arts in Ireland subjected to a vicious campaign of freedom, instigated, no doubt, by the imperialist aggressors of atheistic international Communism.

Simultaneously, persecution, which once held an honoured place in Irish society and inspired so many muses, has been allowed to wither. Here, briefly, are some of the more tragic results:

The theatre: Not an actor, director or playwright arrested since 1957. In twelve months no cry from the stalls of 'stop this filth'.

Literature: It is now so difficult for an Irish author to get himself banned that I am not even bothering to try. Edna O'Brien, of course, must have influence in high places; and anyway she is a woman.

Art: Not a garret to be had. In a so-called Christian society, must young Irish artists be left without a place in which to starve with dignity?

The cinema: *The Family Way* featuring the unutterably sultry Hayley Mills, was shown in Dublin with the film censor's imprimatur, despite the fact that it actively encourages men to have sexual intercourse with their wives.

Television: An unscripted, uncensored, live debate on 'Are Ireland's Eyes Open?' was not merely screened, but was panned by the sex-jaded critics as *boring*!

Times obviously have changed radically in the artistic sphere in Ireland. What has happened?

I believe that those who curbed free artistic expression—and they were not exclusively Churchmen—realized suddenly that all their little children were growing up and were ready to wear long trousers or nylons, depending on their sex, if you will pardon the phrase. To deprive them of these little vanities, it was felt, could well have earned for the parents a thump between the eyes, which might have destroyed the last flitter of their authority. The fact that most of their children were old enough to be married does not matter at this stage. They have been given the key of the door and they are not going to give it back.

* There be.

The artistic scene, as a result, is singularly free from any issue which would have raised even a mild controversy in the days of the great Seán O'Casey; and I am inclined to believe that a few writers, actors and artists generally are feeling a little deprived because nobody has stolen their teddy bear lately. The vast majority, however, have fought a good fight and are delighted with their victory. The changes they have won in the theatre alone over the past decade have been remarkable and the story of the battles, told to me by Phyllis Ryan, who was in the thick of them with her Gemini Group, is exciting.

The darkest days were those of 1957. Alan Simpson, a young producer, was presenting *The Rose Tattoo* at the Pike, a small theatre club in a converted coach house. Despite the fact that the published play had never been censored and was on sale in Dublin, the police warned Simpson that he was breaking the law and should take the play off. Because he was not told what law he was breaking, he refused to do so. He was arrested, jailed overnight and charged later with having produced for gain an indecent and profane performance.

For a year the case ambled with sad hilarity through the courts. The police refused to say who had started the proceedings and ultimately Simpson won. The costs were £2,500 and much of this sum was raised by the 'Rose Tattoo Fighting Fund', set up by the British magazine, *Encore*, and sponsored by such people as John Osborne, Seán O'Casey, Peter Hall, John Gielgud and Wolf Mankowitz.

Two years later Phyllis Ryan was in trouble. With the Gemini Group, which she had founded with Godfrey Quigley and Norman Rodway, she decided to present Tennessee Williams's *Cat on a Hot Tin Roof* in the Gas Company Theatre, Dun Laoghaire, eight miles from Dublin. (The architect who designed this Gas Company office deliberately drew in the theatre; and, though I lived near it for many years, I never thought it odd in any way. Could my home town be the only place in the world where a gas company is married in this fashion to the arts?)

'We were soon in trouble,' Phyllis told me. 'One of the Gas Company's directors' wives fainted, or something. Anyway, Jim Fitz-Gerald, the producer, and I were hauled before the Board, where the directors, in rather disgusted, disinfected voices, began reading extracts of the play to us. We admitted that we had spoken the words out loud in public and they told us we would have to take the play off. We did so because, had we refused, we would have lost the theatre for good.

'About eighteen months later, we had another go, not with *Hot Tin Roof* and not at the Gas Company Theatre. Hugh Leonard had written *Stephen D*, a brilliant adaptation of James Joyce's *Portrait of the Artist as a Young Man*. It portrayed his problems with religion in general and the Church in particular; his abandonment of both; and his final departure from Ireland. We put this on in the Eblana Theatre, which is part of the central Dublin bus station. The Press raved about it, but some of the audiences walked out. They said it was blasphemous. They didn't like the sending up of religion bit. Neither did the Lord Chamberlain in Britain. We don't have one in Ireland, of course, no official censorship of the theatre whatsoever. We never have had. But when we were putting *Stephen D* on in the West End, the Lord Chamberlain chopped the word "Jesus" every time he saw it.'

Stephen D was a big success in Dublin and London. Encouraged by the fact that nobody had been jailed or hanged, Gemini produced a revue, written by David Marcus and based loosely on a long poem in Irish, *The Midnight Court* by Bryan Merriman.

Merriman was a bawdy, lecherous and vigorous poet, who wrote in Irish in the eighteenth century. His 'Midnight Court' consists mainly of a many-splendoured attack by Irish women on Irish men for their sexual inadequacies; and the Gemini Group included most of the Rabelaisian parts in their production.

'We had no real trouble,' said Phyllis. 'Just a few people standing up here and there and shouting: "This is disgraceful". I don't think they liked the bit about what a shame it is that priests can't marry. The bit that goes something like:

> *While others miss the best in life*
> *Because a priest can't take a wife,*
> *Just think of the massive population*
> *This rule has cost the Irish nation!*

Stephen D and *The Midnight Court* were major engagements in a war against the secret censors. Gemini's victories made the road easier for others. When I was in Dublin, for instance, the Abbey was presenting *Borstal Boy*, an adaptation by Frank McMahon, an American publisher, of Brendan Behan's splendidly tolerant record of his early days as a political prisoner in Britain. That was rather incongruous, really, because the book, *Borstal Boy*, was and is banned, presumably because it is top-heavy with rude words. Some of these were toned down for the stage production; but plenty of the raw, ribald text survived and was presented nightly without a murmur of anything except approval. Its presentation coincided, incidentally, with the removal of the ban which prohibited clergy going to the theatre in Dublin; and for many priests Brendan Behan's bawdy piece was their theatrical baptism.

Many evaded the ban, of course. Some used to get themselves invited to dress rehearsals (which did not count, apparently); others had themselves smuggled into the wings illegally (theologically speaking). One such well-known wing man told me: 'It was the nearest I will ever get, I think, to the feelings of a black South African. There outside in the stalls were hundreds of people, rustling chocolates, laughing, applauding; and there was I, breathing the same air, but excluded from their mood and their lives. Come to think of it, I haven't been to the theatre since the ban was lifted and the fruit was taken off the forbidden list.'

Nuns, as well as priests, were given this freedom; and soon afterwards Dublin was dispensing the apocryphal story of the two Sisters who went to see *Borstal Boy* with their Mother Superior.

After the first act, one nun could stand the dreadful language no longer and fled to the foyer.

After the second act, she was followed by the second nun, face scarlet, hands over her ears.

At the end of the play, they waited dutifully for their Superior. When she did not appear, they went to seek her and found to their horror that she was on her hands and knees, groping under the seats.

'I won't be a minute, Sisters,' she said. 'I'm just looking for that bloody rosary of mine!'

Certainly the Abbey is reviving after the years of stagnation which followed its golden era, when it had playwrights like Yeats, Synge, O'Casey, Lennox Robinson, and, later, T. C. Murray and Paul Vincent Carroll; and actors like Sara Algood, Maire O'Neill, Arthur Sinclair, F. J. McCormick and Barry Fitzgerald.

It has started to tour again, visiting London and Florence, for instance. Perhaps even more significant, it has proved itself to be a really National Theatre by bringing the company to small towns and villages in Ireland and even out to the Aran Islands, an Irish-speaking group that form a windswept barrier between Galway Bay and the

Atlantic Ocean. To get from one island to another, they had to hire a
trawler first and then, piano and all, transfer to currachs, incredibly
light boats made from tarred canvas stretched across a wooden skeleton.

'When we were going to Inisheer,' Phil O'Kelly, the manager, told
me, 'they said we needn't bother bringing our piano. The Priest was
away, they told us, and they could borrow his, even though it meant
lowering it out of the top window because it wouldn't go down the
stairs. When we got there, however, we found it wasn't a piano at all.
It was a harmonium. So we had to call out the trawler and the currach
again.'

It was a successful, worthwhile tour, with only one sad little commentary. On one of the islands the players could not understand why
there was no applause from these extremely courteous people. Then
they learned that they were playing in the hall where the island
television set was kept. Once a week or so the islanders paid a shilling
to watch it. It was the only form of organized entertainment they had
ever seen. Nobody applauded the television set; and silence, it seemed,
was habit-forming.

They also toured in the North of Ireland, where the Union Jack still
flies, and advertised themselves as the National Theatre. There Phil
O'Kelly suggested to the Prime Minister, Captain Terence O'Neill,
that some people might regard the National Theatre as that other little
group, run by Sir Laurence Olivier in London.

'They have been over only once,' said Captain O'Neill. 'All we get
from England is money. You must come more often.'

Lack of theatres and lack of money, rather than lack of freedom, are
the main problems in Dublin today. The Royal, which was the city's
largest house, has been bulldozed to make way for office blocks. The
Queen's is about to follow it. The Gaiety and the Olympia have been
saved only by a Dublin Corporation ruling that they must be maintained as cultural assets. Money is a more complicated problem.
Theatre seats are cheap and therefore actors' salaries are low. When
Norman Rodway began working with the Gemini Group a few years
ago, they could afford to pay him no more than six pounds a week.
When Cyril Cusack and Siobhan McKenna returned to the subsidized
Abbey recently to play in *The Shaughraun*, they earned twenty-six
pounds a week.

Not that they had any regrets. Afterwards Cyril said: 'I lost a great
deal of money because of the long run of *The Shaughraun*, but in a

way I'd rather earn twenty-six pounds than £26,000. When you make £26,000, the vultures swoop and suddenly it has gone. When you get twenty-six pounds from the Abbey, it comes in a pay envelope and you can count the notes.'

It is good to hear him say so; but not everyone could afford to talk like that. Micheál MacLíammóir and Hilton Edwards, two men who made an immense contribution to the theatre in Ireland, went bankrupt, and had to be saved by the Irish Arts Council.

'Once we used to produce *Peer Gynt* or *Julius Caesar* at the Gate and have maybe sixty people on the stage,' said Micheál. 'Now I do my one-man shows. It's so much cheaper that way.'

In fact, he has taken his one-man shows and particularly *The Importance of Being Oscar* (a tribute to another famous Irishman, Oscar Wilde) around the world with high success. Hilton Edwards, who was for a while Drama Director of Irish Television, gave Brian Friel's play, *Philadelphia, Here I Come!* its first production in Dublin and subsequently took it to New York, where it holds the record as the longest-running Irish play on Broadway.

Most of Ireland's theatrical talent lives by grazing deep in foreign fields and then returning to work at home for as long as it can afford. Typical examples are T. P. McKenna, Ray McAnally, Jackie McGowran, Eithne Dunne, Milo O'Shea and Donal Donnelly.

A fair commentary, indeed, on the international impact of Irish actors, together with the financial state of the theatre at home, appeared recently in the *Irish Times*. It was written by Séamus Kelly, who doubles for that newspaper in the roles of columnist and drama critic, performing in each capacity, if I may so say, with vinegar-sprinkled grace and charm. I cull the following from his columnist act:

Maureen Toal, who made a tremendous hit when she co-starred with Ray McAnally in Arthur Miller's *After The Fall* during the Theatre Festival, has turned down two very attractive offers to play opposite Cyril Cusack in the premiere of Brian Friel's latest play, *Crystal and Fox*, which is being presented by Gate Productions at the Gaiety on 12 November, directed by Hilton Edwards. Miss Toal had been offered a leading part in a Baroque comedy at the Nottingham Playhouse with Christopher Plummer, as well as a film lead. . . .

Meanwhile, from back in New York, I hear that Miss Toal's husband, Milo O'Shea, has started rehearsals for *Dear World*, in which he co-stars with Angela Lansbury, and which is to open at the Mark Hellinger Theatre on 26 December under Alexander Cohen's production at an estimated cost of three-quarters of a million dollars. (The whole Irish theatre industry could flourish for at least a year on that amount.)

That the forces should be scattered thus is sad, but inevitable, perhaps, in a country with a population of under three million. Now that the freedom fights have been won, maybe the economic war will be waged; and an interesting footnote to those freedom fights, incidentally, is the appointment, as I write, of a new Artistic Director at the Abbey. He is Alan Simpson, of indecency, obscenity and *Rose Tattoo* fame back in 1957. It would seem that victory is complete.

The revolution on the literary front has been even more astonishing for those who, like myself, have returned to the country after an absence of fifteen years. In those days and for some time afterwards, the list of banned Irish authors included Samuel Beckett, Austin Clarke, Patrick Kavanagh, Frank O'Connor, Líam O'Flaherty, George Moore, Oliver St John Gogarty, Seán O'Casey, George Bernard Shaw and James Joyce. Edna O'Brien and Brendan Behan joined them later.

Foreign authors, over whom a green veil was drawn, included Somerset Maugham, John Steinbeck, Graham Greene, Arthur Koestler, F. Scott Fitzgerald, Doris Lessing, Alberto Moravia, Aldous Huxley and Voltaire.

Since then there has been a change in the spirit of censorship, which is operated by an unpaid board of five members, and of the law relating to it. In 1967 a new Censorship of Publications Act was passed. It cancelled all prohibition orders that were more than twelve years old and made this twelve-year limit applicable to all other prohibitions, both then and in the future. As a result, nobody in Ireland is ever very sure at any given minute just who is banned or has been unbanned or why. All they know is how it happened, for there are two methods for greasing the guillotine. In the first place, any member of the public may send a complaint—with a copy of the book —to the Censorship Board. Secondly, customs officers send to the Board any book entering the country which they deem suspect.

Because of a more enlightened attitude, prompted, I suspect, by this sudden realization that the Irish are not children and never have been, the list of censored books has grown shorter; and if the following recently published sample of bannings is typical, the loss of some will create no literary starvation in Ireland:

The Horses of Winter, by A. A. T. Davies; *Confessions of a Kept Man (Male Prostitute)*, as told to John O'Day; *Female Deviations and Lesbian Practices*, by Robert J. Bledsoe; *I, A Woman*, by Siv Holm; *Mr Madam*, by Kenneth Marlowe; *Naked From A Well*, by W. A. Ballinger; *The Reunion*, by Yvonne MacManus; *The Sex and Savagery of Hell's Angels*, by Jan Hudson. I must admit that I have read none of these and some may be, indeed, literary masterpieces; but a few of the titles would seem to suggest otherwise.

On the other hand, a shoal of paperbacks entering Ireland today suggests that the mesh in the censorship net is wide indeed. How about this little lot, for instance: *The Virgin Soldier*, described in the *Sunday Telegraph* as having 'the right degree of aimlessness, sex obsession, drunkenness, bravado, teenage naïvety and innocence'; *The War Babies*, which announces on its cover that it has got 'everything: violence, sex, pathos, sex, humour, sex, racial angles, sex, the devastating effect of war, sex, abnormal psychology and sex'; and *The Microcosm*, a study of lesbianism?

They all appeared on Irish bookstalls at one time or another in recent months, while poor Edna O'Brien and Brendan Behan remain banished.

More startling still is the change in the newspaper and magazine scene. Here I write with some authority, for I spent some time as Irish representative of *The People*, one of my more important chores being to ensure that it did not get banned.

It was a tricky old course to hack, but I stuck it for three years, without, I am proud to report, deportation of myself or the newspaper. The Irish public bought British newspapers in the constant hope that they would find therein salacity denied to them by the Irish newspapers. This seldom happened, of course, because of the hot breath of the censor on my neck, but occasionally I darted briefly over the accepted frontier of decency, merely to keep those hopes glowing. Generally speaking, however, we played it safe. If, for instance, a bikini-clad girl was scheduled to appear on the front page, we measured the expanse of tempting female flesh displayed between top and bottom of the swim suit. If we decided that the Irish censor would deem it sufficient to drive the male population mad with desire, we painted over the gap and the girl appeared in the Irish edition wearing a demure one-piece. Delicate brushwork of this nature must be a dying art now, for not only do navels wink shamelessly from pagan British publications, but a great deal more may be found within the folds of newspapers and magazines published in Ireland.

This is particularly true of the Irish women's magazines. They carry articles and letters that would make their Saxon sisters curl up with the shame of it all. *Woman's Way*, for instance, an excellent little mass circulation journal which describes itself as Ireland's leading woman's magazine, carries fairly basic advice for girls who write because (a) they think they are pregnant, (b) they think they may be too permissive with their boy friends and, occasionally, (c) they think they may have contracted venereal disease.

The number of 'How Far Should I Go' letters is disturbing because it suggests that far too many girls are launched into life without an adequate knowledge or understanding of sex. It is impossible, of course, for the various Mrs Wyses to cope with this problem in a few lines, but I do feel that the following piece of advice to a puzzled teenager could have been more comprehensive.

This youngster, who was having trouble over her good-night kisses, was told (not in *Woman's Way*, incidentally) that she should not do anything which she would not do while saying good-bye to a relative at the airport. The mind boggles at the thought of the scenes, as indecent as they are incestuous, which may be seen any day now by casual observers at Dublin and Shannon Airports.

The medical correspondent of *Woman's Way* wrote an article on frigidity which was so clinical that I doubt if any middle-class magazine in Britain would have published it.

A new arrival on the Irish magazine scene, *Woman's Choice*, included in its first issue an article entitled 'How To Keep Your Husband Happy', in which a woman's orgasm was graphically described. It went on: 'From a recent survey it may be seen that between sixty and seventy per cent of married women experience orgasm "usually or always"; about twenty-five per cent "some of the time"; and between five and ten per cent "rarely or never". There is reason to believe, however, a leading Dublin gynaecologist says, that these are maximum figures and that Irish women may not enjoy the degree of sexual satisfaction these figures suggest.'

If Voltaire were alive today, I wonder what he would have to write to get himself banned after that!

I digress, however, into the petticoat fringe, which is one of the troubles about discussing Irish literature. As soon as the first words hit the floor, the ever-weakening body of censorship is dragged from its sick-bed to be given another pummelling.

How, then, stand Irish letters today? In the last few years they have suffered badly from the death of Frank O'Connor, Patrick Kavanagh, Donagh MacDonagh, Brendan Behan and Brian O'Nolan, a satirical civil servant who wrote brilliantly under the names of Flann O'Brien and Myles na gCopaleen.

Like the actors and actresses and, broadly speaking, for the same reason, many of the remaining writers live outside Ireland. Edna O'Brien, J. P. Donleavy, Tony Gray and Patrick Campbell are in England and Benedict Kiely on various campuses in America. Seán O'Faolin, it is true, remains at home, despite all the ancient, halo'd hatchets hurled at him; but he can be counter-balanced by another of the older school, Sam Beckett, who is more or less a tourist attraction in Paris now, like Montmartre.

From time to time there is a plaintive moan raised about the exiles—'Ireland's literary life blood is draining into foreign gutters' and so on—but I can never see the point of this complaint. With the aid of the new-fangled aeroplane, most of them come back fairly frequently to sniff the air; and, even if they did not, what matter? They still are writing and so far no Irish government has made it compulsory for all Irish writers to write about Ireland, perhaps because most of the cheques are drawn on British and American banks. Irish cheques are small because the purely Irish word market is small. The Irish buy books, it is true, but, as Tony Gray says in *The Irish Answer*, there are not enough of them to keep an author in toothpaste.

The artist, indeed, probably gets a better living than the author in Ireland today, if both are relying on the home market. Industrial growth has provided not only more money, but more opportunities. George Campbell, a member of the Royal Hibernian Academy, told me: 'People have become more aware of art and are better informed about it than ever before. That, I think, is because there is more leisure and more money. They have time to look at paintings, to study them; and they can afford to buy them. Neither of these operations was easy in the old days, when the rent was overdue. I earned nothing from my first exhibition twenty-two years ago. Today it's almost impossible to stage an exhibition without selling seven or eight pictures.'

The buying is being done by a wide canvas of people, though

naturally enough the professional classes and the new industrialists are inclined to dominate the market; and most of them buy because they like what they see, rather than to impress the neighbours. As George Campbell said, the status symbolists buy yachts or ponies.

The glib, the slick or the fashionable, therefore, have less chance in Dublin than they have in larger centres. A man of little talent but many words may survive for quite a while in London or New York, fooling some of the people all of the time. He is in one end and out the other of the Dublin circuit very fast, however, and one big, unfair killing on the way is enough to make his journey shorter still. A pint of bad news, served with skill and drunk with relish, satisfies the thirst of many in Ireland, which is another reason why people are cagey when they buy a picture. Native humour can be acid and laughter is the one weapon that really frightens us Irish.

For all of these reasons, the artist is doing reasonably well in Ireland today. It is true that no more than half a dozen make a good living entirely from art; but youngsters who would have been forced to the wall a decade ago, can survive now by feeding the growing demand by advertising men for good illustrations.

His status has grown substantially, too. With increasing affluence, there has been a flurry of new building—particularly of new churches—and more and more often the artist is being called in to consult with the architect before a line of design is drawn. That certainly makes a change. George Campbell told me, for instance: 'I remember the day when we were called in at the last minute and told that a job lot of statues was needed. As an afterthought, the foreman or someone would say: 'We'll be wanting a few stained glass windows, too. Can you run them up fast?'' '

In the younger artistic industries of the cinema and television, rapid advances are being made in Ireland. Balancing the advantages of cheap labour and magnificent scenery against the scourge of an erratic sun, more and more British and American film companies are operating there.

The bait of cheap labour, however, is growing a little stale, as the locals grow wiser to the ways of foreign film men. When M.G.M. came to Galway to film their £2,000,000 production of *Alfred the Great*, the extras, many of them students from University College, Galway, staged a series of sit-down strikes in an effort to get better conditions. The following statement by one of the strikers makes splendid reading and could well be a blueprint for further action in this particular field of industrial relations:

> The present rate (for extras) is half what is being paid in England. We get £3 daily for a twelve-hour day, compared to £4 10s. od. for an eight-hour day. We also have been working eleven hours on Sunday for £3, which we don't consider enough.
>
> One day fire hoses were turned on us to make us wet and it was estimated that the water pressure was equal to that used in controlling riot crowds.
>
> We do quite a lot of night work and yet we discovered that night watchmen are getting more than us and all they do is sit in a tent all night.
>
> For some of the battle scenes we were put running up and down hills, carrying swords and shields in pouring rain. This was understandable, but for these battle scenes we were covered in make-up 'blood' though there were no facilities for washing it off afterwards. The result was that we had to walk back through Galway covered in this red stuff and looking as if we had been in fights down town.

I remember the days—during race week, for instance—when for some members of the community it was positively indecent to walk through Galway without a stroke of blood. Nevertheless, I applaud the general sentiments expressed in the statement.

So far, however, there is little sign of a native industry being born to produce full-length films for international consumption on a commercial basis. That is a pity because, heaven knows, there is plenty of talent around. Peter Lennon (another exiled Irish writer, indeed, living in Paris) is one man, for instance, quite capable of finding a place for himself and his films in world markets. A couple of years ago he made *Rocky Road to Dublin*, a keen, well-balanced film on Irish life. It played to packed houses in Dublin for weeks and received an enthusiastic welcome outside Ireland, too.

Equally professional are a group of young priests who have formed a company called Radharc (Irish for 'View') and are producing films for television. Each of these documentaries has a deep, social bite, one of their early—and milder—efforts being a close look at the amount of money prised out of young people when they get married in Ireland. I do not imagine, somehow, that it went down too well with some of their more conservative and older fellow-clerics.

So we have the talent—the actors, the writers, the men with know-how and experience, like Peter Lennon and the Radharc boys. Why, then, no film industry? Every time I asked that question, I was told: 'It costs too much. We couldn't hope to produce anything more than short documentaries and even those are dicey propositions. To produce full-length features, we'd need millions.'

Millions are not necessary, not even for full-length features. Lennon's film, which was shot in colour in sixteen days, cost no more than £20,000 and ran for an hour and ten minutes. Anyway, what about all that money that so many people assured me was no problem in Ireland any more? Could it be that the financiers love art only for art's sake and feel that it would be an impurity to invest money in it?

The thought of money brings me to the youngest child in Ireland's artistic sphere: television. I have praised it already for the courageous and efficient way it has removed the veils from so many Irish eyes. I forgot to mention that it has done and is doing so with very few pennies in the kitty.

How about letting this be 'Make Telefís Éireann Rich' year?

12 SPORT

I HAVE a simple plan by which Ireland could become world champions in all sport. It comes in two parts:
1: Squeeze out politics and bigotry.
2: Provide training facilities.

That is all. With the Bestic Plan for World Domination, however, Ireland could send a team of green-ribboned female old-age pensioners to the next Olympics and see them trot home with a string bag full of gold, won mainly in the men's events.

It will never happen, however, because sport in Ireland is in a mess and a ludicrous, lunatic mess at that. The main trouble is the border, which politically severs the bit on the top right-hand side, but has nothing that I can see to do with jumping, running, fishing, throwing, catch-as-catch-can or any of the other activities to which energetic young people devote themselves, given time and a piece of land, or, for that matter, a piece of water.★

It is all very sad because Ireland could—and occasionally, in spite of everything, does—produce some of the best ball players, for instance, in the world. The Irish make some slight claim to having invented the first ball game and there could be an element of truth in that, for there are references to hurling (a purely Irish game) in Ireland as far back as 1272 B.C.

Today they play pretty nearly everything as well as the conditions allow. Consider, for example, the case of Association Football, hereinafter called soccer. Ireland, little spit in the Atlantic that she is, produces two international teams; not a first and second, but one from the North and one from the Republic. It might be imagined that they would not be able to beat an egg, what with the island being so small in the first place and the sport divided in the second. On the contrary, however, these teams take on the big leaguers, England and Scotland, always give them a good game, sometimes shake the professionalism out of them and, once in a green moon, beat them.

That is another point, incidentally: professionalism. The vast majority of the Irish are only semi-pros, playing soccer for a few quid at the weekend, but earning their real living at a variety of other jobs the rest of the time. When they should be training, they are working in offices or shops, digging roads or driving trucks. Yet they can

★ Should your mind have strayed here from sport, I would remind you that the border has nothing to do with field activities of any nature between vigorous young people.

147

acquit themselves well against fellows who eat and breathe the game all the time and are paid as much as £100 a week for the privilege.

Because of the natural ability of the Irish, of course, English talent scouts visit Ireland frequently to keep an eye on them. Whenever they see a likely lad, they sign him up. Throughout the years, Irishmen have made a big impact on English soccer and currently Manchester United, one of the best teams in the world, has three of them: Georgie Best, a winger from the North; and Shay Brennan and Tony Dunne, two full-backs from the South. Just think what a soccer team Ireland could have, if only that political line could be withdrawn from the game, as it is, incidentally, in rugby, cricket, hockey, boxing and Gaelic games. I shall have more to say about these last, however, because they have their own bag of politics and bigotry.

The case of the boxers is particularly interesting, for it demonstrates that, given goodwill and sanity, unity can be achieved. At the Olympic Games in Mexico, Jim McCourt, an Ulster man, who won a bronze medal in Tokyo four years earlier, was one of Ireland's main hopes. Other members of the team came from the South and not a fratricidal punch was flung between them.

Very occasionally, a slightly awkward situation can arise, but nothing that cannot be straightened out by a little touch of tact. That happened the last time the European Amateur Boxing Championships were held in Dublin. At this particular international function, it is the custom for the teams to march into the ring for the opening ceremony, led by their heavyweight carrying the national flag. Unfortunately the Irish heavyweight was a member of the Royal Ulster Constabulary. The Irish team officials held a hasty conference. They agreed that they scarcely could ask this loyal Ulster Unionist, who had sworn allegiance to the Queen, to hold high the green, white and orange Republican tricolour. On the other hand, it was not really feasible for the Irish team to gather on the eve of battle under the Union Jack, which, of course, the heavyweight held dear to his heart outside the sporting arena. It did not take the amateur boxers long to find a solution to this problem, which would have led to baton charges and water cannonades had the politicians been let loose on it. They simply announced that, by way of a change, the fly-weights would be the standard-bearers that year. The Irish fly-weight, of course, was green, white and orange.

On another occasion, the un-partitioned Irish rugby team included a Catholic priest and a Protestant minister. Not one thunderbolt was pitched into the arena, which showed that someone fairly high up either believed in ecumenism or did not watch rugby.

It is in athletics that the real, bloody-minded tangling is evident. In my day—excuse me, if I tread slowly through this particular mine field—there were three athletics organizations in the island of Ireland: the Amateur Athletic Union of Eire; the National Athletic and Cycling Association of Ireland; and the Northern Ireland Amateur Athletic Association.

The Amateur Athletic Union represented the twenty-six Counties of the Republic and was recognized internationally. The National Athletic and Cycling Association represented all thirty-two Counties of the island and was not recognized internationally. The Northern Ireland Amateur Athletic Association was allowed to join with the Amateur Athletic Union and represent Ireland in home international contests, but had to join with Britain for the Olympics and European contests. The Olympic Council recognized the twenty-six Counties Amateur Athletic Union, but spurned the thirty-two Counties National Athletic and Cycling Association, though how it managed simultaneously to embrace an un-partitioned boxer and a partitioned athlete I neither know nor care.

The twenty-six Counties body picked an official team for the Olympics. On one occasion, the thirty-two Counties body picked an unofficial team and sent it to the Games, although it knew perfectly well that its members would not be allowed to compete. They attempted to gate-crash, presumably for the sake of propaganda for the cause, but only the Irish journalists present had any idea what it was all about.

Naturally everyone concerned with this hollow farce felt bitter and twisted, particularly in view of the fact that it had lasted for thirty-two years. Consequently I was surprised to hear that in 1967 peace was in danger of breaking out, that a good, strong table had been found for the warriors to sit around and that a solution had been torn from the backcloth of bitterness.

I shall now try to explain the solution, which reveals in me, I suggest, a devotion under excruciating cross-fire above and beyond the line of duty.

It was agreed that the twenty-six Counties A.A.U.E. and the thirty-two Counties N.A.C.A.I. would merge under the title of

Bórd Luath-Chleas Éireann, meaning the Irish Athletics Board. The Northern Ireland Amateur Athletics Board would be asked to join them. If they felt they could not do so, they were asked to give their members the opportunity of joining the new Board and running for Ireland. Alternatively they could remain within the folds of the N.I.A.A.A. and run for Britain in international events. This formula was hacked out with the aid of strong and patient men, among them the Taoiseach, Jack Lynch, no mean athlete in his day himself.

The N.I.A.A., however, did not want to have any part of the new organization. Neither, for that matter, did the British Amateur Athletic Union, who had been saying for years: 'Look here, you chaps, that bit up there is ours—red on the map, you know. Therefore we can have anyone who lives there for our side ... provided they're good enough, of course.'

So there we were, up to our neck in muck and bullets again, while the rest of the athletic world laughed its handsome head off, if it ever happened to hear about the nonsense, which, come to think of it, was unlikely.

By now it had become wide-screen, vista-vision nonsense. In the summer of 1968, Maeve Kyle, a famous and unpartitioned member of the Irish hockey team, while being an equally famous, but partitioned member of the Irish Olympic athletic team, came down from her Northern home to run in a race at the John F. Kennedy stadium, Santry, Dublin. What followed would have made that liberal President think that the solution of the colour problem in the United States of America was a simple matter, indeed, by comparison.

Maeve climbed into her singlet, shorts and spikes. She went out to the track. Then along came a gaggle of officials, who said that she could not run. They produced rule books and solemn faces. They said she was a member of the wrong organization, from the wrong crowd, or came out with some similar tortuous, hair-splitting twaddle. Poor Maeve, who had won more Irish international caps for hockey than anyone else, who had represented Ireland at three Olympics, a record, I think, had to pull on her track suit and walk away. Making the whole affair even more farcical is the fact that she is from Kilkenny in the Republic and lives in Ballymena in Northern Ireland because her husband happens to come from there.

Surely in the name of the patron Saint of Pole Vaulting or Pigeon Racing they could have asked the decent girl to have a cup of tea and said: 'Be our guest, Maeve. Go out there and run like mad. If you win, we'll give you a prize, though it won't be official, of course.'

Had they done that, the crowd, who had come along on a nice day to see some good running and jumping, would have cheered them all the way from Cork to Belfast and back again. Instead they had to play rule books!

Let us move away from that thoroughly silly scene, though I fear we are approaching one that is just as ridiculous: the arena of Gaelic games. Under the mantle of the Gaelic Athletic Association, there are three Gaelic games. There is Gaelic football, which to an outsider looks like a cross between rugby and soccer, but has much earlier antecedents. Players can run with the ball for a few paces, kick it, punch it. The goal-posts are like a cross between those of rugby and soccer, too, having uprights extending above the net. If the ball—it is like a soccer ball—goes over the bar and between the uprights, one point is scored. If it goes into the net, it is a goal, worth three points.

Hurling has the same scoring system. It is played with a small leather ball that is belted at extreme speed from one end of the field to the other with an unsprung stick of ash, somewhat broader at the base than a hockey stick. It is, perhaps, the fastest game in the world, as I have mentioned in a footnote to my chapter on politics; and the fact that I should have a footnote like that to a chapter like that shows clearly what a delicate task it is to write a book about Ireland. There is handball, which is something like squash without the racquets. It, too, is very fast.

Now, when I was at school, I played rugby, hockey and cricket because we played nothing else officially. Sometimes someone brought along a soccer ball and we belted that around a bit. Had anybody handed me a hurley and showed me how to load it, I would have played hurling as well. I was not fussy.

The Gaelic Athletic Association, on the other hand, is more than fussy. If a youngster who plays Gaelic games is seen playing rugby, soccer, hockey or cricket by a G.A.A. official, a ban is slapped on him and he is drummed out of the organization. His crime: playing a foreign game. Worse still, if he as much as watches a 'foreign' game or goes to a 'foreign' dance—anything other than a céili, which is exclusively an Irish dancing affair, though I suppose non-English folk dances would scrape by—he gets the chopper.

Can there be any excuse for this—to a non-Gael—baffling behaviour?

The best I can say in defence of the G.A.A. is that once upon a time there was a good reason for the ban. An honourable reason. Before Ireland won her independence, the more revolutionary Nationalists were ardent supporters, naturally enough, of the Irish language and Gaelic games. To them, these symbolized their struggle.

The G.A.A. clubs were focal points of rebellion, places stirred by revolutionary talk, centres, often, where plans were laid and discussed. If detectives from Dublin Castle could infiltrate these clubs, men could lose their lives. If those who were members were seen following the games of the British Establishment—rugby, hockey, soccer, cricket— it could mean that they were unreliable. Such men were dangerous and the ban was a reasonable protection against them.

Quite a few All-Ireland hurling medals have been won, however, since the last British detective sat in Dublin Castle. Who now is being protected from whom? Was the security of the Irish republican movement threatened, the future of Irish culture in jeopardy, when Dr Douglas Hyde, President of Ireland, and a life-long member of the G.A.A., went to an international rugby match? I would not imagine so; but they banned him. The only possible parallel I can imagine would be the expulsion of the Duke of Edinburgh from the League for the Preservation of Wild Life (or whatever it is) because he shot a duck. That, however, would be reasonable and proper because the duck could not shoot back.

I cannot understand why the G.A.A. does not bury the ban, if only to protect an otherwise fine movement from the ridicule which circumstances force upon it from time to time. Recently, for instance, Waterford City, a League of Ireland soccer team, was drawn against Manchester United in the European cup series. A visit from the great United was a matter of huge excitement for all Irish soccer fans and particularly for those from Waterford. Such was the interest, in fact, that the venue was switched from Waterford's small stadium to Lansdowne Road, headquarters of the Irish Rugby Football Union, so that as many as possible could watch.

It seemed likely that most of Waterford would emigrate to Dublin for the day; but one man made it known that he would not be there. The Lord Mayor, Councillor William Jones (fine, old British name, that!) announced that he could not attend because he was a member of the G.A.A. The debate that followed threatened to push the pill out of the correspondence columns of the newspapers. The fury of it all would have taken the paint off a gate; but nobody laughed, which was a pity, because laughter here would have spelt hope. In the end, I am happy to report, the Mayor attended the game and so far has reported no ill-effects from contamination.

Is there no hope? I would not say that. It is flickering, if not yet flaming, and it is singeing the green, green Gaels of home. The younger G.A.A. members are not going to put up with this nonsense for very much longer, as I discovered in a rather odd place: mid-Atlantic. Behind me in New York, it was two o'clock in the morning and Terry O'Neill was still serving up great, tender steaks in the Abbey Tavern. Ahead of me in Shannon it was breakfast-time. There I was in a gastronomic no-man's-land, sharing an Aer Lingus Boeing with the London All-Stars Gaelic Football team, a group of Irish emigrants whom I had seen beating the New York Gaels a week earlier.

The boys were singing 'The Holy Ground', which is not exactly a lullaby. I decided that I might as well make fruitful use of my time by conducting a poll on the ban among this captive and articulate audience. The first man I asked—I shall not name him, lest he be burned at the stake—smiled at me, as if I were a small, innocent child, and said: 'The ban? Are you joking? Sure most of us play rugby, when we get the chance of a game!'

I told him to go and wash his tongue and I abandoned the survey.

There are other signs of hope. For a very long time the ban-mentality was represented by those who insisted that all Gaelic games players were clean-limbed youths, drenched with fine Irish sportsmanship and incapable of mean thought or action, while those who played 'foreign' games were a bunch of scurrilous, knuckle-dustered thugs with hate in their hearts for their opponents. That, of course, was untrue. Gaelic games can be skilful and spectacular, as, indeed, can soccer and, to a lesser degree, rugby. All games, however, can be dirty as drain-water and just as dangerous. This the top Gaels of my days in Ireland refused to admit. What was worse, the top Gaelic games writers would not admit it or would not dare to admit it. If machine-guns had been produced on the field, I doubt if they would have reported it for their journals.

I remember, for instance, seeing members of a team, beaten in the All-Ireland Gaelic football final, thumping the starch out of the referee as they came off the field, while the victors tried to fight them off. This unpleasant yet understandable scene took place in front of the stand which held the President of Ireland, Seán T. O'Kelly; the Prime Minister, Éamon de Valéra, with several members of his Cabinet; the Apostolic Nuncio, Dr Paschal Robinson, with several members of the diplomatic corps, plus a fair coterie of bishops.

It was a dramatic incident; but not a line about it appeared in the newspapers next day. Not a photographer moved to record it, and I must say that I cannot blame the cameramen present for keeping their heads down. Some time previously, one brave man, who had tried to photograph a battle on the field for his newspaper, had had his camera smashed to bits; and he had collected a fair hiding, too.

Times, however, are changing. Now the newspapers are writing openly that hurling in particular is becoming so dangerously dirty that it threatens to kill itself. Star players are seriously considering giving it up because, as amateurs, they cannot afford time off work through injuries received on the playing field.

Under the heading 'Is Hurling Doomed?' Raymond Smith, author of two best-selling books on Gaelic games, wrote recently in the *Sunday Independent:* 'I found it difficult to talk to Michael Keating (Tipperary), as I looked at the blood coming from three gashes on his face—one very ugly one above the eye. Then I stood on the steps of the hotel after dinner, looking at players from both teams coming back from city hospitals. Líam Devaney (Tipperary) had a bandage covering eight stitches for a gash on the head . . . Líam Danaher (Clare) had a broken finger . . . John Costigan (Tipperary) had five stitches . . . Pat McNamara (Clare) had four . . . and John Gleeson (Tipperary) had two. There were other players cut, bruised and torn and I do not know, really, if any man came out of this brutal Munster Championship tussle unscathed.'

Smith wrote that because he is an ardent supporter of Gaelic games and does not want to see them die. He or his predecessors would not have been able to write it fifteen years ago.

I must say for Gaelic games players, however, that I have never heard them squeal. There are no histrionics, no mock-agonies, such as are seen at any high-class soccer match, and no ill-feelings that last very long. I have seen Gaelic footballers pole-axed and they have not even stopped the game. Eventually they have staggered to their feet, given their heads a couple of shakes and dived back into battle again. No tears. No fuss. Tough men.

Gaelic games, at any rate, have drawn support from one unexpected quarter. Cambridge University has formed a Gaelic football club and has had the game recognized as an official university sport. Its first President, chosen, perhaps, because she is an authority on bans, is Edna O'Brien.

The reckless founders seem to harbour no fear that Dublin Castle detectives will prowl among their cloisters in search of treason. The Captain, Kerry Kehoe, has announced, indeed, that most of the playing members are rugby players and that the club is being helped financially and otherwise by the Emmanuel College Rugby Club.

While the hierarchy of the Gaelic League were catching their breath in Irish, he went on: 'There are fractionally more Englishmen than Irishmen in the Club. There are also more men from the east of Ireland than from the west. We hope to escape the web of complacency, bred by insularity, which currently enmeshes the conservatives who hold the whip hand in the organization of Gaelic football in Ireland.'

Rules sixteen and seventeen of the Club's constitution state that the official languages of the Club are Irish and English and that applicants for membership are requested to take an oral examination in Irish.

Out of deference, no doubt, to the members of Emmanuel College Rugby Club, the Rules continue: 'Failure to pass this test will be accepted as an indication that the applicant does not have a command of the Irish language. It will in no way prejudice his application. The Club is non-political and membership will not be denied any person on the grounds of race, creed, sex or sporting inclination.'

The potential of the new venture is considerable. Edna O'Brien can punch in some hard training, collect a few All-Ireland medals in her handbag and become Taoiseach. Partition would vanish overnight and President de Gaulle would beg Ireland to join the European Community, promising the while to make Irish compulsory among the Six.

Any other sport? Plenty. You name it and the Irish have it; or, if they have not, they certainly will provide a fair-to-middling attempt at it the following morning.

Golf is cheap, compared with other countries, and played well. Irish players like Christy O'Connor and Harry Bradshaw, hold their own and earn fair livings on the world circuits. It is of interest to note, incidentally, that magic Anglo-Saxon double-think can transform them into Britishers—'you're really one of us, old boy'—at the drop of a niblick, when the Ryder cup team is being picked.

Then there is greyhound racing, which is more a way of life than a sport. This tradition was established during the war, when sport was scarce in Britain and the dog tracks were one of the few attractions available. There was no food to spare for British dogs; so many Irish farmers grew greyhound crops to fill the gap, boost British morale and earn a few shillings. Even an unknown pup could fetch a couple of hundred pounds in those days and one old punter, recalling them recently, said: 'There was scarcely a dog on a British track but was a native Irish speaker and a daily communicant!'

In some parts of Ireland they have terrier racing, a spectacular sight, with pooches of mixed marriages tearing up and down the fields, fighting, making as free as possible with any bitch who happens to pierce the security screen, and generally enjoying themselves.

A more esoteric line of country is frog jumping. In Miltown Malbay, Co. Clare, this summer, the first European Frog Jumping Championship was organized by the local Festival committee. The winner, for the record, was Simple Simon, owned by James O'Friel, aged thirteen. In two jumps, he cleared eleven feet three inches, over two feet better than his nearest rival. The last I heard of him, he was on his way to the United States, no doubt on an athletic scholarship.

I have not mentioned yet one sport, which is nationwide in its appeal and highly popular with young and old of both sexes. It is, of course, funeral-going, and here the Irish can have few peers in the world. The only rule, really, is that entrants should not compete in events involving close relatives, as this would leave them open to charges of, at best, bias and, at worst, nepotism.

One of the best all-round funeral-goers of whom I have heard was Brendan Behan's grannie. She brought him to his first—blooded him, one would say in hunting parlance—and naturally the event remained etched in his memory. This is how he described it to me:

'My grannie never got out of bed except for funerals. She would lie there all day, eating tinned salmon, taking pinches of snuff and drinking porter whenever there was any around. She ate tinned salmon because she was convinced that cooking—all that boiling and roasting and frying—must do food no good at all.

'I'll never forget the day the house was raided because it was known, to say the least of it, to be of republican sympathies. In poured this mob from Dublin Castle and they started searching the place for arms, while my grannie kept up a barrage at them about frightening a poor old widow woman in her bed and she with a bad heart. It was a great act. Those guards, however, had no soul for drama. One of them went over, whipped back the bed clothes, spilling the snuff, and picked out three Lee Enfield rifles. They charged her, too, and she got a suspensory sentence of six months.

'The funeral was a more cheerful affair. Out we went, my grannie and two other old ones all tarted up in black and me, very excited because this was my first funeral. A horse carriage was waiting for us. My grannie thought that any funeral with a trace of a motor-car in the first six past the post was no class at all. Off we went, lying a handy fifth.

'In the first carriage were the chief mourners, bawling their heads off for all to hear. In the second were the in-laws, no more than sniffing because they always thought the poor fellow beyond in the box was a bit beneath the daughter. Then came a few amateur riders, laughing and joking, and after them the professionals, who never missed a funeral. They had the blinds down and were playing solo.

'Then us. We'd gone about a mile when we came to the first boozer. My grannie stuck her head out the window and shouted to the driver to stop for a minute. In the three of them raced, me after them not wanting to miss a second of it, and my grannie shouted: "Three balls of malt* and three pints of stout, mister, and in a hurry for we're at a funeral."

'Your man behind the bar pulled them up fast and down went the balls of malt, like oysters. Up came the pints, a bit more slowly, but we were out in five minutes flat and there was my grannie, leaping into the carriage and yelling: "Folly that fewngeral! Can't you see we're fading?"

'He whips up the horse and we made good time at a half-gallop. Three pubs later and we were lying third, with little left in the race except the chief mourners and the corpse and we could see the mourners were flagging. In the end we won at a canter, which goes to show what I've always said—class will tell.

'My grannie kept going to funerals until she was quite old, getting up out of bed each time, but in the end it was the distance that got her. Few could touch her in a sprint, but she hadn't the stamina for the long hauls any more. It was just as well, really, because she had been barred from Glasnevin Cemetery and that was her favourite. Warned off the course, you might say, for barging in the snug at Doyle's Corner.'

* A ball of malt is a large whiskey, important embrocation for any funeral.

If I were asked what I thought would be the national sport of Ireland's future, I would say without hesitation—funerals. In this new affluent society, all other sports are losing support. School-teachers have told me that there is a big falling-off among pupils, who normally would play Gaelic games, soccer or rugby. They have money for a bit of decadence now and they prefer it to jumping around in the mud on a cold day.

Funerals, however, have a wide appeal and—an important point, this—training facilities in Ireland are excellent. As I said at the beginning of this chapter, unless we have decent training facilities, we will never be in among the medals.

13 HORSES AND COURSES

WHILE thinking up ideas for this book many months ago, I jotted down the following trick question for myself: 'Given the choice of a horse or a woman, the Irishman will examine both, tooth and fetlock, and choose the horse unless the going is particularly soft. True or false?'

The answer I now know. It is: false. The Irishman is not all that wild about women; but neither does the sight of a horse make him swoon. Given the choice, indeed, he probably would drift away and go to the cinema, to which he is extremely partial because, unlike either horses or women, it is cheap, relaxing, undemanding and safe. On the other hand, he might slip into a pub and watch colour television. This technicolored gruel is served up by publicans in many parts of the country now and it is widely held that it improves the drinks.

The theory that all Irish males have not only a warm, rugged, manly affection for horses, but some divinely inspired knowledge of them has been accepted for decades by the world and, indeed, by the Irish.

I can find little evidence to support it and have come to the conclusion that it is a piece of cavalry-twill-clad propaganda, encouraged by the Department of External Affairs to make Ireland lovable. Who could hate a nation which loves a horse?

It is true, however, to say that the Irish love what they can get out of the horse and here I list but some of these assets:

Considerable export earnings from bloodstock, which keep the tills jingling and colour television in the pubs.

The gambling entertainment industry, operated by an enormous, nation-wide chain of bookies' shops, which enable punters to make their wagers without setting foot on grass, which, their mothers have always told them, is wet, dangerous and frequently immoral.

A labour force which is being nudged aside now by the tractor, but which for generations relieved the farm labourer of the chore of pulling the plough personally.

An excuse to abandon work and gallop off to a race meeting, in which the horse, though sweating blood for all present, will play but a minor part.

At a race meeting, I admit, it is possible to witness an Irishman in love with a horse for a few brief seconds—the time it takes for it to pass the post in front of the others. Upon its noble head he will lavish, at the top of his voice, a poetry of extravagant endearments, the like of which his wife has never heard from him and which, probably, she would be shocked to find languishing beneath his rough façade.

Love and hate, however, seldom counter-balance each other. This free expression of warmth and feeling will be overwhelmed by the cruel words being flung at the heads of the less successful horses. If a favourite should fall, break its leg and be shot, for instance, a genuine horse-lover would shed a tear. The Irish shed abuse so harsh that cremation is scarcely necessary.

I am working on a new theory, indeed, that priests break their bishops' rules and attend local race meetings because there is so much destructive emotion in the air. It has been argued that they go lest a horse should fall, and a jockey should approach so close the valley of death that he would need spiritual comfort. I think there are further reasons. Generally speaking, only one horse can win each race. The vituperation that is thought, muttered or shouted at all the gallant losers is so severe that it could not only bring on a lethal apoplexy, but plunge the user into a plateful of mortal sin. It is not comfort that would be needed then, but a quick fire-fighting job.

Commerce, whether it be in the bookie's shop or in the dealer's mart, governs the Irishman's feeling towards the horse. If there be money in the animal, his love flowers.

Some years back, for instance, there was a major scandal because it was discovered that the Irish were exporting horses to Belgium, where they were killed, cooked and eaten. Worse still, they were travelling in such diabolically bad conditions that some died on the way and had to be flung overboard. How a nation which claims more or less to have invented the horse could approve of such a trade I do not know; but I do know that the Department of Agriculture loftily disclaimed all knowledge of the fate of the poor beasts, despite the fact that undeniable evidence, pictorial and otherwise, was produced; and it was months before the campaign to end the trade succeeded.

It may be argued, of course, that the Irishman reveres the horse so much that he has placed its image on his coin of highest value, the half-crown. It may be said that the real heart of Ireland in this particular field is revealed to the world once a year at the Dublin Horse Show. Certainly the Horse Show is an international shop window; but shop is the operative word and the real business is transacted, not in the jumping enclosure at Ballsbridge, but at the bloodstock sales across the road. Certainly all that week there are jumping contests not only for the world's finest riders, but for unknown youngsters from all parts of Ireland.

What, however, is love and what is status-seeking? In England the suburban cavalry flourish and multiply. A pony in the paddock or a riding hat in the hall can be worth two cars in the garage in the eyes of the neighbours. Ireland has not reached that level yet, but affluence could close the gap. How many daddies have tossed a coin between the pony Seán or Maureen rides at Ballsbridge and a mohair suit? Which would go down better in the Martello Room of the Intercontinental Hotel down the road from the arena—the sharp suit or the carefully casual story of the pony in the shop window? At this year's show, incidentally, an unfortunate horse fell, was injured and had to be shot in full view of the audience. A moan of anguish, genuine and spontaneous, swept the stands and terraces. All the same, I could not help wondering what the mood might have been had it been leading in the 3.30 at Naas.

The Dublin Horse Show, in fact, is a social event, a few days out, a fashionable canter that is good business for local haberdasheries. Is a more genuine emotion about the horse found, then, away from it all, in the rural communities, where it deserves a real status? Personally, I have yet to hear a Co. Kildare farmer, crooning across the Curragh Plain: 'Old faithful . . . we roam the range together.' I believe that he regards his horse as a symbol of work, as I regard my typewriter; and I am not really wild about typewriters. Yet, despite all I have said, I agree that the horse lies at the root of events which give a great deal of pleasure to Irish hearts: race meetings. It is, however, only a part here of a flamboyant canvas, the texture of which varies from meeting to meeting.

My favourite is Galway, a fine, respectable, five-star orgy, so awesome at its more abandoned moments that at times I think the horse must have been invented specially for it; or perhaps there was a photofinish between the arrival of the pair of them and they got together inevitably and naturally. I went there last with a flotilla of Galwaymen and this destroyer escort was necessary, for here is a hazardous course in anybody's boots. With us was a Galway girl from London, seeing it all for the first time and wondering whether she would ever see Charing Cross again. We parked the car in a field that was carpeted with them already. A task force of tinker-women moved in on us, babies lashed to their breasts with vast shawls, lips moving by reflex in mahogany faces.

'The blessin' of God on you, sir, and on you, my lady . . . spare a copper, sir, and may you win two hundred . . .'

My lady! It was pure Elizabethan. I dug in my pocket and said: 'Two hundred what? Guineas?'

'Of course, sir . . . and the blessin' of God on you and on you, my lady . . .' But she was not talking to me any more. Another car was spilling its contents onto the grass and the show had to go on.

On towards the turnstiles. An old, old man, lay begging in the sun, a dark bottle in the crook of his arm, a woman's bathing cap on his head. Another tinker, low-sized but square, swung skilfully into my path. 'A penny for the holy picture, sir, and may you find the winner . . .'

She thrust out a picture, the size of a postage stamp, a veteran, I would say, of many a race meeting. Séamus beside me said: 'The mark of her thumb is on the back.'

Into the arena. Over to the bar—the Small Bar, which was less crowded than the Long Bar, less spectacular, perhaps, but more functional. We gazed at Big Brother from afar and Séamus said with sad pride: 'It's the longest bar in Ireland. Used to be the longest in the world until the Japs built a bigger one. If you stand at one end, you couldn't recognize a friend at the other.' A pause. Then in a low, far-away voice, he added: 'And that can be a help.'

We sniffed the air, studied the scene. Richard, veteran of many Galway races and with the scars to prove it, said: 'It's quiet this year. Very quiet.'

'Why?' I asked. 'Has the Bishop been complaining?'

'No more than usual,' he said. 'I think the drink prices have civilized us a bit; and this year, of course, there's no Tote.'

It was true that the lack of the Tote caused by a strike of the operators, was a cloud in the air. It meant there would be no each-way betting. It meant that the women could not creep quietly away to have their sly bets on the side. With solemn respect, we looked down at the boarded-up little Tote (like the bars, there is a big and a little), and Séamus said: 'God, it used to be great for the women, that little Tote. They'd sit out here on the little wall, while the kids played round them, and they'd have their drink in the bar and their bet. It was lovely.'

'All that,' I said, 'and the races, too.'

'What?'

'They watched the races, too.'

'God, no! They didn't bother about the races. Just had their drink and their bet and the good fresh air. Wasn't that enough for them?'

It was almost unbelievable, but it was true. The poor old horses, churning chunks out of the course for our benefit, were only a small part of the huge panorama with its carnival, its stalls, its fortune-tellers, its three-card tricksters, its longest bar in Ireland, its big Tote and its little Tote. With a few drinks and a few bets and a sandwich here and there, all busied along by the good, fresh air, who wants horses? Bill, another of our team, never watched one race throughout the two days I was there. Séamus put his bets on for him while he sat on the little low wall, a bottle of beer in his hand.

'Do you go often to the races?' I asked. 'Are you fed up, watching?'

'I've never been before,' he said. 'I just enjoy sitting in the sun here. And betting on my children's names and so on just to pass the time.' He was not even a serious drinker, a man who drank a bottle of ale more or less for the sake of politeness. He just liked his bit of sun and the scene.

I needed more. I wanted not only to know who won, but to see it winning. At the beginning of each race, I walked down to the course. The others—with the exception of Bill—came with me out of politeness.

Maybe they were right. It was a scene that has left many chunks in my memory, but not one of them bears a horse's name.

I remember the woman in smart blue and white, sitting on the little wall beside the little bar and the little Tote, tumbling over backwards, turning a neat somersault, and climbing back up the bank without dropping a word from her sentence.

She was quite sober.

I remember a small, round man in cavalry twill trousers and a check coat, leaving the lavatory under the stand, teetering at an angle of thirty-five degrees back to the bar while struggling to button an obstinate fly, overbalancing as he climbed the steps and being pushed back to something near vertical by two punters who never even raised their eyes from the race cards they were studying.

He was not quite sober.

I remember the two young nuns, dimpling under their wimples, as they stood in the bar, orange juices clutched in pale, white hands, eyes laughing, but lowered demurely.

Then the sudden, stark announcement that crackled over the public address system, jerking my mind back to the orthodoxy of London a

million miles away: 'Will Miss Elizabeth O'Riordan of Swiss Cottage
please report to the Posts and Telegraphs office?' What was wrong in
that well-combed area? Who was sick? And what could she do about
it now?

I remember the bored professionalism of the beggar, no more than
ten years of age, scuffing his professionally bare feet in the grass, as
Séamus asked him: 'What do you want a penny for?'

'To buy shoes.'

'What do you want shoes for on a fine day like this?'

'The thorns do make me feet bleed . . .'

He knew he had made no sale, but the ritual had to be honoured.
When it was over at last, he moved without resentment to the next
hurdle, a plump, prosperous man with a large pink carnation and a
plump, lethargic girl, showing an acre of thigh. 'Givvus a penny,
sir, to buy some shoes . . .'

A large, bronzed priest, whiskey glass swallowed by an ample hand,
was gazing over the shoulder of a Garda sergeant, who was marking
his race card for him. Utter concentration, as the law gave its solemn
evidence about the character of the horses, while I wondered whether
I would ever see the like of it at Epsom, and Séamus muttered: 'Did I
ever tell you the time I marked the Sergeant's card, working hard to
sabotage him?'

'What happened?'

'I gave him six winners and never had one myself. That was bad
enough, but what choked me was the way he treated me as a friend
ever afterwards.'

We filed out past the dark suits and white, white shirts and flat, stout
caps that had known the thunder of many hooves, past the fruit-sellers,
shrill with the jitters as they tried to flood a fading market with their
big American apples, past the old man with the bathing cap, still
cradling his bottle. Out into the night and the start of the races, for
which the horses themselves were no more than appetizers. By ten
o'clock we were in a packed Galway hotel, watching a Belfast enter-
tainer giving the English guests the Butlin Red Coat treatment, the
'Knees Up, Mother Brown'. We could not get out and it was just as
well, for a minute later, a tall, gentle girl was singing in Irish 'The Last
Rose of Summer' to a room that is suddenly hushed.

By eleven o'clock we were far from the tourists, far from the
chrome, deep in the country in a pub where the only genuflection to

the new, dynamic Ireland was a Coca-Cola advertisement on the pale buff walls.

No soft seats here. Just plain deal tables and forms—benches. Not even a bar in this room. Just a square hole in the wall, a sodden, stained serving-hatch through which flowed an endless supply of liquor to the granite men of Connemara, who that night were the forces of occupation, towering, steely men in hand-woven suits of grey, eyes a bit glazed because it is late, but dancing still to the tune of a wheezy jig from a mouth organ.

'The girls are gas here,' Séamus whispered into my ear. 'Very obliging. All of them personally tested by the management, they say.'

One of them passed us, a tray of drink on one flat hand. She was slim and tiny, with a well-scrubbed, schoolgirl face. She wiggled through the crowd, bottom winking, tray in constant jeopardy, her whole demeanour modest and demure. A dancing Connemara man, both blurred feet off the ground, twisted like a limbo dancer and thrust a huge hand up her skirt. She squeaked with surprise or rage or shock or pleasure and ducked behind a table, spilling not a drop. He was still dancing, as she passed again, tray empty this time. With one swift, mighty swing, she clattered him on the backside with it, then darted like a kingfisher past me, squealing: '*Jeezus . . . let me out before I'm reaped!*'

The Connemara man grinned after her. Then, lurching across the floor to the Galway girl from London, he managed a little bow and said: 'Would you care to dance, please?'

With truth and equal courtesy, she said: 'No, thank you. I don't dance.' He repeated his bow and retreated with a smile, back to his jig and a secret slug of poteen, a colourless whiskey which these men from the jagged West coast make themselves.* Wild men they are, but mannerly. They will fight with knives until they drop; but the first harsh word must fall from the stranger.

Then it was three o'clock in the morning and we were fifty miles away, heading West again from Spiddal, once a quiet, Irish-speaking town, now a-glut with tourists, its bars brash with brandy and bacardi and cigars. We had driven there to drop off one of the party, getting lost on the way and missing the Atlantic Ocean by a couple of whiskers.

Séamus said: 'I think it's time we had a drink.'

'They're closed,' I said. 'It's three.'

* It can be good and it can be terrible. Never, never buy it from strangers.

'This man never closes. The lock on his door is broken.'

'Why doesn't he mend it?'

'He's mending it tomorrow. He's always mending it tomorrow.'

Half an hour later we were in the pub with no lock, eating salmon from tins we had opened with knives and, incongruously, drinking tea. Back in Galway City, the horses were in bed, sensible animals that they were, for they had a long day ahead of them. The sad part about it was that nobody, except the bookies and the jockeys and the men who owned the race course, would be all that worried, if they decided to have a lie-in for a change. That, of course, is an exaggeration. On the course, the horse is taken for granted, just one link in a great, coloured paper chain; but take him away and there would be murder, for the chain would sag to the ground. Like a close friend in Ireland, he is accepted as part of the furniture, but never put on a pedestal.

He is a source of pride, too, when he wins; and this he has been doing since the war with sufficient regularity to split the stiff upper lips of English breeders, owners, trainers and jockeys.

Yet here again, the horse—with the possible exception of Arkle, who endeared himself to the Irish world, not merely because he won them money, but drank Guinness, too—takes second place in public esteem to the trainer. Men like Paddy Prendergast, who three times has topped the trainers' lists in Britain, and Vincent O'Brien, whose horses have won three Grand Nationals, three Cheltenham Gold Cups, three Cheltenham Hurdles and one Arc de Triomphe Stakes, are hailed as wizards and afforded all the respect which their alchemy deserves.

Without him, the country's economy would take a knock. In 1967, 11,398 horses were exported for £4,310,000. Of these only 2,571 were thoroughbreds, but they earned over £3,300,000 of that total. So obviously many people love Irish horses and for the simple reason that they are damn good. They are better than others because the limestone in the land gives them great, strong bone. They do not break down easily. They are better, too, because of the wind and the rain which may pummel people into the ground, but keep grass growing most of the time. Irish horses have a good start in life.

There is, however, another reason for their international acclaim and success. Captain Michael Hall of Goff's, the world-famous blood-stock auctioneers, told me: 'The Irishman has an intangible quality, when it comes to breeding and rearing good horses, an innate knowledge. I know farmers who can barely write their names, but, when it comes to horses, they are men of talent and deep knowledge.'

The industry, always solid, expanded dramatically after World War Two. Always famous for its steeplechasers, Ireland suddenly became important to the rich bloodstock fanciers who settled in the country and used their ample cheque books shrewdly. The result was dramatic. Captain Hall told me: 'Ragusa, for instance, was bought at the sales here for 3,800 guineas. No horse has ever won more as a three-year-old, racing in Ireland and England. When he retired, he had won £146,578 in stakes and now he is standing at stud, making a pile of money. What he is worth is anyone's guess.'

It was Captain Hall, who handled that sale of Ragusa for 3,800 guineas. I asked him if he had seen the colt's potential. Chewing on a pipe, held together with insulating tape, he shook his head and said: 'I don't think so. I sold Hard Ridden for 270 guineas. Later he won the Derby. Arkle, the horse of the century, perhaps, certainly in the glamour stakes, went for 1,150 guineas. No other jumper has ever won so much—or, possibly, been loved so much as Arkle. Did I sell him personally? I don't remember because one sells so many. I recall selling Hard Ridden only because he was bought by Sir Victor Sassoon. I wondered at the time why such a rich man was bothering to pay 270 guineas for such an unlikely horse; then I remembered that he owned the sire, Hard Sauce. I suppose that gave him an interest in the son.

'Did I back him? No. Never do. It's a mug's game.'

Having spent all his life with horses, he has no doubts about the main source of Ireland's equine wealth. He said: 'The small farmers are our hard core of sellers. They outnumber the big studs and, while we could not do without either of these categories, we still rely on the farmer for the bulk of our horses. For him it is a sideline and a good one. He grows his own feed—hay, oats and so on—and rears his horse comparatively cheaply.'

For the small farmer, the horse, indeed, is a valuable crop. I saw the proof of that last August along the crinkly roads that lead to Clifden, away out on the Atlantic nose of Co. Galway.

It was the day of the Connemara Pony Show, the annual commercial and social tribute to a game, hardy little animal that for years was neglected. From all over the countryside the farmers and their sons and their daughters were bringing in their wares, sometimes in expensive horse-boxes, but mostly riding them, for the grass lies thin in Connemara. No matter how the ponies could afford to travel, however, each bore the stamp of that intangible quality, which Captain Hall mentioned, that innate knowledge. Today that quality, that knowledge fetch high prices. I stood by the wayside, talked to a farmer, who somehow managed to claw a living from twenty-seven rocky acres, and watched him look with envy at his neighbours who had ponies to sell. 'Some of them will fetch at least a hundred pounds,' he told me. 'Ten years ago, you wouldn't have got ten pounds for them. But now the foreigners are buying them for their daughters.'

By 'foreigners' he meant wealthy Germans, who had been buying plots and building bungalows, Celtic funk-holes for Teutons, divorced from an ultimate deterrent of their own. I said to him: 'Do you mind the foreigners coming here and buying land?'

He took a long, last drag on his cigarette, flicked it onto the road and said: 'Why would I mind them? They're paying money, aren't they? I remember the day when you couldn't give away that old rock there. Now, they say, strangers are fighting to pay £1,000 an acre for the privilege of owning it.'

Why, indeed, should he mind? It is easy to be sentimental and patriotic and outraged in the comfort of Dublin about outsiders buying chunks of Ireland; but that man lost money on his few cattle last year. His son behind a New York bar must send him a small, but regular remittance and a few pounds a month come from his daughter in Birmingham. I do not like to see Germans owning pieces of Connemara or Kerry or any other part of Ireland; but I do not have to hack a living from land where there is more rock than soil. Those men who must, men like that farmer, are more impressed by the size of a bank account than the colour of a passport; and, as I say, who can blame them, when their living is bad? The blame, surely, must lie with a system which allows it to be bad. That is why the horse is respected in Ireland, if he is not loved. He earns his keep, wins the bread, brings a hundred pounds into a wasting home on the day of the Connemara Pony Show.

Donkeys, too, are shooting up the social and economic scale. Once they could be bought for the price of an American dollar. Now they are fetching as much as fifty pounds. One dealer told me: 'They're getting scarce now. Becoming status symbols, if you don't mind. Being exported. Joining the jet set.'

Soon, maybe, they will rank with a mohair suit; and my farmer friend will not mind about that, either.

I WAS having a drink in John Britton's pub, when he decided to emigrate. He walked out, turned right, right again, over a little bridge and across the street to a red pillar box, where he posted a letter.

When he came back, I said to him: 'Why did you go foreign? Why give money to the wicked imperialists, when you've got a perfectly good, green Minister for Posts and Telegraphs of your own?'

He went behind the bar, jerked a head towards the back window and said: 'Up there it costs me fourpence, second-class mail.' Nodding towards the front window, he went on: 'Down there it's fivepence. It's a matter of economics.'

That, from my observer's post on a bar stool in Pettigo, Co. Donegal, was what the partition of Ireland was all about.

The border, a man-made, invisible line which waggles its way round the edge of six Ulster Counties, runs through this village of 250 people and six pubs. Some things are cheaper if you go orange, some things cheaper if you go green.

Stand on the bridge over the River Termon that is stuffed with trout, and for no charge at all you can have one foot under the mantle of the Union Jack and the other beneath the Republic's tricolour. The tar macadam bit is Co. Fermanagh, the concrete, Donegal.

If you want petrol, drive over the bridge and tank up in the garage at the other end of it. Orange petrol is a better buy than green, or at least it was at the last budget call-over.

If you want a drink, tank yourself up in John Britton's pub, which really is in no-man's-land between the two customs posts. Green liquor is a solid investment compared with the other stuff. Anyway, if you wanted to be loyal to the Crown, you would have to go to the village of Kesh five miles away because Brennan's, the only pub on the northern side, fell into the Termon a few years back.

As John said, it is a matter of economics; and that could well be true about the entire crazy, unhappy problem, which has stirred so much bile, and spilled so much blood. When the standard of living in the south becomes better all round than that in the north, the diehards of Ulster could fade away and the line that runs through Pettigo could fade with them.

I crossed the line that day and walked towards Pettigo's northern Check Point Charlie with the Tourist Board sign nearby, reading: 'Welcome to Ulster.' On my left was the shop where John Britton had posted his fourpenny letter, and over it 'Tullyhoman Sub-Post Office'.

Tullyhoman. When they rolled out the border in 1922, the Sub-Post-mistress decided that life was going to be confusing with two police stations and two customs posts, all called Pettigo. To have two Post Offices in the same family would have been ridiculous. So she named hers Tullyhoman, which has a nice lilt to it; and there it is in all its bewilderment and rather lonely because nobody ever uses the name.

In the red, geographically, are the Presbyterian and Methodist Churches. There is no mention of Tullyhoman on their notice boards, Just Pettigo. In the green are the Protestant Church of Ireland and the Roman Catholic Church.

I walked back past the Southern customs posts and through the village. Outside a shop was a notice: 'Lough Derg and Irish souvenirs sold here. Stop here for Lough Derg minerals, water biscuits, oatcake and rock, religious goods, souvenirs. Crazy Price souvenir shop. Bargain offer. If the owner of the shop is needed, call at Egans, fifty yards further up. Sale on.'

Lough Derg and its holy island. Place of penance and scene of one of the most rigorous pilgrimages in the Catholic world. There it was, only a couple of miles away, rubbing its raggedy rocks against this border, stained with religious bitterness. I wondered how the water biscuits tasted.

On I went to the southern outskirts, to a road sign that read: 'Paite Goba—Pettigo. Go Mall—Slow.' I was in the deep south, now, into the bi-lingual country. So deep, indeed, that they used the Gaelic script that had been abandoned by the rest of the Republic some years earlier. I wondered whether it was deliberate, a defiant shout of nationality to the foreign rulers a hundred yards away.

Then I went back to John Britton's pub. The situation seemed less complicated in no-man's-land. Yet, when I probed a little, it was even more confusing. His wife, Bridget, who comes from Westmeath in the midlands of the Republic, teaches in school in the north during the week. On Saturdays and Sundays she helps him out in the pub.

His garden is in the north, separated from the house by the river. 'I don't do much with it now,' he told me. 'I can't. I can't even bring a few spuds across because of a Ministry of Agriculture Order to stop blight. It's the same with eggs. Fowl pest, you know.'

'Which Ministry of Agriculture?'

'Both. Does it matter? They're very strict about it, anyway, though in Pettigo you couldn't live if you tried to do everything legally.'

The cross-border traffic goes on all the time with customs men on both sides behaving sensibly. They are not going to stop someone who slips over to N. J. Johnston's shop across the bridge and buys a razor blade for fivepence less than he would pay in the south. A trunkful would be different. It is the same with butter, which is substantially cheaper in the north. A pound or two will not be confiscated, but people with crates will be in for a probing.

On the bridge a Guard was gazing down into the Termon. I said to him: 'What else do they smuggle besides butter these days?'

'Not much, really,' he told me. 'Motor car parts are worthwhile; but it's been quiet since the cattle prices levelled out. When that happened, they closed the Royal Ulster Constabulary barracks over the road there. There just wasn't enough business for them.'

I asked a question which in Britain or in the Republic, for that matter, would have been offensive, tactless, but here, at the cross-roads of creed, was natural, like an inquiry about the weather. I said: 'What's the religious situation here?'

'Mostly Catholics south of the river. Mostly Protestants north.'

'Do they get on well?'

'Fine. No bigotry and it was always that way. They smuggle to each other, you see. It's the money that counts in the end.'

Down in Brennan's Guest House, Mrs Frances Mangan served me with tea and brown bread, which Ulster women bake better than anyone else in the world; and Donegal, remember, is part of the ancient Province of Ulster, though a County of the Republic. So are Cavan and Monaghan, the six remaining Ulster Counties being under the Union Jack.

On the wall a legend on a plaque read: 'May you be in heaven a half-hour before the Devil knows you're dead.' On the neat, clean tables were table mats, showing Soho Square and Berkeley Square and Buckingham Palace. I had called to see Mrs Mangan because her mother had owned the pub which had fallen into the river.

She took me to the window, showed me the gap where once it had been and said: 'We were the only ones with a pub on the northern side. During the war we did a terrific business because we could get most of the unrationed stuff—sweets, nylons, eggs and so on. I'll never forget Bimbo White, an Australian R.A.F. man. He used to eat twelve eggs at a sitting.

'All the troops came to us. They called my mother Ma Brennan. Our pub was as far as they could go, of course, because they needed civvies to cross the border, though sometimes we used to lend one of them an overcoat and he'd slip across. But they didn't have to move from us. We had the biggest whiskey quota in Fermanagh.'

Mrs Mangan is a widow now, for her husband, a Commandant in the Irish Army, died a couple of years ago. Her sister is married to another Irish Army Officer and lives in Dublin; and that, I think, coats this sad, artificial situation with further irony. Here are two women, brought up in a republican tradition. Yet during the war they grew up surrounded by British soldiers and airmen who called their mother Ma Brennan, confided in her, told her their troubles. Middle-aged men now, they still come back in the civvies they once needed so badly. They call on Mrs Mangan and chat about the old days. There is no bitterness. There never was at this level.

Yet bitterness there is, flowing not so much across the border, but between people in the north. It is not just a matter of religion or a matter of politics. It is an unappetizing blend of both, bigotry without the charity of faith, loyalty without the hope of tolerance.

When did it begin? The seeds were sown with the Reformation. The plant that sprang from them withered elsewhere, but in Ireland it was fertilized by persecution, which denied Catholics all rights; and the border, which sprang from the Treaty of 1922, forced the growth still further.

Does it still flourish? There are signs, small signs that the leaves are withering around the edges; but it is a hellish, hardy plant with years of stoic life in it yet. There is a basic difference in character. In the north, cinemas, dance-halls and pubs are closed on Sunday, though Michael Emerson, Director of Belfast's Festival, is fighting hard against this puritanism. Swings in the park are chained lest children shatter the Sabbath with laughter; and there is no football. Some years ago, indeed, there was embarrassing trouble when a Northern Ireland soccer team was asked to play a Continental team on a Sunday.

In the Republic, Sunday is a holiday. There are dances, films, soccer The pubs are open, a factor, incidentally, which has an impact on all border pubs, like that which John Britton owns. On Sundays they are packed with north of Ireland drinkers and Mrs Mangan told me:

'You see more Guards here than you would in O'Connell Street in Dublin.' On week-nights, too, they close at eleven-thirty, an hour later than their counterparts in the north; and I felt the impact of that one night when I drove from John Britton's across the border to Kesh five miles away. Throughout the journey, headlights dazzled me as thirsty drivers headed south for the extra hour.

I laughed at the time; but unfortunately these are paradoxes with little humour lurking behind them.

In the north about two-thirds of the population is Protestant and one-third Catholic, though the gap here is narrowing; and even that simple statistic filters its way into politics. The Nationalist Party, thoroughly Catholic, sees a voter in every pram. The Unionist Party, proudly, aggressively Protestant, says: 'They won't use contraceptives; and in the south they're not allowed to buy them because of the Church. Now do you tell me that Home Rule isn't Rome Rule?'

My reaction was not all that it should have been. As I pondered the problem in Pettigo, I asked: 'There aren't by any chance two chemists' shops here, are there? One on either side of the Termon?'

Already I was picturing the scene on the bridge, with the stream of drinkers heading south and the wave of seducers washing north; but I was told rather stiffly: 'There are no chemists' shops in Pettigo.'

There seems hardly any facet of life that is not touched by a twist of religion; yet I remember when it was all so much worse, so much more twisted. I remember going to live in Belfast, when I was a child in the Thirties. The polite little boys used to ask me: 'What school do you go to?' The less polite would say: 'Are you a Protestant or a Catholic?' Those without grace at all used to beat the hell out of me first and ask questions afterwards.

Within a few days I had learned to run. In fact I was a Protestant, but that made no difference to the other kids. They simply knew that I was from the south. They had been taught by their mothers that southerners were Catholics and Catholics were bad.

In the south, on the other hand, everyone knew that I was a Protestant, but nobody bothered very much. Privately they found it incredible that anyone could reject the teachings of the Catholic Church; but they held nothing against the curious ones who did. They were rather proud to have them around, in fact, choosing a Protestant, Dr Douglas Hyde, as their first President, and electing a Jew, Alderman Robert Briscoe, as Lord Mayor of Dublin. I went to school with his son, Billy, whom we called Moses because he was the only Jew we had; and that, I think, shows how much religious strife there is in the Republic.

When I married a Catholic, a few eyebrows were raised in the south and a few heads were shaken over the problems of mixed marriages; but no more. When I took my wife to Belfast, however, and introduced her to elderly relatives of my mother, the contrast was sharp. They were kindly old ladies, who were very polite to the poor girl; but obviously they were shocked because they had never had a Catholic in their house before and never had expected such a cloud to fall upon them.

Later they wrote to my mother: 'A nice girl. What a pity!' Ever afterwards they referred to me as 'poor Alan'. It was as if my wife had a crippling physical disability; or, more accurately, perhaps, as if she were a black South African in Johannesburg, and they were Dutch settlers.

In the past ten years, the situation has improved considerably, though the yardstick of progress is inclined to bewilder outsiders. In this oppressive atmosphere, an inch can seem like a mile. Unionists, for instance, stressing that times were changing, told me proudly that Catholics and Protestants had met together in Derry to discuss the city's economic problems. Nor, they said, was that all. Captain Terence O'Neill, the northern Prime Minister, had sent a telegram of sympathy to the Vatican when Pope John died; and during a meet-the-people tour he actually had visited a Catholic school. Non-Irish may shake their heads and wonder what was so great about all that; yet it was truly significant in this area, where so long bigotry was absolute.

Great problems remain, of course. The Nationalists point to two of them: rigging of local Government constituencies and discrimination where houses and jobs are concerned.

The gerrymandering of constituencies is made clear in Derry, where there are three wards. In the North Ward, which elects eight Councillors, there are 4,268 Protestants, who are automatically Unionists, and 3,672 Catholics, synonymous with Nationalists. These eight seats, naturally, go to the Unionists.

In the South Ward, there are only 1,226 Protestants and 14,688 Catholics. Eight seats to the Nationalists by an overwhelming majority.

In Waterside Ward, their are 3,297 Protestants and 2,248 Catholics. Here there are four seats, which go to the Unionists.

Thus a city with 20,608 Nationalist voters and 8,791 Unionists elects twelve Unionist Councillors and only eight Nationalists.

With Unionists holding power in local authorities, it is inevitable perhaps, that Protestants get preference over Catholics when it comes to allocating houses, even when they are in the minority.

The Unionists are on stronger ground when they defend themselves against charges of discrimination where jobs are concerned. If a man should want to employ a Protestant rather than a Catholic, they say, surely it is his affair.

They say little, however, about the fact that the northern Government at Stormont in Belfast and the local authorities are, perhaps, the biggest employers in the area. Invariably they hire Protestants. In addition, British and foreign firms are opening factories in Northern Ireland, attracted by concessions similar to those offered in the Republic. A heavy preponderance of these factories is being placed in areas in which the population is predominantly Protestant. This is reflected in the unemployment figures. In Antrim, 1·6 per cent of men are out of work; in Ballymena, 3·6; in Lisburn, 3·6; and in Bangor, 4·1. All these are Protestant areas.

In Derry, 17·1 per cent are unemployed, in Newry, 17·5, in Enniskillen, 20·6, and in Strabane, 24·1, nearly a quarter of the adult male population. All these are Catholic areas.

Unionists argue that the sites are chosen by the incoming industrialists, not by them. The Republic, however, seems to be able to diversify its new industry so that it will help areas where employment is needed. A further argument that industries must be near a port does not stand up very well, either. Derry, after all, is a port.

There is another anomaly which the anti-Unionists are trying to have removed and that is the archaic business vote. Its strange operations were explained to me by Gerry Fitt, leader of the Republican Labour Party and quite a remarkable man. He is an Alderman of Belfast Corporation, a Member of the Northern Ireland Parliament at Stormont and a Member of the British House of Commons at Westminster, to which Northern Ireland is entitled to elect twelve members. His friends refer to him as Alderman Fitt, M.P. and Bar. They also refer to his many delightful daughters, of course, as the Miss Fitts.

Foreigners may think it odd that Alderman Fitt's Labour Party is not the official opposition to the right wing Tory Unionists in an area with such heavy unemployment. In fact the situation is much odder than they imagine, for, as well as the Republican Labour Party, there is the Northern Ireland Labour Party. Again, inevitably, religion is involved, for Alderman Fitt's party represents, broadly speaking, Catholic Socialists, and the other, the Protestants. The fact that Fitt managed to attract Protestant voters from the strongholds of the Shankill Road in Belfast was and is regarded by students of northern politics as an important swing and a major breakthrough.

Naturally and, of course, ideologically, he is against the business vote, for it is based on capitalism. In his home in Belfast, he told me: 'Anyone who has a limited company with a £10 valuation is entitled to a vote on that account, apart altogether from any vote he may have in his personal capacity. If the valuation is £20, he gets two votes, right up to six votes for a £60 valuation.

'Even if you live in Belfast, you can vote in Derry, provided you have a big enough business there. If you have a very big business, you can vote six times. Yet nobody is allowed to vote in these local elections unless he pays rates. So every time the Unionists build a house, they build a vote—and naturally they are going to make sure it doesn't go against them, that a safe man becomes the tenant. Is it any wonder that Protestant Liberals are the most unhappy people in Northern Ireland? Compared with the Unionists, the British Tories are left wing intellectuals. That is why we want the Race Relations Act extended to Northern Ireland. We have a colour problem right here—orange and green.'

It might be said that Gerry Fitt, being an opposition M.P., was exaggerating, that he was making propaganda, that the situation could not be quite so bad as he made out. Those who expressed doubts about the state of democracy in the north, however, were able to produce strong evidence in favour of their case in Derry shortly after I had spoken to Gerry Fitt. That evidence was shown on television in millions of British homes and shocked many, including the Prime Minister, Harold Wilson.

Civil rights workers had planned a march through the city, in protest against discrimination in houses and jobs and against the business vote. The Minister of Home Affairs, William Craig, banned the march through the Waterside Ward and, when the marchers reached the boundaries, their path was barred by police vehicles. Fighting broke out. The police drew their batons and waded into the crowd. Water cannon were turned against the demonstrators and, as the newspaper pictures revealed the following day, there were some very unsavoury scenes, one shot showing a policeman striking a young woman with his baton.

Gerry Fitt, who had been in the vanguard of the demonstrators, received a heavy blow on the head very early in the proceedings and had to have three stitches to pull the wound together. Eddie McAteer, the Nationalist leader, was hit on the shoulder. Altogether thirty people were hurt and fifteen were arrested, but what shocked most people was the manner in which the police acted.

Three British Members of Parliament, John Ryan, Russell Kerr and his wife, Ann (who was having quite a ration of riots, having just returned from Chicago) were behind Fitt when he was hit; and afterwards Kerr said: 'I was appalled by what I saw. Frankly, I had never thought to see the like of it in a part of the United Kingdom. We intend to make a report to Mr Callaghan, the Home Secretary.'

Craig not only denied that the police had been brutal, but praised them for their action. Few observers accepted his version of the events, however; and the following day a leader-writer in *The Times* wrote: 'The refusal of Mr William Craig, Northern Ireland Minister of Home Affairs, to hold an inquiry into police methods in Londonderry cannot be the last word. His assurance that the police used no undue force echoes exactly that of Mayor Daley in Chicago last month. . . . This demonstration was planned to protest against gerrymandering of electoral boundaries, which few deny is widespread in Ulster and amounts to a scandal in Londonderry.'

Certainly Mr Wilson was not happy about the state of affairs in Northern Ireland. Three months earlier he had stated that the situation there could not continue indefinitely. Now he went further. In reply to questions in the House of Commons, he said that he would discuss the disturbances with Captain O'Neill; and he added: 'I have on a number of occasions paid tribute to what Captain O'Neill has carried through in the way of liberalization in the face of very great difficulties; but I don't think anyone in this House is satisfied with what has been done and, in particular, the feeling that he is being blackmailed by thugs, who are putting pressure on him, is something this House cannot accept.'

When Captain C. P. Orr, a Unionist M.P. at Westminster, tried to defend the police action, Mr Wilson said: 'Up to now we have had to rely on statements of yours and others on these matters. Since then we have had British television.'

The reference to the pressures on Captain O'Neill were welcomed by north of Ireland Liberals, who were well aware of his growing isolation from other members of his Party and his Cabinet. This cleavage had become really serious when the northern Premier invited his Dublin counterpart, Seán Lemass, to meet him in Stormont after the way had been paved by informal and secret meetings between backbenchers of both Parliaments. Captain O'Neill had anticipated this trouble, indeed, for he had issued his invitation without consulting his Cabinet colleagues.

That meeting dramatically relaxed the tensions that had existed between north and south since the border appeared, and gave rise to a faint hope that somehow, sometime a solution might be found to the stalemate which existed between them.

When I discussed the meeting with Lemass, he told me: 'My concept was that we were not going to achieve unity or anything else by pressurization, whether it was economic, military or what have you. We had to build up a climate of opinion which would allow us to look at the situation. Captain O'Neill had the same idea, but it was much easier for me. I had nobody telling me what I should do and what I should not do. He had his extremists. It would be slightly unfair to him, if we expected him to move as quickly as we did.

'I think that a better climate is building up, perhaps to a point where we can discuss partition. He, of course, is thinking in terms of social changes, rather than constitutional changes; but, when we break down the old prejudices, at least we can talk about constitutional changes in a more practical way.'

There was, however, one immediate reaction to the talks. Mr Lemass told me: 'I got an enormous flood of letters from people up there, from Presbyterian and Church of Ireland ministers, some saying that they felt as if they had been released from jail. One wrote: "Now I can cross the street and talk to my Catholic neighbour".'

This feeling that religion was being used by the politicians to perpetuate bigotry, rather than politics being used by the religious, was confirmed when I interviewed Ireland's Cardinal, the Most Reverend Dr William Conway.

A tall, well-built, thoroughly informal man in his early fifties, he said to me: 'The Protestant churches and their ministers, whom I know well, are generally much more ecumenist than they can afford to appear. There have been quite a number of very friendly meetings taking place between groups of priests and groups of ministers. We will have one soon in my Archdiocese, though it will be held in Drogheda, south of the border. I think our Protestant friends would agree that it would be impossible to hold it in the northern part.

'It is the politicians, not the Protestants, who are responsible for the break. The Protestant clergy are fine men, very courageous men, considering the way they are inhibited by the political strait-jacket.

'It is true that young people offer hope. They are thoroughly sick of the Catholic-versus-Protestant rows and I think that is a good thing. Personally, however, I am rather disappointed that more action has not resulted from all the encouraging words. Captain O'Neill is virtually without support in his own Cabinet and his own party. I think he is genuine and sincere, but he is a lonely man.'

He paused, pulled a pipe out from beneath his cassock and said: 'I am sorry that so little that is concrete has sprung from the promise of five years ago. When I return to the north, I still feel that I am coming back to an antediluvian atmosphere . . . an atmosphere close, tense, unbending.'

It is true that the hopes which sprang from the meeting between Captain O'Neill and Mr Lemass, and later between the northern Prime Minister and Mr Lynch, Mr Lemass's successor, do not seem quite so bright now. Nevertheless, there are healthy signs, in spite of the scandal of Derry. Shortly before that unpleasant affair, for instance, Co. Down won the All-Ireland Gaelic Football final at Croke Park in Dublin. That a team, not only from Ulster, but from one of the Counties, governed from Belfast, collected such an exalted trophy was, to say the least of it, interesting. It revealed, for instance, that there were an awful lot of Nationalists in Down and that most of them were highly enthusiastic Gaels, who would have little sympathy with the northern Government.

Yet the Lord Mayor of Belfast, a Unionist, of course, gave a civic reception for them because, irrespective of their politics, religion or culture, they had brought sporting honour to the Province. That would not have happened five years ago.

Are there any other grounds for hope? I can offer two, though both are slightly negative. One student of Queen's University, Belfast, told me: 'There's hardly an undergraduate here who is not sick of politics and religion.'

Then there was the view of Denis Barritt, a Quaker social worker, a liberal, a man of tolerance and gentleness. When I asked him for his thoughts on the future in Northern Ireland, he said: 'While there is death, there is hope.' He was being neither over-pessimistic, nor unkind. He meant that the old guard, the die-hards, who held power through pogrom, riot and bigotry, are old now and soon must die. Some of their ideas may die with them and, perhaps, the young men of Queen's University, sick as they are of Northern Ireland's current brand of religion and politics, will move into the arena.

I hope so, though I must say that, when he spoke of death and hope, my mind went back to the square in Pettigo with its war memorial that has nothing to do with the wars of 1914–1918 and 1939–1945. The inscription was: 'In proud memory of Patrick Flood, Bernard McCanny and William Kearney, who died fighting against British forces in Pettigo 4–6–1922, and of William Beasley, who died of wounds, 6–6–1922.'

Died for what? A tiny village that today has two sub-Post Offices, one red, one green? Maybe if the Dublin Government took a penny off the price of letter post and we all closed our eyes, it would help. What price bitterness, however? How much does it cost to have the stain of bigotry removed? Here, I believe, the twin detergents of time and education are more effective than money.

[Since this book was first published, the lonely Captain O'Neill has been forced to resign by opponents within his own party. Extremist resistance against 'one-man-one-vote' remains strong, though the Civil Rights movement has become now a significant political force.]

15 THE EMIGRANT

I'm a decent boy just landed from the town of Ballyfadd.
I want a situation; yes, I want it mighty bad.
I seen employment advertised. 'Tis just the thing', says I.
But the dirty spalpeen ended with: 'No Irish need apply!'
                      —American ballad, circa 1880.

THERE was a boarding-house keeper in London who put a notice in her window, reading: 'No coloureds. No Irish. No children. No dogs.' She was, presumably, one of a select group with a yen for unmarried, Protestant, animal-hating Caucasians; and there must be only a few of them left.

The 'no Irish' tag, however, once was prevalent in both Britain and the United States of America. It certainly made life no easier for the emigrant, but it did not stop him climbing on the boat, for in the past century several million people from Ireland have crossed either the Atlantic or the Irish Sea. In the past decade alone, half a million have left, many of them for good, and that makes a sizeable dent in a population which for a long time has been under the three million mark. How does today's emigrant fare? How does he compare with those who went before him?

The pre-war emigrant had a rough time and sometimes he became rough enough in return to merit those 'no Irish need apply' notices. He did not want to leave home, but was forced out by economic conditions. He was poor and he was lonely in an alien culture. He drank to cure that loneliness, finding many of his fellow-countrymen in the same pub and in the same emotional state. On their collective shoulders they carried a vast historical chip, an inferiority complex, which led to aggression and newspaper headlines which read: 'Irishman on drink charge . . . three in hospital.'

His drinking, together with the fact that he was sending money home, made him poorer. His education was slight, his temperament careless; and hangovers did little to improve his efficiency. Hence the ethnic censorship in some lodging-houses. Hence the true stories of a dozen Irishmen sharing one room and paying outrageous sums for the squalor—often to another, much wealthier Irishman, who owned the house.

That, at any rate, was the English scene. In America it was different. There he found a new country, instead of old enmities; and with a pick and shovel he helped to build it. He earned fast and he spent fast, gathering a reputation of being a great, big, lovable heap of fighting, drinking, laughing fun. This legend Hollywood clutched to its ample bosom and nourished so well that even today some second and third-generation Irish Americans feel it a patriotic duty to keep it alive, a debt they owe both to the land of their ancestors and the land of their adoption. When I was in New York gathering material for this book, for instance, my announcement that I did not drink was followed on occasions by a few minutes' vigorous discussion. 'An Irishman who doesn't drink! Well . . . whaddya know!'

In America, the Irish invented police, politicians, and James Cagney, seasoned with little Nelly Kelly, by courtesy of Judy Garland. They invented, also, a few gangsters, thanks to prohibition which made a few of them rich, a few of them blind and a few of them dead. Many of the immigrants came from the poorer parts of the west of Ireland, where the illegal still industry flourished; and the liquor they made in America to dampen those dry days was less bad than much of the lethal gruel produced by those less skilful or dedicated.

They banded themselves into Irish County Associations, which helped new immigrants find jobs and their feet; into Emerald Societies; and into the Friendly Sons of St Patrick, which at one time was so powerful that it was reputed to be able to make and break cardinals. They launched Tammany Hall and the Irish vote, a headstrong maiden that had to be courted strong and constantly. A few had power and a few had money. The rest swung along behind on a Hollywood legend and a prayer; and that was how the Green Derby belt was born.

Ireland was very far away—unattainable for most. Memories grew dim and the gaps were filled with cosy little dreams of a green, green isle and grey, grey mothers and cute little white thatched cottages, with the boyos and colleens dancing and laughing to the scrape of a fiddle, while the old farm-horse, which won the Grand National every year, jumped over the moon for the joy of it.

Ireland was sick, but very few could go back to take her pulse or give her medicine. The best the immigrants could do was send back money, the American remittance, which even today is an important Irish import. They could pay regular tribute to their dream, of course, too; and this they did in monumental fashion every St Patrick's Day.

In New York on 17 March, the whiskey is green—even the Scotch. The Italian spaghetti is green. The tears are green as every radio and television station proclaims for what seems like twenty-four solid hours that it is a Great Day for the Irish. Fifth Avenue was painted green until Mayor Lindsay put a stop to that nonsense.

The face of the emigrant is changing, however, making the whole, strange picture very different and much nearer to the home-based truth. The Irish vote, for instance, scarcely exists today in the United States. It has splintered.

Even when the sickness in Ireland passed, the Green Derby belt might have continued to flourish with its shillelagh under its arm and its twinkle in its eye, passing this tradition of Celtic mist down to its children and to its children's children. After the war, however, came a new wave of immigrants, boys and girls who were uninterested in fighting old Fenian battles or brooding over other facets of ancient history. They were reasonably well educated and so they did not need the help of the County Associations, unpaid and admirable employment agencies though they were.

Most important of all, many of them came to the United States to integrate, rather than live in a nationalistic ghetto of the mind. They wanted to become citizens; and so the thick umbilical cord withered and soon will be no more than a tenuous thread of genuine sentiment. This slenderizing process is being speeded by Aer Lingus, which offers cheap excursions to Ireland. The older ones are going home now, often for the first time for twenty or thirty years, and they are returning to the United States with a picture of reality.

The gap between the generations, however, still is wide. The old folk cheered Joe McCarthy and his witch-hunts against the wicked Reds. The new folk are drawn to Eugene McCarthy and Paul O'Dwyer, a fine liberal from Co. Mayo. One generation mistrusted Bobby Kennedy because he raised the status of the Negro, thus threatening the status of the Green Derby. The other generation mistrusted him because he was not progressive enough, soon enough.

The new immigrants have a confidence that their predecessors never knew; and they are spared the rough battle which the oldtimers had to fight. Nevertheless, they face plenty of problems.

Mrs Moyra Casey from Roscommon, a schoolteacher in New York for nearly twenty years, told me: 'Some arrive with their honours leaving certificates and are disillusioned when they find that nobody is interested in that sort of qualification. They could go to night school and get qualifications which would land them white collar jobs, but few do. They go into construction work or get jobs in bars, where they probably earn a good deal more than they would sitting behind a desk.'

Moyra herself came out with a B.A. degree from University College, Dublin, and a Higher Diploma of Education. She had, also, a certificate stating that she was qualified to teach through the medium of Irish, though she did not flaunt that very much. She found that her qualifications, which had been fine in Ireland and England, were not acceptable in New York schools. So she had to go back to college to get herself an American M.A. This she did and today she is teaching in Scarsdale, one of the more fashionable New York suburbs.

Moyra was one of the first of the new immigrants. She is fond of Ireland, but is an American citizen. She is a founder-member of the New York National University of Ireland Club; but she and her fellow-members are not at all partial to green spaghetti.

'We have a dance on St Patrick's night,' she told me. 'But green is worn only if it is a girl's best colour.'

Does that mean the death of little Nelly Kelly and her old softie cop of a dad? Not quite, but it is one of several bullets in her big, kind heart; and latest bulletins on the state of her health are cheerfully depressing.

One came to me from Matt Guinan, an Offaly man who succeeded the famous Mike Quill as President of the Transport Workers' Union of America. He told me with scarcely a sigh of regret: 'The image of the Irish worker in New York is changing. He has more education. He is no longer choked with sentimentality. He is blending into the environment, becoming more American than Irish, jiving, or whatever they call it now, instead of dancing jigs and reels. And a fair number are moving out of New York, too. As soon as we get them better wages and conditions, they buy themselves little houses in the suburbs and start voting Republican.'

This was confirmed by Deputy Inspector Pearse Meagher of the New York City Police Academy, a remarkable and amiable Irish-American. Though born in New York, he not only speaks Irish, but can play the Irish pipes. He founded the New York City Police Emerald Society Pipe Band and for twenty-six years has been a member of the Friendly Sons of St Patrick Glee Club, which was founded by Victor Herbert. All his seven children are learning Irish dancing, of which he was no mean exponent himself in his younger days.

He was speaking, therefore, with unique authority, when he said:

'The Irish no longer have a big base in New York. Their numbers here are dwindling. They don't seem to be having so many children. We don't have so many first generation families here. They are marrying outside Irish circles, too, and so there is a shadowing of ethnic identification. Then there is the flight to the suburbs since the Negroes and the Puerto Ricans moved into the old Irish areas. As a result, Irish dance-halls are failing in the city. The Irish Counties organizations, which once had great vitality and political influence, are shrinking, as the old people die off and new arrivals go their own way. Even the police force is feeling the wind. Once it was overwhelmingly Irish; but not any longer.'

He is sad to see the change, for it means a decline in the Irish cultural activities which he supports so strongly. Yet he is not over-pessimistic. . . .

It is true that there may not be so much Irish dancing in New York nowadays; but it is achieving a new social status. The wealthier Irish-Americans, who moved to the suburbs, have brought their hobbies with them. Now Long Island businessmen are having their daughters and sons taught Irish dancing and are even becoming interested in Gaelic games.

While the two-ulcer men of Westchester County tap their feet to jigs and reels, what is happening to their brother-Celts who could not afford the move? They, I regret to say, still sit in their old, dark, mahogany pubs, glowering through the door at the new, dark, mahogany faces which pass in the street outside. They no longer bother to mutter: 'There goes the neighbourhood!' So far as they are concerned, the neighbourhood has gone.

Sometimes they stroll off, as I did one Sunday, to Gaelic Park to watch some hurling or Gaelic football. There the green flags still flies high but it is not really rampaging itself to tatters. A solitary police car was parked outside the stadium. I asked the sergeant in charge whether he was expecting trouble and he said with a grin: 'We never get trouble here any more. Can't think what's happening to you Irish.'

Nuns in sunglasses at the turnstiles gave an occasional gentle jingle to collection boxes that bore the rather confusing and, to American eyes, unflattering inscription: 'Please help the African Missionary Sisters from Cork, Ireland, to establish a house in U.S.'

My mind still boggling at the thought of missionaries descending on Manhattan with beads and Bibles, I accepted a green pamphlet from a middle-aged man. It was headed: 'UNITED IRELAND PUBLI-CITY COMMITTEE . . . BETRAYAL . . . DECEIT . . . JOBBERY.'

The text contained a violent attack on both Dublin and Belfast Governments, summed up in one brave flamboyant line: 'We have seen the leaders of the Dublin Oligarchy kiss and embrace their counterparts in Belfast, notwithstanding the rampant discrimination being practised against the Nationalist population of the gallant land of Owen Roe.'

The crowds were thickening, brightened here and there with a splash of red hair and now and again a green frock. Mums and dads were there, some towing four kids with a fifth in a pram. It was all very festive and, despite the trappings, not frantically nationalist. I found myself gazing sadly at a poster which read: 'Benefit dance in aid of the nine children of the late Teresa Finn, formerly of Co. Monaghan, with Matt Connolly's Majestic Show Band.'

Inside the stadium, the Stars and Stripes flew high. The teams were led on by an accordion band. The game was started by Brother Gregory, a member of a religious Order; and, for the record, the London-Irish All-Stars beat New York Selected in one of the tougher contests I have seen for some time. While it lasted, Brother Gregory came in for a reasonable quota of abuse and half a dozen players were pole-axed, only to rise minutes later without trace of a grudge. It was all good, clean fun, but hardly, I felt, a springboard for the resurgence of Irish power in New York. I wondered if the new immigrants would support it and decided they would, if the day were fine.

What do the newcomers do with their time? There are half a dozen dance-halls where they gather in New York, but not for Irish dancing. I went to one of them, Jager House at Eighty-Fifth Street on Lexington Avenue and entered to a fanfare of 'My Wild Irish Rose'. There was not a non-Irish face in sight, but the atmosphere—apart from the Rose above and a slight dash of 'Danny Boy'—was far from Celtic. Nor was it New York. Or London. Or Dublin. Or anything akin to the Sixties. Couples moved rather stiffly around in old-fashioned waltzes, as if they were back in the Thirties at a tennis club hop.

More and more of the new Irish in New York frequent bars, to which, believe it or not, they go, not so much for the drink, but to enjoy the social life. These saloons are catering for what they call the swinging twenties, the figure referring, naturally, to the age of the customers, rather than the date. They are places to which girls may go unaccompanied without being misunderstood, for the proprietors go to great lengths to ensure that the indiscriminate lecher conducts himself properly and that less desirable girls do not slide in for a swift piece of business.

Quite a few of these places are owned and run by young Irishmen, who are demonstrating, incidentally, that New York's streets, if not exactly paved with gold for the immigrant, still cradle a few dollars. Gerry Toner from Belfast and Terry O'Neill from Cork, for instance, arrived in town about four years ago, fairly broke. Today they own three of these swinging saloons and are on the lookout for a fourth. They both are in their middle thirties, both left school at the age of fourteen and both failed to get decent work in Ireland, which was a pity for Ireland.

Terry worked in Cork as a messenger boy for a year, then in London as a delivery boy. When he was sixteen and a half he joined the army. There he won himself a boxing title and a trip to Suez for that dismal campaign, before returning to Cork to work in the docks.

Gerry started off as a commis waiter in a Belfast hotel before getting a job on the *Queen Mary*. There he met Terry, who had given up being a docker in favour of being a 'pearl diver'—a dish washer—on the boats. After that the pair of them worked for a couple of years in the Stork Club, New York, before deciding to return to Ireland and buy a pub.

'We went to this bank and asked for a loan of £2,000,' said Gerry. 'The manager wanted to buy my car, but he laughed at the thought of lending us money.'

At that stage Terry tried to get himself a job as a barman at Cork Airport. They did not even reply to his letter. So back they went to New York, where they got work again as waiters. They saved hard, for they were determined to get their hands on a saloon of their own, and finally they were offered the Green Derby.

'It was a typical old Irish saloon,' said Terry. 'A shambles. But we managed to scrape up enough for the first down payment and did it up ourselves.

'The only part we could do nothing with was the floor. It was terrible. So to cover it up we sprinkled it with sawdust, like they used to in the old days in Ireland: and next thing we knew the punters were clamouring to get in just to have a look at the stuff.

'We did well, in fact, despite the fact that the place went on fire three times. The brigade used to know its way round to us and other saloon owners were getting quite jealous because they thought we copping a load of insurance. They began to ask us if we'd slip around and do a job on their places.

'In fact those fires were costing us a barrel of money in loss of goodwill and business, though everyone else was taking it calmly. Early one morning one of the fellows who worked for us saw the place on fire and didn't he ring me and say: "Don't worry, but the Green Derby's blazing."

'Don't worry! I came over in my underpants!'

Eighteen months later they had made enough to expand. They bought the John Barleycorn, one of the few Chinese restaurants ever to go broke in New York four times in succession, despite the fact that it was in the heart of the city's Steak Row.

Terry and Gerry exorcized the Chinese aura and imposed an Irish air instead. Twelve months later, they bought their third saloon, which they named the Abbey Tavern, after a well-known ballad house in Howth, Co. Dublin.

'We've branched out into other business, too,' Gerry told me. 'We've a real estate corporation and a vending machine corporation. We don't really need to work, but we like it. When we opened first at the Derby, we were so short of readies that I had to keep on my job. Now we employ about eighty-five people.'

Hard work is only one part of their formula for success. Others are excellent meals, served at most hours of the day or night with charm and at reasonable prices. This combination has attracted some unexpected customers.

'Bobby Kennedy had his office just up the road,' said Terry, 'and one day he walked in for lunch with his entourage. He seemed to like the place, too, because after that he came in quite a few times; and last time he brought along our own Prime Minister, Jack Lynch.

'Then there was the night that the Archbishop of New York came in. Dr Cooke. He stayed for hours, listening to the ballad session.'

Broadly speaking, the Irish have a fair grip on the liquor business in New York. Malachy McCourt runs a place with the discreet old Irish name of 'Himself' on the corner of Eighty-Eighth Street and Lexington Avenue. John Joyce has bought two pubs in ten years. McSorley's Ale House, one of the best-known bars in the city, is strictly for men only—but it is owned by a Killarney woman.

But the daddy of them all, perhaps, is Jim Downey's Steak House, a watering-place for every star on Broadway and a haven, incidentally, for many an unknown Irish actor or actress without the price of a meal. Jim has subsidized hundreds of them—and, what is more, ninety per cent of the money he loaned has been paid back. He prefers to be known as a good saloon owner, rather than an Irish saloon owner, perhaps because the last time he stressed his nationality it got him into a spot of bother. That was during the War of Independence, which landed him in jail. When he came out, he got involved in the Civil War and that landed him in Manchester with half a crown in his pocket. His comrades had deemed it advisable that he should leave Ireland in the middle of the night rather than have his head blown off.

Just forty-two years ago he arrived in New York, survived the depression and bought a pub for a couple of thousand dollars. On the night he opened, he was offered ten thousand and refused it. After that he bought a second place. 'I got it from an Italian bookmaker,' he told me. 'He used to rob the till to play the horses.'

By 1950 he had made two fortunes and lost one. When I asked him how he lost it, he said with superb and beautiful simplicity: 'I spent it.'

His latest venture—and his last, he says—is the Irish pavilion at 130 East 57th Street on the corner of Lexington Avenue. It is being run by Mrs Rosaleen Fitzgibbon, and it is a neat expression of sentiment, as opposed to sentimentality. Displayed for sale there are some really first-class Irish-made goods—Galway crystal glass, Connemara marble, Crock of Gold stoles and sweaters, Irish silverware and solid gold cuff links and bracelets. Irish books are available, too, recordings by Irish writers and actors—Austin Clarke, Paddy Kavanagh, Jack McGowran —and paintings by Brendan Behan's widow, Beatrice.

With a bit of a growl, Jim Downey told me: 'I'm not putting up this pavilion because I want my name in the paper. I'm doing it because when I left Ireland, I'd no bloody shoes. If I can sell this Irish-made stuff here, it'll give work back home and maybe a few more people will be able to stay there, which would be more than I was able to do.'

He is a remarkable man with a remarkable story. Unfortunately there is little opportunity now for any ambitious young man, following in his footsteps or in those of Terry and Gerry or any of the others, for that matter. New immigration laws have virtually stopped Irishmen (or Britons, for that matter) working in the United States unless they have some skill that is badly needed.

It is, come to think of it, another way of saying: 'No Irish need apply.' And that, I feel, is a pity because the last group to get in before the curtain came down could be the best crop the country has ever had.

At least there is some logic about these new American laws. We may not agree with them, but we know what those who framed them were trying to do. The British, on the other hand, have acted in a way which the rest of the world would call typically Irish. They make it difficult for Commonwealth citizens from the West Indies, Kenya and wherever to enter the country, despite the fact that some hold British passports. The Irish opted out of the Commonwealth long ago; but, when they turn up, they are welcomed. I am not even asked to show my passport when I arrive at London Airport from Ireland.

Until comparatively recently it might have been just possible to argue inadequately that Irish affairs were the responsibility of the Commonwealth Relations Office and then to paper over the cracks in this petal-thin argument by mumbling something about 'special relationship', which, incidentally, I have always thought sounded rather immoral and decadent. Even that minute loophole, however, has disappeared now, for our affairs have become the chore of the British Foreign Office, which would imply, rather heavily I would have thought, that we were foreigners. Yet, if any innocent Irishman ever should be stupid enough to ask where he could apply for a work permit, he would be told with an engagingly intimate smile: 'Don't be silly, old boy. You're really one of *us*!'

Undoubtedly there is a touch of the Caucasians about it and the path might not be quite so smooth if the Irish immigrant in question were flaunting a particularly heavy suntan; but, apart from that unpleasant facet, the whole situation is ludicrous. It could be, of course, that they are anxious to ensure a regular supply of white generals, diplomats, judges, doctors, senior civil servants, road builders, nurses, barmaids and third-rate tenors. Whatever the reason, there are about a million Irish in Britain today and of these about 300,000 live in the London area. That makes London the third largest Irish town, the first two being Dublin and Belfast.

Because the two countries are so close together, emigration from Ireland to Britain is inevitable and probably always will be. This the Irish Government seems to accept; and two years before he died, Donogh O'Malley, then Ireland's Minister for Health, told members of the National University of Ireland Club in London that they should play a fuller part in the political and social life in Britain.

He was speaking to them at their annual St Patrick's Day dinner and he stressed that they could not be citizens of both Britain and Ireland simultaneously. 'You are not exerting an influence on British life commensurate with your numbers,' he told them. 'This may be because of a fear of betraying your Irish heritage, but you must reject maudlin sentimentality about the old country.'

How many immigrants manage to integrate in this manner? I would say that a fair proportion do so, though obviously there remain some who insist on waving their nationality around their heads like a cutlass. There are, too, those, who, because of their background, find England utterly alien; and these are the sad ones, wide open to exploitation, as Father Athanais, a Franciscan priest, author and lecturer pointed out in Dublin recently.

The poorly educated Irish, he said, were tired of study, having found out how little use it had been to them in Ireland after putting in five years at convent or college. They preferred the easier path of entering virtual slavery, when what was presented to them was the choice of going on the bottle and working in a factory.

They are the Irish who sleep twelve to a room, who send prim landladies scurrying for their 'no Irish need apply' notices. Their numbers will dwindle as the educational opportunities Donogh O'Malley later gave to Ireland begin to bite; but always there will be a few.

Similarly, there will be always a few girls in danger because they are incapable of settling far from home, let alone integrating. Their background has left them inadequate and their sense of insecurity is wounding.

During and just after the war, some unscrupulous British firms took full advantage of these girls, not only advertising in Irish country newspapers in the hope of scooping the cheap labour pool, but sending recruiting officers to the rural areas. I met one; and, when I asked him about his job, he said with cynical candour: 'I'm in the white slave traffic.'

The formula was simple. These firms offered wages which were exceptionally high by, say, West of Ireland standards, but enough to offer little more than a sub-existence in London. The moral dangers are glaring in a situation like that. A girl from a village of pocket-handkerchief size is dumped in a strange city. Until the moment she climbs on the boat train, everyone knows her business, knows when she goes to the cinema or to a dance and, more particularly, who went with her. Now she is alone, away from all those eyes and ears. Inevitably she is homesick, trapped in dreary digs or a mean bed-sitter, unable to go out because she seldom has the price of a meal once she has paid the rent. If anyone should offer to take her out, to show her a good time, she will go, after, perhaps, a couple of cliff-hanging refusals. If the bill is presented ultimately in the form of a shared bed, she will pay. There are no parents to scrape at her conscience with shrewd questions; no parish priest peering at her through the presbytery window; no parish pump gossips to whip up scandal; and she is lonely.

To protect girls like that, Catholic rescue societies meet the boat trains from Ireland at Euston Station in London with advice about jobs, accommodation and the hazards that loiter around in the big city. Many slip through their net, however, and a few end up as call girls.

Always there has been a fair proportion of Irish prostitutes in London, as one detective in the Dublin vice squad discovered when he went there on his honeymoon before the Street Offences Act swept the girls under the carpet. On his first night there, he was walking down Piccadilly with his brand-new bride. Suddenly from half a dozen doorways came the cry: '*Jasus . . . the bold Mickser!*'

He was surrounded by a cluster of girls who once had been on his arrest rota back home, but who since had emigrated in a desire to improve themselves with a little extra loot. They clutched him, eyes damp, squeezing him for the latest news of the old crowd back on the home beat. They, too, were lonely.

It is true that they were in business before they left Ireland; but others are recruited after they arrive. These boys and girls who cannot adjust are in the minority, however. The average young Irish immigrant of recent years is absorbed easily enough into English life because he has what the others lack—a fair education and a sharp intelligence. Like his counterpart in New York, he differs greatly from his pre-war predecessor.

The personnel officer of a large contracting firm which employs acres of Irish labour told me: 'Once we would scarcely hire an Irishman unless he wore a muffler to cover his lack of tie. It was part of the uniform, a certificate to show that he knew the trade. Now the lads we take are well-dressed. They spend money on clothes instead of drink. They are ambitious, too, anxious to become gangers. Some have been so good that they have joined our permanent staff and travelled all round the world on major contracting jobs.'

Now the Irishman is quite choosey about his digs, spends as much time in the dance-hall as he does in the pub, gets himself a steady girl friend, marries her and settles down in a council house. He will do his football pools, dig his garden and usually will take a little more interest in local politics than his British neighbour. Generally speaking he votes Labour. His interest in politics, all politics, has been developed in Ireland, bred into him, indeed, and he cannot understand why the English are immune from the disease. He may drift away from his religion for reasons similar to those which guide the young girl from the village off the rails: there are no parents to nag him about going to Mass, no parish priest appearing round the corner and giving him a look that says: 'When did you make your last confession?' When he marries, however, he is likely to bring his children up as Catholics unless there is particularly vehement opposition from his wife, which would be unlikely in Britain today.

Why, however, does he go in the first place? The easy answer—and I have given it already—is that he is forced out of Ireland by economic conditions; but I am coming around to the view that the complete answer is not here. It is true that a degree of prosperity in Ireland has cut emigration substantially; but still a large number of boys and girls leave home every year.

History, too, could have spawned a tradition. There were the Wild Geese, King James's Irish soldiers, who chose flight to France and Spain rather than surrender when the Williamite forces drove them to the sea. The Irish names of their descendants can be found today in French telephone directories, the most easily recognizable of them, perhaps, being Hennessy, the brandy people. It may not be entirely a coincidence, either, that the maker of a Spanish sherry is Rafael O'Neale, for the Irish, as I have said earlier, always seem able to produce reasonable liquor.

The famine, of course, in the five years that followed 1846, carved a further million from the population, sowing its seed mainly in America. Here it was a case of leave or die, as the last verse of a cruelly sad ballad, 'The Famine Song', reveals:

Oh, we're down into the dust . . . over here.
Oh, we're down into the dust . . . over here.
We're down into the dust
For the God in whom we trust
Will not give us bread or crust
Over here . . .

Those who left established bridgeheads for relatives and friends still scraping a fragile living from the dust; and thus in a way emigration became something of a heritage.

Yet it could be that I found another piece in the mysterious jigsaw of the Irish emigrant's mind, when I went to Ballyconnelly on the Atlantic Ocean in Connemara to visit John and Kathleen Mullen and John's sister, Bridie, all three of them home from New York on holiday. John drives a bus for a living and Kathleen works as a clerk in a Wall Street law firm, though she is thinking of taking a job as a waitress, for the money is nearly twice as good. We had met in Jager's dance-hall, where they told me how they had known each other in Ireland, but decided to get married only after they had met again almost by accident in New York; and, when I discovered that they would be home on holiday when I was due in Connemara, I said I would call.

The drive to their home in Ballyconnelly must be one of the most magnificent in Ireland. The road is good, if twisty, thrusting the Twelve Pins Mountains into view on the left and the right and sometimes dead centre. Lakes are littered all along the route, calm and aloof, cradling tiny islands with tiny, ruined churches that mark the dedication of monks centuries ago, when the rest of Europe was dark. The fields are ragged and humpy, sparse and hungry, the aggressive rock of the mountain jutting through like teeth; then suddenly they give way to the sea, to the Atlantic, to yellow, midget beaches with here and there a black, tarred-canvas currach, upside down in the sun, like a basking seal. Seaweed, which may coax some life from the thin, sick soil, is spread to dry in a sun that seems to shine even when it is raining.

It began to rain as I drove, throwing a rainbow across the road so close, I swear, that I could have opened the boot and thrown it in. I came to a road off to the right and a sign that pointed up a hill to a monument in honour of Alcock and Brown, the Atlantic flyers. I drove up to see it, a vast chunk of stone, shaped like the tail of the Boeings that came so much later. British tourists had autographed it liberally—'Joe Brown, Birmingham', 'F. W. Mason, Kilburn', 'Mary Mac-Donald, Edinburgh'—but they had spared the inscription; and I read:

This monument honours the achievement of John Alcock and Arthur Whitten-Brown, the first men to fly non-stop across the Atlantic Ocean on the morning of the fifteenth day of June, nineteen hundred and nineteen. They landed in their aircraft five hundred yards south of this point, having left St John, Newfoundland, sixteen hours and twenty-seven minutes before. The aircraft was a Vickers Vimy biplane, powered by two Rolls-Royce Eagle VIII engines of three hundred and fifty horsepower each and the average speed was one hundred and fifteen miles per hour. Dedicated this fifteenth of June, nineteen hundred and fifty-nine. Tá a ngaisce greannta ar chlar na spéire.

Tá a ngaisce greannta ar chlar na spéire—'Their noble deeds are inscribed in the sweep of the skies.'

I looked out over the Atlantic, which they had beaten, and then I walked down to the spot where they had landed, past thatched cottages, happy with fresh paint, the colour of seagulls' eggs. The road dwindled to a path that soon was swallowed by soggy bog. A white, primitive obelisk marked the landing place and it was hard to believe that it had ever happened.

How could a plane land here, where the soggy turf blends into jagged rock and deep, sombre pools, the whole vista bulky with meandering, hostile hillocks? What made them climb into that Vickers Vimy biplane, with its Rolls-Royce Eagle VIII engines and toss themselves from the nose of Newfoundland over an ocean that had never been crossed by air before?

Why do the Irish emigrate? Alcock and Brown might have been able to answer that question that day in June, nineteen hundred and nineteen.

A FTER all that, what are the Irish really like?

The natural modesty which permeates the fibre of all Irishmen prohibits me from answering that question myself. What better could I do, instead, than quote from two advertisements, inserted by Bórd Fáilte, the Irish Tourist Board?

The first appeared in *Private Eye,* a satirical magazine in Britain. It read:

'The natives are warm and gay and friendly. Many have been educated in England and will understand you readily. The others are even more approachable and have merry twinkles in their eyes; but watch this lot!'

The second comes from the *New Yorker* and was written by the splendid Adrienne Claiborne, mistress of the controlled non-sequitur and, for that matter, of the Celtic character. In a very short time she learned to understand us thoroughly—a gargantuan task—and even after that still liked us. She wrote:

'There is that in the average Irishman, which makes him behave in a pub like nothing so much as a shy and independent, though reasonably friendly, cat, when confronted by a well-intentioned stranger. And, if, in that situation, you already know how to make friends with the cat, then you already know the whole technique of making friends in a pub with an Irishman.

'But, if you do not already know, then we hope you will not take it amiss, if we offer a single pointer: let the Irishman come to you, which he (like the cat) will do, drawn by a natural and friendly curiosity, if you but offer him time and the appearance of an amiable indifference. For, if you make the first move, the Irishman will (like the cat) retreat in alarm—either literally, or by hiding behind the façade (which he hopes will please you) of the stage or old-time-American-movie Irishman. . . .'

If that does not make Paddy purr, he is not a cat, but a churlish pig, who deserves to be banished to live in the kitchen of one of the crumbling, old, thatched, cardboard cottages, that can be found in those old-time-American-movies. Indeed, it is a lethally accurate compliment, such as only the Irish would appreciate.

ACKNOWLEDGEMENTS

Now I come to the deepest and most dangerous ditch of all. Hundreds of people helped me while I was gathering material for this book. I am deeply grateful to them all; yet, as I sit down to name them, I am chilled at the thought of omitting some whose contribution was substantial, but who will slip through the wide-mesh net of my memory. If that should happen, will they ever forgive me, for I am jaded? Because of this fear, I was tempted to chicken out on the entire acknowledgement business, but that would have been churlish indeed.

I would like to thank my colleagues in the newspaper, television and public relations industries, with many of whom I worked a few aeons ago. Each of them helped me on a variety of subjects, sketching in the background before I delved more deeply. My anchor-man on many occasions was Tony Lennon, Chief Librarian of the *Irish Times*, who, incidentally, managed to find time in between files to collaborate with his brother, Peter, on the film, *Rocky Road to Dublin*. Then there were Líam MacGabhann, Michael McInerney, Mary Maher, John Horgan, Sydney Robbins, Peter Byrne, Paddy Downey and Séamus Kelly, all of the *Irish Times*; Pan Collins and Seán MacReámoinn of Rádio Telefís Éireann; Caroline Mitchell of *Woman's Way*; Líam Robinson, Irish representative of the *Sunday Express*; Roy Lilly of the *Belfast Telegraph*; Andy Boyd, trade union official and intrepid Belfast freelance; Séamus O Túathail of the *United Irishman*; David Shanks of *Nusight*, a mature and out-spoken magazine, run by students; Herbert Brennan and Hilary Weir of *Scene*, a mature and outspoken glossy; a formidable team from Aer Lingus—Jack Millar and Bart Cronin in Dublin, Gerry Geraghty in Limerick and Carl O'Sugrue, Tom Kennedy and Bill Maxwell in New York; Tim Dennihy, Joe Jennings and Frank Finn of Córas Iompair Éireann, the Irish transport company; Martin Sheridan of Córas Trachtála, the Export Board; Dick O'Farrell of the Industrial Development Authority; Aidan O'Hanlon of Bórd Fáilte, the Tourist Board, and Seán White of its New York office; Des Fricker of the Department of Agriculture; Honor Edgar of Sam Edgar Public Relations; and Dot Tubridy of Waterford Crystal Glass.

On the theatrical scene, Phyllis Ryan, Michaél MacLíammóir and Phil O'Kelly were there to help me and to entertain me. George Campbell, R.H.A., gave me sound advice about the art world; and on the Irish language front, Dónal Ó Moráin of Gael Linn, Caoimhín O'Cinnéide, and Con Howard guided me in courteous English.

Everyone, of course, talked politics, but those from whom I sought and got specific information included Seán Lemass, T.D., a former Taoiseach; George Colley, Minister for Industry and Commerce; Senator Garrett FitzGerald, Senator Jack MacQuillan; Alderman Robert Molloy, T.D.; Brendan Halligan, Donal Nevin and Mick O'Riordan, all from the Republic; and Gerry Fitt, M.P., Michael Barritt, Betty Sinclair and Martin Burns, all from Northern Ireland.

The industrial front was fluid and explosive. I recall with pleasure being helped by Séamus Kavanagh of Galway Crystal Glass; Vesta V'Soski and Alma Joyce, both of the V'Soski-Joyce carpet factory in Oughterard; Major The Hon. Phadrig Lucius Ambrose O'Brien (now Lord Inchiquin), who sadly yet amiably was winding up his Connemara Sea Food company beyond Clifden before buying a car in Munich, where his daughter was about to be educated, and driving to the Greek Islands; Hector Grey, who circles the globe, even unto China, in search of novelties, which he buys for hundreds of thousands of pounds and which he sells on the metal bridge in Dublin every Sunday, servicing the rest of the world, more or less literally, on weekdays; Sona Sercik, the cheerful, imperturbable British-educated Czech who runs the Galway-based Steinbock Fork-Lift Company, which the Americans bought from the Germans; and Murrough O'Brien of the Tara Exploration and Development Company, one of the groups which have found minerals beneath the green, green grass of home.

Agriculture and fisheries? Father James McDyer, of course, with his remarkable revolution in Co. Donegal; Marcus Clements, who sold the family heirlooms to promote farming, forestry and tourism in Lough Rynn, Co. Leitrim; Maurice Moore, James McLeod, Michael Rogers and Padraig McGee of the Donegal Co-operative Fisheries, Ltd., in Killybegs; and Colm McDevitt, Chairman of the South Connemara Fisheries Co-operative, the man I did not find when I turned right at the Atlantic Ocean because he was in Paris.

Tourism? Ken Besson of the Royal Hibernian Hotel, who began his career in the kitchens of one of Paris's grandest hotels, helping an otherwise entirely Communist staff cook for the bluest, most capitalist blood in Europe; Billy Huggard of the Butler Arms in Waterville, Co. Kerry; George Carpenter, once a rebel Olympic fencer, of the Club Hotel, in Glenbrook, West Cork; Rory Murphy, Moira Colleran and David Byrne of the Great Southern, Galway, and Ignatius Murray and Dermot Mulcahy of its sister in Bundoran, Co. Donegal; Kruger Kavanagh, who once worked with the Zeigfeld Follies before settling down to run his guesthouse in Dunquin, Co. Kerry; and Marius Van Cooyk, Dutch Manager of the Skelligs Hotel in the Kerry Gaeltacht. All the staff are native Irish speakers, except Marius, and he is learning.

Many priests helped me with a wide variety of subjects, a fair proportion of which had little or nothing to do with religion. I would like to thank particularly Father Peter Canning, Father Fergal O'Connor, Father Michael Keane, who runs a marriage bureau at Knock, Co. Mayo, Father Mike Walshe and his pupils at Dun Laoghaire Technical School, Father Tom Stack, who introduced me to Sister Marius O'Byrne, O.P., and Sister Margaret McCurtain, O.P., at Muckross College in Dublin; Father Frank Lenny, the Cardinal's Secretary in Armagh, who arranged an interview with Dr Conway for me only a couple of days after they had returned from Bogota; and, of course, to the kindly Cardinal himself, who told me that he was not so much tired by his travels as he was by the sight of the work that had piled up on his desk in his absence.

In New York, which the blasé ones told me was a tough, unyielding city, I found warmth and friendship wherever I went. I can scarcely thank twelve million people (or is it eight million?) and therefore will have to make do with the following short list: Mr and Mrs Jack Casey, who first guided my faltering, old-world footsteps; Gerry Toner and Terry O'Neill of the Abbey Tavern and two other bars, and Des Crofton, their manager in the Abbey, whom I last saw helping out on his holidays behind the bar of his father's pub, the Stage Door Inn in Galway, during race week; Jim Downey, of course, monumental man that he is, and Rosaleen Fitzgibbon, who runs his Irish pavilion; Nat Goldstein and Pat Reynolds of the *New York Times*; Paul O'Dwyer and his nephew, Frank Durkin, who found time to see me in the middle of their brave battle for Eugene McCarthy in the Presidential campaign; John Malone of the F.B.I., Matt Guinan, President of the Transport and General Workers' Union; Jack McCarthy, veteran commentator on the St Patrick's Day parade; Deputy Inspector Pearse Meagher, who plays the Irish pipes; Joe Kennedy, who has brought the Irish language, music and dancing into the wealthier suburbs; and, of course, Adrienne Claiborne, who sells Irish rain and cats in the *New Yorker*.

There are so many others: Dr Peter Fahy, Student Advisor, Consultant Psychiatrist and Special Lecturer in Social and Preventive Medicine, University, Dublin; Commandant Pat Canavan, Secretary of the Galway Race Committee; Captain Michael Hall of Goff's Bloodstock Sales, with not merely photographs of famous horses he has sold around his office, but snippets from their tails, too; Donald Douglas, a medical representative, who refused to sell the pill on principle because he was a Protestant in a Catholic country; Jimmy Young of the Group Theatre, Belfast; Mrs Bridie Flanagan of Ballymoe, Co. Galway and her son, Sylvester, who was my guide on a couple of hazardous expeditions in the area; Mrs Agnes Devine of Roscommon town, a shrewd commentator on most aspects of Irish life; Mrs Monica McEnroy, who battles with cheerful zeal for Irish women's rights and who told me: 'They call me a ferocious committee woman, of course'; John and Bridget Britton and Mrs Frances Mangan, who helped me to understand the riddles of divided Pettigo; Mr and Mrs Padraig Kennelly of Tralee; Tony Gray, who once worked with me in Dublin and now, like myself, freelances in London; David Ascoli of Cassell, who thought of the idea; and Mary Griffith of Cassell, who saw it through the mangle without raising a hand in anger, except in self-defence.

My sincere thanks to the lot of them; thanks, too, and cringing apologies to those whose names I have omitted (they can get me the second time round); and more thanks, together with unqualified admiration, for Hoppy, who in six months never failed to find parking space for me in St Stephen's Green, Dublin.